ROPE TO WIN

The History of Steer, Calf, and Team Roping

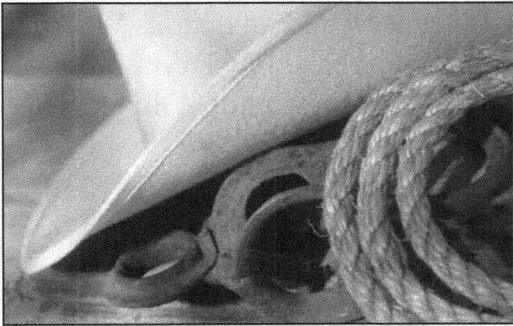

Gail Hughbanks Woerner

EAKIN PRESS ✦ Fort Worth, Texas
www.EakinPress.com

Illustrations by Gail Gandolfi

Copyright © 2007
By Gail Hughbanks Woerner
Published By Eakin Press
An Imprint of Wild Horse Media Group
P.O. Box 331779
Fort Worth, Texas 76163
1-817-344-7036
www.EakinPress.com
ALL RIGHTS RESERVED
1 2 3 4 5 6 7 8 9
ISBN-10: 0-9789150-2-X
ISBN-13: 978-0-9789150-2-5
Library of Congress Control Number 2006939216

Cover: Cowboy Hat and Rope Photo © Photographer: Olivier Le Queinec | Agency: Dreamstime.com

CONTENTS

FOREWORD

My life has been blessed by the opportunity to associate with some remarkable people. Among those I most enjoyed and from whom I learned the most are men who made a living with a rope in their hand.

It has been my observation that men who rope and train roping horses to compete at an elite level have much more to offer than may be obvious from their résumés. The rapid art and science of roping calves and steers has provided them a means of understanding—and explaining—life. Though they aren't roaming the countryside offering their philosophical musings from raised podiums, they are sometimes willing to share their thoughts in the practice arena with a fellow willing to listen. I was fortunate to rope with some who were willing to share themselves in that way. They became and remain my heroes.

I met Allan Johnson at Elbert, Colorado, when my dad was taking delivery on Hereford heifers near Colorado Springs. I was about 14, just learning to rope calves, and Allan invited me to come rope with him and his sons for a few days. That became an annual trek for several years. Allan was a good athlete and horseman with a gentle, consistent spirit, and I immediately trusted him. He seemed always trying to do the right and honest thing, using his special abilities.

As I progressed, Allan was pressing me to be less tentative. "Don't wait for it to be perfect; rope when you get there!" he said. I realized later he wasn't just talking about roping calves. When situations and opportunities arose that didn't allow time for lengthy cogitating and analysis, I could hear Allan's advice and became more inclined to take a shot when I sensed I was close. Sometimes I missed; but sometimes I didn't and my life is clearly richer for his counsel.

Allan invited Bobby Seals from Pampa, Texas, to have a calf roping school at his place one summer. I was excited to be invited, and enjoyed getting to know Seals. While he was no longer a young man, I thought he was amazing. I watched him rope one of the first calves I ever saw tied in 8 and change, and he never seemed to hurry. Through the first couple days of the school, I thought I was doing great. I was being careful to get into position and rope every calf, remember all my lessons to block and flank, and take two wraps and a hooey on every tie to make sure I didn't lose one. Walking to the arena on the third morning, Bobby came up beside me and said, "Chuck, how about doing something exciting today, rather than being so damned consistent?"

At first taken aback, the smile on Bobby's face said, "OK, you know how to do this. Why not take some risks and have a little fun?" As the river of life flows on, I've tried to remember Bobby's advice to try something out of the ordinary sometimes. He was unimpressed with anyone who simply repeated the same routine year after year, and I hoped not to live my life in a way that would disappoint him. I can still see him smile when I do a "hey, watch this!" move at work or play.

One summer before I was old enough to drive, I was staying a few days at the Banning Lewis Ranch near Colorado Springs while my dad was looking at cattle nearby. The Banning Lewis neighbored legendary Hugh Bennett's ranch, and Hugh invited me over to rope calves with him one afternoon. He had a big sandy arena, and after we had roped five or six calves apiece Hugh noted I was tracking those calves a lot farther down that arena than he though I should before I roped. "Man, if you're going to rope," he counseled, "go like you were killin' snakes!" He put some "Chihuahua" spurs on me that had the biggest rowels I'd ever seen and said, "Now, I know you're going to be there fast enough, so just rope the same way!" We ended the afternoon drinking lemonade on the front porch, talking about horses, dogs and life and I came away with an important lesson: Live life like you were "killin' snakes"—with enthusiasm, purpose and energy. Hugh certainly did, and I've tried to remember how he chose to pursue things he really cared about, and then used his many talents to achieve all that was possible. By the way, I came home with a great dog that day, too!

During my college years when I was trying to prove my independence, my dad traded a few horses with pro cowboy and rope horse trainer A. Clark Brown at North Platte, Nebraska. I'm not sure if it was by human or heavenly design, but Clark and his wife Dorothy became like second parents to me. They put good calf horses under a lot of accomplished and aspiring ropers, including World's Champion

Calf Roper and All-Around Cowboy Paul Tierney. But many of us who had the privilege of their company as we were entering adulthood look back and realize they were putting a foundation for living under us as well.

I say "had the privilege" because everyone knew that being invited to rope with Clark meant you had to pass some sort of unwritten exam, and he was completely unreasonable by the emerging standards of the 1970s. We all knew that disagreeing with his advice was a very bad idea; though it was kind of fun to see someone else do it just to hear how cleverly Clark would proceed to disembowel them. And we knew that getting a haircut (remember, this was the '70s), wearing a long-sleeved shirt, boots and a hat (not a baseball cap) would save you merciless teasing. He didn't make it easy, but once he took you in, something special happened.

On down the road after ranching for ten years, then diving into politics, I called the Browns one day to ask if I could "escape" the political scrapes in which I found myself and come to their place for the weekend. It was like I'd never left. After sending me to bed without an alarm clock, I woke the next morning having slept far later than I would ever have dared in the old days. I came running down to the kitchen, and Dorothy assured me there just wasn't any reason for me to get up earlier, and that I would find Clark at the arena if I maybe wanted to rope some calves.

Clark and his son Ray were riding a young horse I'd bred at the time, so I was pleased for an invitation to run a few on him. Shortly, I was backing into the box for my first run. My bay horse ran astraddle of the calf, I roped, stepped off, felt the jerk of my horse's stop and started somewhat tentatively down the rope. It had been awhile since I'd tied any cattle down, and I was being cautious, I suppose. Well, my horse was tuned and went flying back, bringing the calf to me more rapidly than would require any fancy anticipation of his moves. To my surprise, my horse drug the calf right square up the middle of me, knocking me on my back beneath the calf, then drug us another five or six feet, filling the back of my jeans with fine Platte River Valley sand. As I lay there assessing the situation with the calf laying on top of me, Clark came quickly waddling across the arena on his badly bowed legs. When he reached me, he leaned over and asked, "Are you hurt?" "No, I don't think so," I replied. "Well, then get up and tie this calf. You look funny under there."

Embarrassed, I did so, and as I got back on my horse and rode ahead, he untied the calf, then stood there holding the piggin' string. "If you'd be aggressive and just handle him like you know how, you wouldn't get run over," he said as he tossed me my string and walked away. "Think about it!"

Driving back to life in a coat and tie, I realized that grouchy ol' man had done it to me again! He had used a calf roping run to tell me about life. I was being too cautious in my life among politicians, and was being "run over" as a result. I knew what needed done; I just wasn't being aggressive about it. As I look back across my many experiences with Clark and Dorothy Brown, I realize they invested themselves in much more than making me a better roper. They tried to make me a better man.

These mounted philosophers are my heroes. When I learned that talented writer and rodeo aficionado Gail Woerner was doing this book on great ropers, I was ecstatic. Every young fellow in my generation who loved to rope had a dog-eared copy of Willard Porter's wonderful *13 Flat* beside his bed. But many great ropers and great horses have come and gone since then. A new chronicle is in order to provide both an accurate, contemporary history of the sport and a source of inspiration to young folks still looking for heroes. They find too few in today's world. Some of the gifted cowboys on these pages qualify in both ability and character to serve as proper examples for honorable living.

Thank you, Gail, for telling their stories.

CHARLES P. SCHROEDER
Executive Director
National Cowboy &
Western Heritage Museum

PREFACE

A simple piece of rope has been the catalyst for cowboys on horseback to lose sight of everything else, forget their responsibilities, and even "go a little crazy." It starts out as a simple chore. "Hey, go rope that sick cow." And before you know it there is another cowboy who thinks he can rope faster and better than everyone else. That brings on a challenge and in no time those cowboys are practicing their roping night and day. The passion which this length of hemp instills in these ropers is amazing. In fact those trying to rope better and faster have come to admit it might even be an obsession!

Calf roping, steer roping, and team roping are all official competitive events in professional rodeo today. Since cowboys began handling cattle all three types of roping have had a purpose in their daily work on a ranch. The sport evolved from the ranch. The speed and accuracy of a horseback cowboy, or cowgirl, at roping an animal has been challenged and improved year by year.

Observing a roper prepare to rope is like watching a world renowned musical conductor preparing to play a masterpiece. The cowboy's concentration, focus and mental awareness toward themselves, their mount and the task at hand, is all consuming. As for the roper, once that gate is opened and the chase is on, anything can happen. But regardless of how fast, how accurate, and how well the roper does, he will always try to improve and do it better the next time. Do they ever reach perfection? In the roper's mind, the answer is, "No. Next time I'll do it better."

PREFACE

INTRODUCTION

The world of roping is diverse. Cowboys in the early days on the ranch seldom left on horseback without a rope tied to their saddle. It was a necessity, and would probably be needed before the day was over. A calf who couldn't keep up with the herd was roped and carried across a cowboy's saddle as the mother trailed behind bawling for her newborn. A young bull that needed to be steered and branded, or a sick or injured cow, would be roped by two cowboys, one roping the horns, the other the hind feet, so they could get the bovine down and treated. These tasks and numerous others required a roping. Cowboys and cowgirls were always trying to improve on their roping technique, their ability to throw a more accurate loop.

A roping competition is never dull, especially if you are aware of the effort and hours of practice in which the competitors have gone to in reaching their ability to compete. In addition to their ability to throw a more accurate loop, it is also important that it is done with speed as the roper must complete his task in the shortest amount of time.

All types of glitches can occur and often do happen. The rope may break, the horse can stumble, the calf outruns the horse and rider, the piggin' string gets tangled, the steer gets up before the rider can dismount, the calf kicks so furiously his legs can't be tied, and so on. The variables that can put a "hickey" into an official roping time are numerous, and never expected, but must be addressed.

It was the ninth round of the National Finals Rodeo in 2001 and the calf roping event was just about over. The calf shot out of the chute and the barrier snapped open as Cody Ohl's horse shot from the box in hot pursuit. Ohl's loop was thrown. Missed! In a millisecond the chase continued and his second loop was ready. It was thrown! The calf was caught. As Cody Ohl quickly stepped off the right side

The "Try" of Cody Ohl is what makes a champion.

—Photograph by and courtesy of Dan Hubbell

of his mount his right leg gave way. He fell to the ground on his back. Something was terribly wrong with Ohl's right leg! The taut rope, and Cody holding the rope, caused the calf to fall as well. The cowboy could see the calf was caught by his two hind feet. Ohl struggled to his feet putting his weight on his uninjured leg he circled the calf while reaching in his pocket for his knife. He cut the rope, held on to it and the calf, who had regained his footing, then dragged Ohl a few feet, as he was still hanging on to the catch rope. Struggling, Ohl awkwardly made his way to the calf. He lifted the calf off the ground and laid it down, balancing on his one strong leg. He tied the calf's three legs as quickly as he could. Then he rolled over onto his back and lay beside the calf, his arms went up over his eyes—it was evident he was in excruciating pain. His time tying the calf was forty point nine seconds!

Seventeen thousand fans, sitting on the edge of their seats in the Las Vegas Thomas & Mack Stadium watched this amazing display of "try" by this young roper. No one could ever remember seeing such toughness and true grit as Ohl displayed in getting his calf tied. He already had the calf roping championship in his pocket before the ninth round. He would have won the gold buckle without tying this calf.

But that wasn't Ohl's plan. He is a cowboy who continued to complete his job in spite of injury, pain, and adversity, as witnessed. The "heart" this man showed in that display of determination to finish the job could only be placed in the highest echelon of his profession. A world-class champion!

Cody Ohl, at the top of his game, had just suffered a severe injury according to Dr. Tandy Freeman, top sports medicine doctor for the Justin Healer Program that treats injured cowboys. Freeman is the premier healer of cowboys, and tops in his field of sports medicine. He was the first person to reach Ohl, as he lay on the arena dirt. As Ohl was carried from the arena on a stretcher, the entire viewing audience gave the roper a standing ovation. He had torn his anterior cruciate ligament and his medial cruciate ligament, and would be out of commission for at least the next six months.

By the way, Ohl not only won the World Champion Calf Roping title that year but also won the All-around Cowboy of the World Championship, too.

Just as a roper of note will attest to the fact that they didn't get where they are today without the help from many people, I, too, have many people to thank for helping me get this book completed. My husband, Cliff, has been a constant support and without his encouragement I am sure the pages of the manuscript would still be scattered all over my home. Imogene Veach Beals has been a constant source of information since I first began this project and never seems to tire of my incessant questions and requests for help. The facts and information in this book have been drawn together by the efforts of many, including Sherry Compton and Harla Kadrie at the PRCA office. Others who must be recognized are Jim Aplan, Chuck Schroeder, all the photographers who generously supplied me with remarkable photos, as well as fans of rodeo who came forth offering photos, and all the cowboys and cowgirls who took time to visit with me during this project.

CHAPTER ONE

RANCH CHORES SPAWN A SPORT

The horse was a must for the early day ranch cowboy. But another equally important tool a cowboy had to own was a piece of rope about thirty feet long. Roping livestock from horseback has been the chore of the American cowboy since the beginning of "cowboy times," just after the Civil War. Numerous unbranded cattle roamed the country, especially in Texas. A person could gather quite a herd for himself if he could capture these cattle and put his brand on them. The Johnson County War in Wyoming during the late 1800s happened because of "freelancing" cowboys who had dreams of gathering enough cattle to eventually own their own ranch. Roping was an important means to capturing the loose animals.

These unbranded cattle were called mavericks, named after Samuel A. Maverick, a Texan who was given 400 head of cattle by a man who owed him $1,200. Maverick left the cattle in the hands of a "free negro," located on the Gulf coast, who did not bother to keep the Maverick brand on the newborns. Eventually an unbranded cow, in this coastal area, was said to be "one of Mavericks." The term "maverick" eventually spread across the country.[52]

Tripping was the logical way a cowboy could get a cow stopped. Tripping was done by roping the animal, getting the rope around the back of the animal and knocking him off his feet. The fall would stun, or knock the wind out of the downed animal momentarily while the rider could dismount, tie him and then take care of the business at hand.[8] Early day ranches had vast areas of open range, not fenced as we know it today. Therefore the ability of a cowhand to stop a calf, a cow, steer or bull, even a wild mustang or horse, for the purposes of branding, doctoring, or other reasons, with a lasso, was one of the most important requirements of a cowboy's job qualification.

The rope has been found to have been used long before the cowboy came into being. In fact, history of the rope records show the use

1

of the rope to catch livestock or capture wild animals, in order to tame them, began with the pastoral people of the ancient Middle East. These nomadic stockmen trailed their herds wherever they went. In this way, the use of a rope in handling stock spread throughout Asia, into Europe and Northern Africa.

The rope was also used as a weapon of war. Xerxes, King of Persia, led an immense army into Greece in 480 B.C. The army was a wandering tribe known as the Sagartians, 8,000 mounted expert ropers, who used a noose as a weapon.

The first known contests, held in ancient Greece, included bucking horses and bulls, wrestling a bull, and throwing a noose. A wall engraving in the temple of Seti, at Abydos, Egypt, depicts a scene of Rameses II and his son roping a scared bull for sacrifice. The bull had been roped by the horns and a half-hitch is around one hind leg.[22]

Until horses were introduced by the arriving Europeans, America had no native horses. The Spanish Conquistadors would not allow their workers—the Indians, mestizos or mulattos—to ride horses. It was considered a privilege and something only the hierarchy could do. This demand was soon relaxed and changed when the owners learned that it was much easier for their workers to manage livestock when mounted.[20]

The earliest records of roping in America was through Spanish and

Cowboys dragging a calf to brand, Wyoming, 1890s.
—Photograph by C. D. Kirkland, Cheyenne, WY. Courtesy of Jim Aplan

Ropers, ready to work. Note the size of their loops.
—Photographer unknown. Courtesy of Jim Aplan

Portuguese introduction of the horse to the Americas. A rope, with a running noose, was tied securely to the horse's tail. Then a loop large enough to go over the horns of the animal was placed on the end of a pole. This method was called "using the laco." The first record of throwing a rope by hand (a "gaza") was in 1624. But they continued using the reata tied to a horse's tail for another hundred years. Determining this method to be unsatisfactory, the saddle horn was finally invented. The early Spanish saddle had no saddle horn. Then they tried tying the rope around the horse's neck before they began to "dally a rope" around the saddle horn.[22] "Dally" is a form of the Spanish word *dar la vuelta*—to give a turn.[36] Vaqueros in Texas, near San Antonio, were recorded as working cattle on horseback and using ropes as early at 1767.[A8]

Pictographs were found in California in 1846 of Indians on horseback roping elk and bears. Comanche Indians were also expert at roping. Even some Comanche women would rope, witnessed by an army officer, who saw two young Comanche women chasing a herd of antelope. Each caught one with her rope on the first try.[22]

The very first material used to make a rope is unknown. Speculating, it is assumed man found materials that grew around him, such as bark, certain plants, reeds, and eventually strips of leather from animal hides to use. The rope was twisted, braided or held together in some crude manner. Rope made from the papyrus plant along the Nile River has been found in Egyptian tombs dating back 3,500 years. Many professions have needed rope, such as ships, the oil industry, railroads, trucking, and farmers and ranchers, just to name a few.[38] The vaqueros of Mexico use the rawhide *reata* and some use the *maguey reata de pita*, made from the agave plant. The *maguey reata* is not as strong as the rawhide, and is used as a dally rope.[A16]

THE COWBOY ROPE

One type of rope used by the cowboy in the United States came from The Plymouth Cordage Company of Massachusetts.[2] The cordage business had begun in the U.S. as early as 1640, but it was not until much later that machinery was used to make it.[38] The company began manufacturing rope in 1824 and their primary customers were boat and ship companies. A small amount of rope went to farms and shore use, but it was minimal. The manufacturing of rope goes through four stages: preparing the fiber, spinning the yarn, forming the strands, and finally laying the rope.

The very first Plymouth Cordage Company price list that showed a quote for "lariat" rope was dated July 31, 1895. Obviously they had been selling rope used for lariats previously, but not specifically made for that purpose. The company made what was called "Yacht Rope" of the highest grade of manila fibers obtainable, which was used for running rigging on racing yachts. It was creamy white in color, with a sheen almost like silk. It was stronger, tougher, and better in appearance than any other manila rope. In 1905 a salesman for Plymouth Cordage made a trip through the southwest and had some samples of Yacht Rope he was taking to the Pacific Coast. While in Dallas, Texas, at Padgitt Brothers Saddlery, he showed them a sample and they ordered lariat made out of the same kind of stock. The order said, "Lariat made from Yacht rope stock." The factory then named it "Plymouth Yacht Lariat," and repeat orders followed. Other manufacturers made this same type of rope and the title, Yacht Rope became the grade of manila fiber.[2]

The material used is the best grade of manila (abaca) fiber, which is grown in the Philippine Islands. The fiber comes from the stalk of

Wyoming cowboys roping their horses out of a lariat corral holding the remuda along the Yellowstone River in Montana, 1880.
—Photograph by Keystone View Co., Meadville, PA. Courtesy of Jim Aplan

the abaca tree, which is similar to the banana tree, but does not bear fruit. The best grades of fiber come from the center of the stalk of the best trees.

Originally, all lariat was 7/16 inch in diameter. Later 3/8 inch lariat was ordered for roping calves. Around 1912 further refinements in size were required, and the Plymouth Cordage Company began making a 3/8 inch full and 7/16 inch full, both of which were slightly over exact size. Cowboys eventually used 30, 33 or 26 thread rope. Steer ropers used 36 thread; calf ropers can use as small as 27 thread, which is the smallest suitable for this type of use.

Early day photographs often show a long, large coil of limp rope hanging from a cowboy's saddle. Hard use and aging would result in breakage, thus shortening the length. Splicing a rope was also not uncommon. The term for this sailing ship rope was sometimes called "seago."[53] The length of time a good rope will last depends entirely on the roper, his use of the rope, and how well he takes care of it. A careful, conservative roper protects his rope against weather, keeps it out of the dirt, cleans and stores it in a canvas or metal bag, when not in use. If he allows slack in his rope it would last longer. The roper who lets the rope take the full shock of the catch will have to replace his rope sooner.[2]

The braided rawhide reata was the closest thing to a hard twist rope, made by the cowboys by using strips of green cowhide. Some

Cowboy throwing a huge steer in Wyoming, 1890s
—Photographer C. D. Kirkland. Courtesy of Jim Aplan

became quite proficient at making these rawhide ropes. When dried hard they would hold a loop without much effort from the cowboy. However, they were hell to hang on to and could severely burn the hands of the user. The Mexican maguey rope, made from the agave plant, was also hard on the hands. Both of these types of ropes were not as strong as ropes used today so it was necessary that the cowboy learn to rope these cattle "artfully," much like catching a big fish on a light line. The secret was in the cowboy's trip.

The trick roper has a completely different set of criteria for his ropes than the competitive roper. When Montie Montana was asked about his ropes, he said he used Samson Spot Cord and Mexican maguey ropes. He said his first rope came from Hamley Company in Pendleton, Oregon. It sold for 12 cents a foot for a Number 12 Samson Spot Cord, and ten to fifteen dollars for a seventy foot maguey rope.[19]

Regardless of how the rope is used it is very sensitive to temperature and humidity. It was not unusual in the early days for a roper to have his rope carefully packed in his duffle where he carried his clothes. Some would even place them on the motor of a car to keep them warm and pliable. Eventually the roping bag or can became a must. Without it, change of climate, which happens often when cowboys are traveling from rodeo to rodeo, can cause a rope to become stiff and not be as accurate and usable as needed.

Roundup on the Sherman Ranch, Geneseo, Kansas, 1902.
—Photograph by Keystone View Co., Meadville, PA.
Courtesy of Jim Aplan

THE EVOLVING COWBOY

During the early nineteenth century the cowboy as we know him began to be known. After the Civil War when soldiers began to return home jobs were scarce. Many found work helping herd the Texas Longhorns to northern railheads in Kansas, Nebraska, and the Dakotas. Numerous cowboys were needed to help gather the huge numbers of wild cattle scattered over south and central Texas and herd them up the trails. The people in the eastern part of the U.S. had little or no beef due to the war. If they could get the cattle to a railroad to ship them back east, they got a much bigger price. During a trail drive the primary job of the cowboys was to keep the cattle together and calmly moving up the trail. Occasionally there were a few runaways in every herd. They would try to break out and go on their own, especially when passing an area where there was cover or rough terrain. Cowboys learned to rope and bust these runaways and if they repeated their "break for it" the cowboy would bust them again until they learned to stay with the herd. Killed or crippled cattle on the drive ended up at the chuck wagon so the crew would have beef to eat.[51] The trail drives played out after about twenty years, but the cowboy had found many other ways to use and improve his skills. Ranches grew larger and larger, and required more hands to check and care for the stock. There were no fences and few corrals, therefore, roping was a necessity any time the stock needed to be examined.

Cowboy on a single rig saddle, carrying plenty of rope!
—Photographer unknown. Courtesy of Jim Aplan

Branding a maverick, 1890s Wyoming. You might call this "early day" team roping.
—Photograph by Kirkland. Courtesy of Jim Aplan

Some cowboys, however, were found to do more roping than necessary. When the ranch owner wasn't looking, some hands practiced their roping skills on unsuspecting livestock. Animals were expected to gain weight prior to being sent to market. Those who didn't were a puzzle to their owners, until they discovered the after hours ropings being held by the hands, causing the stock to run the preferred weight off.

Competitive roping evolved directly from the ranch cowboy's daily chores. Whether it was calf roping, steer roping, or team roping, a cowboy with a talent to rope would be called on often to collect and contain the stock.

EARLIEST CONTESTS

Cowboy contests, rodeos and frontier days began to be held in various western locales and ranch hands from the area got a chance to show their abilities in front of friends and neighbors. Santa Fe, New Mexico, had a roping contest and horse races in 1847. In 1872, Cheyenne, Wyoming, had a steer roping competition. In 1882, during the Texas State Fair at Austin, a silver-trimmed saddle valued at $300 was given to the cowboy who roped, threw and tied a steer in the fastest time. Ten cowboys competed for this prize.[10] Dr. Bruce Classen wrote an article, "Rodeo 100—Looking Back," about the first rodeo in North Platte, Nebraska, 1882, which included buffalo riding, bronc riding and roping.[A2] The Prescott Arizona Cowboy Tournament was first held in 1888. A horse race and bronc riding were held, but the big event of the day was the steer roping competition. *The Arizona Journal-Miner* newspaper reported, *"A prize of a cowboy outfit, valued at $125 was offered and there were nine competitors—One steer at a time was cut out of the herd and driven by a vaquero at breakneck speed, across the open ground to the dead line; then at the drop of the flag the contestant, stationed about one hundred yards behind, shot out after it."* Juan Levias won with a time of one minute, seventeen and a half seconds, with the steer getting a 100 yard start.[25]

The first Cheyenne Frontier Days was held in 1897. The advertising posters announced many races, pitching and bucking horses, and *"Roping Contest. Purse $50. To be given to the man who ropes and 'hog ties' a steer in the shortest time, five per cent to enter. First man seventy-*

Cowboy prepared to go to work. Taken in front of a mud-roofed house, Miles City, Montana.
—Photograph by R. C. Morrison.
Courtesy of Jim Aplan

five per cent, second fifteen, third ten."[26] In the book *Daddy of 'Em All* by Hanesworth, published in 1967, he reports: *"Steer roping in 1898 was quite different from today. Larger and heavier steers were used. They were given a 150 foot head-start on the roper, who after catching the steer had to 'bust' the animal, dismount, and tie him with three feet crossed. He then had to remount his horse before giving the 'finished' signal to the judges. It is no wonder that Duncan Clark, the winner, required two minutes and thirty-five seconds. Under rules in existence today, with lighter steers, nylon ropes and a start of 30 feet on the roper, a good time is 21 or 22 seconds."*[23] Milt Riske's book on Cheyenne Frontier Days reported that in the second year (1898) Hugh McPhee won the steer roping, and again in 1900 he won with an amazing time of 40 seconds, much faster than Clark's two minute plus time the first year, but the rules had changed. "Clark had had to 'bust' his animal, return to his horse and remount."[14]

Also in 1900 the scoreline was shortened to 100 feet.[26]

HUMANE ISSUES, NOT HARDLY

The wild west shows that became so popular in the 1880s were also havens for cowboys who could rope and ride and perform these skills for audiences across the country. By 1885 more than fifty wild west shows were touring the country. In 1886, Buffalo Bill's troupe performed at Staten Island, New York. *A complaint of cruelty to ani-*

mals reached Henry Bergh, the founder and President of the American Society for the Prevention of Cruelty to Animals. Bergh went, in person, to investigate the charge. However, not even the 'father' of the American humane work could find anything wrong. He said the Indians were very careful of the horses."[10]

The rodeo and wild west shows have always been plagued with complaints of cruelty to animals. Down through the years it has been proven time and time again that most people involved in rodeo competitions are more protective and careful with animals than anyone. It makes very good sense they would be—they make their living from these animals. Roping competitions and exhibitions have been especially targeted by animal rights groups. To the person who has not been exposed or raised around animals through ranch-life or farming, seeing a calf or steer roped and jerked to the ground may look inhumane. But experienced ranchers, farmers and people who have experience with stock know these critters are tougher and more resilient than many realize, and rarely does an animal get injured during these events.

Pawnee Bill's Wild West Show in 1887 presented several Mexican ropers performing charro roping. Among them was *lazador* Jose Barrera. *Lazador* is a Spanish word meaning roper. In 1897 Buffalo Bill's Wild West extravaganza invited twelve rural Mexicans, led by the *charro poblano* Vincente Oropeza, who performed his *"Floreo de Riata."* Buffalo Bill's Congress of Rough Riders of the World pronounced Oropeza the best *lazador* in the world.[20]

YOUNGSTERS DISCOVER THE FASCINATION OF ROPE

Mulhall, Oklahoma, in the 1890s, must have been a boon to youngsters who found the rope and its miraculous abilities. However it might also have been a scourge to the members of the community who became the target for these youngsters and their piece of hemp. Lucille Mulhall learned to rope very early, out of necessity. Her father, Zack Mulhall, was gone from home so much of the time it was up to the rest of the family to run their ranch, brand cattle, and doctor them. Colonel Mulhall also put on wild west events in which he expected his children to participate. As a teenager, Lucille's expertise with a rope so impressed President Teddy Roosevelt, he recommended to Zack that he take her all over the country so people could see her talents with a rope.[42]

Sammy Garrett was also an early day roper, born in Mulhall in 1892. His dad kept throwing his rope away because he was afraid Sammy wouldn't learn a trade and be able to support himself. Little did dad know that Sammy would spend his life making a very good living with a rope. He was a top flight trick and fancy roper, as well as a top contender in roping competitions throughout the country.[4]

Chester Byers and his family moved to Mulhall when he was three years old (1895) and eventually he and Garrett teamed up to harass the neighbors and catch "anything or anybody" they could. Byers also became a world-class trick and fancy roper, wrote books on the subject, and won many awards with his roping prowess.[7]

Clyde Miller, also a Mulhall youngster, could throw a rope with the best and both Garrett and Byers claimed that Miller, who was older, helped their careers blossom in roping when they were still "wet behind the ears." Although both Byers and Garrett were best known for their ability to manipulate a rope in many ways, both of these cowboys were good competitive ropers in calf and steer roping and contested, as well as performed, at rodeos across the nation.[4,7,A28]

Marv "Slim" Girard, a youngster living back east, began his interest in roping through his fascination with Will Rogers. *"Dad stood by in dismay, pondering my sanity, while Mom ducked flying loops as I turned her home sweet home into a roping arena. Hunks of hemp rope turned up missing from the nails where Dad had hung them, and Mom's clothesline got so short she took to hanging clothes inside to dry,"* reported the "cowboy crazy" kid, as the neighbors had titled him.[16]

In 1897 the Festival of Mountain and Plain, held at the Denver Wheel Club Park, a wild west show and circus performer, Arizona Charlie Meadows, billed himself as a "grand specimen of the real cowboy" and gave an exhibition of lassoing and throwing of bulls. *The Rocky Mountain News* description of his demonstration was close to what is today called steer roping.[10]

Joseph McCoy wanted to do something special to promote his cattle shipping yards in Abilene, Kansas, for cattle buyers from Chicago. He put together an event in 1898 including roping buffalo.[A8]

In 1899, the Denver National Stock Show, under the program committee headed by C. E. Stubbs, held a "rough riding tournament" and invited Teddy Roosevelt, governor of New York at that time. Each western state or territory was invited to enter not more than two riders to compete for the national championship and prizes.[30]

Competition in roping and other cowboy sports before 1900 were spotty at best, but as the new century dawned it was evident rodeo would only grow and improve. Cowboys had a taste of testing their mettle and they were ready for more!

OW Ranch cowboys ready for roundup, on Dutch Creek, east of Sheridan, WY, 1895. This ranch was owned by John B. Kendrick, Governor of Wyoming and later a U.S. Senator.

—Photographer unknown. Courtesy of Jim Aplan

CHAPTER TWO

RODEO SPREADS

The business of roping and tying cattle for branding and doctoring requires great skill and comes from long hours of practice. It also requires daring horsemanship, alertness, a true hand and a quick eye. A great deal of pride is manifested among cowboys who have accomplished such skill.[A4]

The competitions for cowboys at the turn of the century were still few and far between. Occasionally spontaneous matches were held. Steer ropings, called "fairgrounding" were held.[3] The reason for the word "fairgrounding" was because most of these meets were usually held at a local fairground, if one existed. These competitions were also called "steer bustings." Cowboys were determined to compete. If there were no rodeos in the area, they would invent a competition.

When Europeans came to the west and encountered the Mexican vaquero they learned *dar la vuelta* from the vaquero, which meant to take a turn. Most often they worked together, one at the head of the steer and one on the heels.[47] This could have been the beginning of what is now called "team roping."

Cheyenne Frontier Days modified the steer roping event by 1900. The "start" the animal was allowed was decreased to 100 feet. Five-year-old steers were still used, however, and many ropes snapped as the "trip and bust" was made.

During that year (1900) Hugh McPhee, of Cheyenne, roped, busted, and tied his steer then remounted his horse in a record time of 40 seconds. Gradually the committee changed to the use of younger and lighter steers. These animals were more fleet of foot as well as much quicker to regain their feet when thrown. The older steers were also less clever at dodging the ropes thrown by contestants. With the advent of younger steers the start given the animals was decreased in 1908 to a sixty foot scoreline, in 1914 it diminished again to a forty-foot scoreline for steer roping and twenty foot for steer wrestling and

Clay McGonigal was an early day steer roper not afraid to bet on his own skill and he seldom lost.

—Photographer unknown.
Courtesy of *Hoofs & Horns*

in 1921 to thirty feet for all timed events.[23]

Clay McGonigal was known for his outstanding roping skill. In Tucson, Arizona, in 1901, he roped and tied a steer in 23 seconds flat.[2] One of McGonigal's most remarkable feats was in Muskogee, Oklahoma, in 1907. Confidently, he bet Bob Gentry, who was considered at that time, the champion steer roper in Oklahoma, $1,000 that he could rope, throw and tie eleven steers in the same time that Gentry could rope and tie ten steers. McGonigal's first steer took him one minute and 55 seconds, but he tied the next six in less than 30 seconds each. He tied his eleven steers in seven seconds less time than Gentry took to tie his ten steers.[A4]

Another top flight roper at this time was J. Ellison Carroll. He was tall, good looking, and with a trim, athletic figure and tremendous grace and speed. All he wanted to do was rope. But there were too few riding and roping contests to keep him busy, so he traveled about the country much of the time, getting up roping matches with anyone who would rope against him for a side bet. During his trips through Oklahoma and Texas, he defeated so many ropers in matches that it became hard for him to get anyone to bet against him. A matched roping was held at San Antonio, Texas, on December 31, 1907, between Ellison and McGonigal, two of the best ropers of the day. The reputation of these ropers was fairly equal and the betting was heavy. The side bet was $2,000 for ten steers each, and it lasted two days. Carroll roped one steer in sixteen seconds, with a sixty foot start, and ended winning the match and the $2,000.[1]

Steve Birchfield, entered a steer roping contest, with twenty-six other ropers, held at Meyers corral, near Deming, New Mexico. The prize for first place was $100, second $25, and third paid $10. The steers grew up on the open range and were as unrestrained and wild as deer. They drew names from a hat for order in which to rope. Birchfield won first with a time of 27¼ seconds, Butch Smith was second with 35¾ seconds and third was Alex Wilson with 40¼ seconds.[A4]

THE FIRST TITLED COWGIRL

Foghorn Clancy, the first rodeo announcer for rodeo, remembered seeing a polo match, at Kansas City, in 1902, between experienced polo players against a ragtag team of cowboys followed by a riding and roping competition. In the steer roping Lucille Mulhall only seventeen, made better time than most of the men entered. She had the dash and daring of a man twice her size, for she never hesitated to tie onto the biggest and wildest steer. She had the knack of throwing her trick rope over and really giving the longhorns a 'fairground bust'—that is, she threw them so hard they seldom got up before she could tie them down. Lucille's prowess and skill at roping and riding gave her the very first title of "cowgirl." The title was coined by Will Rogers, who later became the world–renown entertainer and roper, when he was just a young man starting his career. It was undisputed that Lucille was by far the foremost lady steer roper of the world. Her skill with a lariat made her famous on two continents. Once while still in her teens Theodore Roosevelt came to an event put on by Zack Mulhall and saw Lucille rope a coyote. He claimed it the greatest stunt he had ever seen a girl perform![1] Her talent allowed her to catch six to eight horses with one throw. For over twenty years Lucille was often in steer roping competitions pitted against twenty to thirty men. She didn't always win, but generally had a very respectable time.[42] In 1920, at a steer roping in Ardmore, Oklahoma, against a group of men she did make the fastest time and won.[2]

Other early day cowgirls who had a special knack at roping were Bertha Blancett Kaepernik and Mabel Strickland. When Mabel DeLong met Hugh Strickland, in 1918, little did she realize they would marry and that he would teach her to be a top flight steer roper. His apt student would rope against men in roping jackpot contests and was so successful that several of the top roping men suggested she

Doubleday photo of Mabel Strickland steer roping. She often competed against men.
—Courtesy of Jim Aplan

Cowboys at a 1906 roping contest at Cleveland, Oklahoma Territory, October, 1906.
—Photographer unknown. Courtesy of Jim Aplan

steer rope in exhibition. In other words, they preferred that she not rope against them![44]

NEW RODEOS, ROUNDUPS AND COWBOY CONTESTS

The first Dewey, Oklahoma, roundup was held in 1908. Henry Grammer, one of the best of the early Oklahoma cowboys won the steer roping. Blue Gentry landed somewhere in the final prize money.[1] A show in Fort Worth called "The Wild West and Range Country Life and Expert Riding Demonstration," was held on Tuesday, March 17, 1908. It was part of the Breeders & Feeders Show. From the vantage point of almost a century of growth, prosperity and development, this single event takes on a particular importance. It was the "grandfather" of the modern Fort Worth Rodeo. Most of the events staged during this single performance were not new, but it was their unique combination in this unusual setting that made this particular night momentous. They held a Grand Entry, a demonstration of cutting horse ability, hurdle jumping, bronco "bustin," rope riding, and the highlight which was watching Bill Pickett bulldog a steer using his teeth. However, no where could a record be found of any roping events.[11]

1912 Dewey, Oklahoma, Roping and Riding Contest on July 4th.
—Photographer unknown. Courtesy of Imogene Veach Beals

Note how big the steer is that A. J. Vey is roping at Pendleton, Oregon.

—Photographer unknown. Courtesy of Jim Aplan.

Mike J. Sokoll, immigrated to the United States from Hungary, with his family. They settled in Pennsylvania and after attempts at many jobs, in the steel mill and the coal mines, for which he was not suited the youngster went 70 miles to Pittsburg to see the 101 Wild West Show. He not only saw it, he stayed, got a job in the cook tent and traveled with them. When their season was over and the crew headed back to the 101 Ranch in Oklahoma, Sokoll went too. Whenever he was not working he was fiddling with a rope, attempting to learn to trick rope. Mexican Joe, a performer, took him under his wing and taught him enough about trick and fancy roping he was finally hired to be part of their roping team, in 1908, to included Tex McCloud, Chester Byers, Sam Garrett, Mexican Joe and Hank Darnell. Sokoll met Henry Grammer, a winning roper, in 1909. Sokoll was only fifteen, and Grammer was twenty, and he revered him as a god on horseback. Sokoll said Grammer was the only roper he ever saw who could swing his noose clockwise or counterclockwise and settle it around the animal's neck perfectly. Fred Beeson was also champion calf roper of the time. Sokoll remembered they would often rope calves on weekends. Everyone would put a dollar in the pot and winner take all. Once Beeson got too much Choctaw beer and chased

Frank Hart, famous Dakota cowboy, throwing the trip, at the Interior, South Dakota Roundup.

—Photo by Doubleday. Courtesy of Jim Aplan

his calf across the pasture, coming back, without roping the calf, he admitted he saw two calves and didn't know which one to rope.[17]

W. S. Bonnell, of Mayetta, Kansas, started roping at an early age and perfected a method of tying a calf faster than anyone up to that time. His horse, named Romer, was a top roping horse, but unusual as roping horses go. He could rope calves or steers and knew the difference without a neck rope. He would keep his head to the calf, but when roping steers he would drag the animal as long as needed. Bonnell roped a calf at Cedar Vale, Kansas, on August 30, 1909, in 25 seconds, with the calf getting a 50 foot head start and two men on horseback following the calf and whipping him. When the calf was tied the judge would whip him with a quirt trying to make him break loose from the tie. A time of 35 or 40 seconds would generally win with these rules. Bonnell traveled with the 101 Ranch Show for several seasons, and worked with Mulhall. In 1912 he was one of the five men having the best average in steer roping. In Canada he was called on to show his expert roping abilities for King George and Queen Mary of England.[A4]

BUSTIN' A PROBLEM

Steer roping at Cheyenne Frontier Days in 1909 was not considered a contest because of a disagreement on rules between the Wyoming Humane Society and the Rodeo Committee. The argument concerned the 'busting' of the animal. However, they did announce that Ed McCarty was declared the champion.[14] It wasn't until 1913 that steer roping returned, during that time team tying replaced the steer busting.[47]

Steer roping was not considered inhumane by ranch cowboys. It was a necessity long before ranches had pens, corrals and fences. When a sick or injured animal needed to be checked or treated the cowboy had no alternative but to rope and tie it. But the Humane Society had a different opinion. In 1910 the Wyoming Humane Society, after a conference with the Cheyenne Frontier Days committee, permitted team roping in which one roper caught the animal around the head while the other "heeled" him (term for catching the hind feet). The roper then dismounted, tailed down the steer and made the tie. Both ropers then released the steer and the time was taken.[23] Meanwhile in Texas the cowboys learned from the vaqueros how to somersault steers by holding to their tail. The cowboy instead used his rope and began "steer tripping."[47]

Cheyenne Frontier Days had a slightly different approach in 1911 in the team roping event. Both ropers caught the animals as in 1910 with one dismounting to tie a ribbon around the steer's neck. Both ropers then released the steer and the time was taken. In 1912 the committee was instructed to continue team roping but the newspaper of August 15th said that the old-style steer roping was being held. The steer busting was discontinued on the last day because the Frontier Days committee, cooperating with the Humane Society, decided to eliminate the event. Frank Maisch was designated the World Champion Steer Roper. By 1913 all criticism of steer roping had subsided and the old style event was again allowed.[23]

The rodeo boom to Calgary came in 1911 and 1912 and the men interested in holding a rodeo contacted Guy Weadick to organize and produce it for them. Back in 1908 when Weadick went to Calgary with the Miller Brothers 101 Wild West, as a trick roper, he approached H. C. McMullen about staging a week long rodeo. The Canadian did not think the time was right. The first rodeo opened on Labor Day, September 2, 1912. $20,000 in purses was announced. $1,000 in cash, plus a new saddle and silver belt buckle, was offered for the champion calf roper, the bucking horse rider and the steer wrestler. More than 25,000 people saw the show each day including trick and fancy riding,

Getting ready for a steer roping contest at Pendleton, Oregon, 1916. Note: Jackson Sundown, Nez Perce Indian who won All-Around that year, at far left, preparing to rope.

—Photographer unknown. Courtesy of Jim Aplan

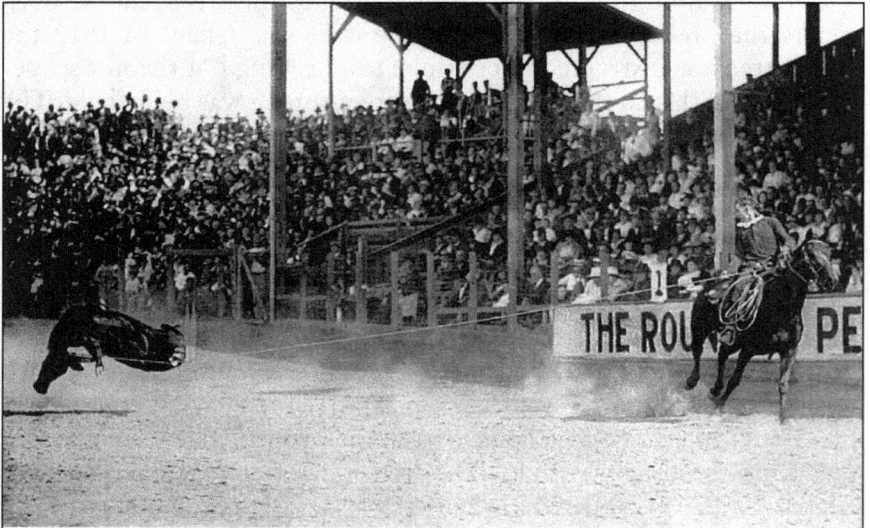

Chester Byers, World Champion trick roper, as well as a very competitive steer and calf roper. Taken at Pendleton, Oregon, in 1918.

—Photo by Doubleday. Courtesy of Jim Aplan

a stage coach race, steer roping, a cowgirl relay race and so on.[9] Ed Echols, later to become sheriff of Pima County, Arizona, won the World Championship Steer Roping at Calgary in 1912.[A4]

GOLD IN THEM THERE HILLS?

Dewey, Oklahoma, advertised *$24,000 Gold, Prize List* for their July 2, 3 & 4th Rodeo, 1914. The roping contest purse was $1,125 in gold, divided as follows: 3 Day Average: First $300, Second $200 and Third $100. Day Money would be: First $100, Second $50 and Third $25. The entry fee was $25. The Bronco Riding Contest had a purse of $750 with an entry fee of $15. The Wild Horse Race purse was $525 with an entry fee of $10 for three days or $5 for one day.[A28]

The Pendleton RoundUp steer roping champ in 1912 was Jim Roach with the fastest time of 55 seconds for two steers.[13] Eddie McCarty won it in 1913 and again in 1918.[18] In 1914 Tommy Grimes won and took the $1,200 purse and a $350 saddle made by local saddlemaker, Hamley.[14] Sam Garrett went to Pendleton in 1914 and did a roping exhibition for which he was paid $300, but he also entered the competition there, and won the Police Gazette's Gold Belt for Champion All–Around Cowboy.[4] George and Charlie Weir, of Arizona, were also steer roping winners. George won the RoundUp event in 1915 and 1916 and Charlie won it in 1917.

During this time period trick roping was a competition at many rodeos. Sammy Garrett won the World's Championship Trick Roping at Cheyenne Frontier Days in 1916. He also won the All–Around at Billings, Montana, that same year. He again won the Trick Roping Championship at Cheyenne every year from 1920 through 1927. Finally the 'powers that be' ruled him out of the competition, but hired him to do exhibition trick roping for the next five years. In 1912 Cheyenne hired Cuba Crutchfield to stand on his head and rope a galloping horse. There were many ways to show the abilities and talents of trick roping. The announcer at a Sidney, Iowa, rodeo counted 168 good catches before a miss was made by four trick ropers in six performances.[8]

Charles Furlong reported in his 1921 published book, *Let 'Er Buck*, about ropers, *"The star ropers are particularly well-proportioned, clean-limbed men—take for instance, the wonderful trio there, George and Charlie Weir, and Eddie McCarty. McCarty is well known at Cheyenne as one of its prime movers and organizers. He won the world's steer roping championship here in 1913, also in 1918, and has always been in the finish, his best time for a single steer being 26 2/5 seconds, made with a total of 55 4/5 seconds for his two steers in 1918 when Fred Beeson, a marvel at roping, beat him out in 47 seconds. Beeson's best time for a steer was 20 seconds flat that year, which stands as the top record here.*[18]

The 1916 Cheyenne Frontier Days was a Mecca for steer ropers. The prizes were the biggest in the country and all the best steer ropers were there to compete. In addition to the money prizes there was a lot of honor that went with winning at Cheyenne. The winners were being considered world champions because of the great numbers of top ropers always entered in this contest. A young fellow from Lenapah, Oklahoma, named Fred Lowry, won the top money that year. He was just a kid and it was one of his first trips any distance from home. But he out roped one of the biggest and toughest fields of steer ropers ever assembled at a contest in that era. He went on to become one of the world's greatest ropers. He came back to Cheyenne in 1921 to win the calf roping contest, then he won the steer roping again in 1924, 1925, 1927 and 1929. By 1930 he had won large sums of money in the steer roping and calf roping events. This was during the time when steer roping events began to diminish due to criticism by various groups as to its cruelty to the steers. If you can believe, calf roping replaced the steer roping event without complaint. Prominent saddle-maker, Monroe Veach, of Trenton, Missouri, designed a special roping saddle according to Lowry's specifications and named it the "Fred Lowry Roping Saddle."[1]

THE EAST GETS A TASTE OF RODEO

The New York Stampede, was put on by Guy Weadick, that same year. It was held at the Sheepshead Bay Speedway, in Brooklyn, and was the first big eastern rodeo. It was a milestone in rodeo and gave the sport a tremendous amount of publicity. Few cowboys had available transportation so Weadick arranged for groups of twenty-five or more to travel on trains coming from Cheyenne, at the close of Frontier Days, one train from Fort Worth, and another from Iowa.

Postcard photo sent by Clarence Luper, in Clovis, New Mexico, 1912, to his sister, Grace, in Clarita, OK. "Hello sister. How are you. I have been out on a hunt and just came in and had these made. You tell mama to send any shirts. Be a good gal and write soon."

—Photographer unknown. Courtesy of Jim Aplan

Bee Ho Gray, World's Champion Trick Roper, Vancouver, B.C., 1914. He is known as the originator of the three loop catch.

—Photo by Marcell. Courtesy of Jim Aplan

Lucille Mulhall was known for her outstanding roping abilities. She roped a coyote and President Theodore Roosevelt was very impressed.

—Photo taken near downtown San Antonio, 1917, by Doubleday. Courtesy of Jack Long Collection

Tickets were furnished which included a free baggage car for their horses. Weadick had found financial backers to offer prizes to total $50,000. Unfortunately, due to a streetcar strike and an epidemic of infantile paralysis, which was a devastating illness in those days, the rodeo was a financial failure. When it came time to pay the winners they were not paid in full. Weadick did his best to collect but the financial backers were unwilling to pay the full amount. What was paid was still more than any other contest that season. It was always said that Weadick's rodeos were tough contests and no place for weaklings. The Cowboy Steer Roping was won by Henry Grammer, 2nd was Fred Beeson, and third was Johnny Murray. The Cowboy's Trick Roping competition was won by Chester Byers, 2nd by Bee Ho Gray and 3rd by Tex McLeod. The Cowgirl's Trick Roping was won by Florence LaDue, 2nd was Lucille Mulhall and 3rd by Emily McLeod.[A4]

The Prescott, Arizona, Cowboy Tournament always considered the steer roping a popular event. It was one of the original competitions held in 1888. The steer back then had a scoreline of 100 yards. In the early 1900s Arizona passed a state law, not prohibiting steer roping, but to prohibit the "busting" of stock that did not belong to the cowboy or his employer. It is said this came about because steer ropers, practicing before an event, often practiced on the animals owned by dairymen, and the dairymen were the ones to see that the law was passed. Goats were used for a short time, but cowboys weren't too interested in this replacement competition. Breakaway steer roping was on the program in 1915 and 1916, but the cowboys eventually decided it was too easy. The last breakaway competition was held in 1939. The first calf roping was held at Prescott in 1917. It was called "World Championship Calf Tying Contest" and offered $2,000 in prizes, including day money. The Arena Director for that year explained, *"This is not a tying contest forbidden by law. No calf will be thrown by means of horse and rope. Calves will have a forty foot score, caught by rope, but not thrown. The cowboy must dismount and throw the calf by hand. All calves must be securely tied, 'three bones crossed.' Should the tie be contested the calf must be left on the ground for five minutes."* H. Eubanks, of California, won in 1917 and collected $750 plus some day money with a three calf time of 97 seconds. The event was not held again until 1920.[25]

The first two decades of the Twentieth Century were learning

—Illustration by Gail Gandolfi

stages in the development of rodeo. Often the rules varied from rodeo to rodeo. In roping the scorelines were different, some as long as 150 feet, and short as 30 or 40 feet. Occasionally a rodeo producer would disappear before the winners were paid off. On many occasions the judging was biased. But regardless of the problems the cowboy faced he was there to compete and the chance to prove he was a better steer roper or a calf roper than his opponents was his main objective. Sure he needed the prize money. But deep in his gut he knew the money was incidental, being announced the winner was his goal. He was there to stay!

ROPERS OF THE TIMES

HENRY CLAY McGONIGAL. Born at Old Sweet Home, Lavaca County, Texas, on September 24, 1879. The family moved to Odessa when Clay was a small boy. His father raised good, fast horses, and he rode early in his life. He also spent his early days working on ranches in west Texas. He was a good bronc rider and a great roper. Although

Unknown roper catches a good-size steer.

—Photographer unknown. Courtesy of Jim Aplan.

Photograph taken from B & M Railroad of cowboys and rope corral holding horses near Sheridan, WY.

—Photo by H. R. Locke & Co., Deadwood, SD. Courtesy of Jim Aplan

there were few rodeos in his day he found a way to compete whether it was roping at an organized rodeo or at a matched event.

McGonigal married Annie Laurie Johnston at Sealy, Texas, on January 16, 1904, and they had one son, Clay, Jr., born at Midland, Texas, May 15, 1905. He worked as a cowhand for several big outfits in the northwest, but later he ranched for himself in Texas, New Mexico and Arizona.

His career took him to steer ropings all over the United States, Canada, Mexico and South America. At Tucson in 1901 he broke the record by roping and tying a steer in 23 seconds, with a 100 foot score-line. At Hot Springs, Arkansas, in 1904, on a 60 foot score, he tied a steer in 21½ seconds. At Juarez, Mexico, in 1910 he tied a steer in the same time, on a 30 foot scoreline. At Chicago, in 1916, again on a 30 foot scoreline, he tied one in 18⁴/₅ seconds. The term "to do a McGonigal" was a sweet kind of praise to reach a roper's ears in those days. He was an artist with a rope.[2] When steer roping was eventually outlawed in most western states he began entering calf roping events.

In 1919 he won first place, and $1,000, at the Arizona State Fair in Phoenix, with the best time for three calves.

McGonigal was killed at Sacaton, Arizona, on October 24, 1921, when he contacted an electric power line carrying heavy voltage. He was buried in the McGonigal family plot at Lovington, New Mexico.[A4,3]

J. ELLISON CARROLL. In 1862 he was born in San Patricio County, Texas. He moved to the Panhandle of Texas and herded cattle until the late 1890s. He also ranched in Greer County, Oklahoma, for a time. During this era he made a name for himself "fairgrounding" steers.

In 1904 he and Clay McGonigal met and had a three day steer roping. Each roped 28 head and Carroll averaged 40.3 seconds to McGonigal's 46.1 seconds average. The steers reportedly weighed between 800 and 1,000 pounds. In 1905 steer roping was banned in Texas, but Carroll, undaunted by the law, took his competition to Oklahoma.

He also ranched with his brother, R. M. Carroll, in Oklahoma, but eventually returned to Crockett County, Texas, where he bought 20 sections and established the 07 Ranch. He was truly a cattleman of the old school. He had also been a trail driver during that brief era. He started the Big Lake Meat Market, served two terms as sheriff of Reagan County and several years as a county commissioner. He died in 1942.[1]

CHAPTER THREE

THE RIP-ROARIN' TWENTIES

The 1920s began with a bang. Rodeos were being held in more and more towns in the west and cowboys were anxious to compete. New names were rising to the top ranks in every competition, especially in the roping events. At Pendleton RoundUp in 1920 Ray Bell, from Wyoming, had an average on two steers of 62$\frac{3}{5}$ seconds to win the championship.[18] Cheyenne Frontier Days, that same year, crowned

Group of cowboys at New York, 1925. Left to right, front row: #1 Bugs Yale, #2 Jake McClure, #5 Floyd Gale, #8 Everett Colborn, #9 Bob Crosby. Middle row: #3 John Bowman, #4 Rusty McGinty, #5 Dick Shelton, #6 Everett Bowman, #7 Hugh Bennett, #8 Mrs. Hugh Bennett, #9 Earl Thode, #11 Floyd Stillings, #12 Dick Truitt. Back row: #2 Carl Mendes, #6 Smokey Snyder, #7 Burel Mulkey.
—Photographer unknown. Courtesy of Jack Long Collection

Fred Lowry of Lenapah, Oklahoma, a double winner when he won both the Steer Roping and the Calf Roping.[14]

The Arizona Record, local Globe newspaper announced, *"The first cowboy to tie his calf in twenty seconds or better would win an Overland automobile."* The car could be seen in the display window of the local Overland Agency. The challenge attracted lots of attention. Local waddies conditioned their roping arm whenever their employer, the ranch owner, was not around. Some cowboys even bought stop watches. Unfortunately no cowboy won the car. Lee Robinson won the calf roping with a time of twenty-four seconds flat.[A17]

Homer Stokes, a Burwell, Nebraska, resident returned home from Norton, Kansas, where he saw a rodeo promoted by John Addison Stryker (who later became an outstanding rodeo photographer). Thinking this type of event would be good for the Burwell community, he solicited local businesses to donate $25 each to hold a similar event. The site chosen was the Shultz farm east of Burwell.

The town road-grader prepared a race track, which was enclosed by steel posts and poultry netting. A grandstand for 200 people was built. The bandstand from town was hauled to the farm. The rodeo was held September 28-29, 1921, charging spectators thirty cents admission. A profit of $500 was made.

The businesses participating incorporated and sold shares at $50 a share. They bought eighty acres, sold half the land at a profit, raised a crop of oats on the remaining forty acres, harvested it, then began a permanent building program. Burwell citizens went to nearby towns to promote their rodeo. The program included roping, saddle bronc riding, baseball games and horse races. Local ranchers furnished the livestock.[33]

A HORSE WITH A HEART

The love a cowboy has for his horse was demonstrated at the Chicago World's Championship Rodeo, put on by Tex Austin in 1920. Big tents were used for stalling the saddle horses and Joe Gardner had tied his roping horse, Skunk, in one of them. Anyone who knew of this horse knew he was one of the best steer roping horses the rodeo arena had ever known. He didn't look like much, he was slightly swaybacked, was sort of flea-bitten grey and ugly. But ugly or not, Joe loved that horse and he was a good enough horse to win the admiration of everyone else who knew him.

Joe noticed the flies were very bad in the tent, and he immediately hired two boys, each working eight hour shifts, to keep the flies off Skunk. This may sound like pampering, but it was smart tactics, for flies can drive a horse wild. The better the condition of the horse the better he would work. He carried Joe to the steers so fast and with such precision that Joe won the finals in steer roping, then the championship and a check for $1,000.

Joe was dying, and knew it. He asked his old friend, Dave McClure, to take care of Skunk for him. Dave was as proud of Skunk as Joe had been. Joe died about eighteen months later. Dave never roped off Skunk, for he could see the great horse was beginning to show his age. He retired him and saw to it that he was well cared for.[1] In 1926 McClure and Foghorn Clancy, according to *Billboard*, took Skunk to the '89er Rodeo Days, in Guthrie, Oklahoma, to "let all the spectators see the horse, and let the horse see the rodeo." He was 26 at the time. McClure was truly looking after the comforts of the horse in his declining years.[A1]

Respect was also something that cowboys had for their horses. Hugh Bennett recalled, *"We kids had to make our own fun, and we had fun ever day. That was because every day we did the same thing. We roped*

Bob Burke steer roping at Pendleton, Oregon.

—Photographer unknown. Courtesy of Jim Aplan

whatever got in front of us. We had the best dad in the world. He knew that if we were roping we weren't into something we shouldn't have been. He was also the greatest horseman. I'll never forget, he used to tell me to never touch the rein if I didn't have to. Leave the mouth alone, 'cause the horse only had one, and if you broke those bars in his mouth, he was through."[24]

CALF ROPING BECOMES A COMPETITION

The Fort Worth Rodeo held calf roping, steer riding, bulldogging and saddle bronc riding in 1922. Day money was paid, and riders competed for purses ranging from $300 down to $20, with added money given to finalists on a percentage basis governed by each event. Rodeo bucking stock was shipped in from Wyoming for the event, which was something of an innovation in 1922, as most rodeos relied on stock from local ranchers. Verne Elliott and Eddie McCarty were professional contractors providing the bucking stock. They had begun to develop a reputation across the nation for their stock, which was considered the finest.[11]

Tex Austin produced the very first Madison Square Garden Rodeo, held in 1922. Bob Crosby, a top-rate New Mexico roper, arrived by train, carrying his saddle, gear and a suitcase. When a taxi driver told him it would cost $5 to get to the Garden, he took the streetcar for five cents. In addition to the roping event, Crosby hazed for Richard Merchant in the bulldogging, and Merchant hazed for him. They added Charlie Johnson to their team and entered the wild horse race. Crosby eared down the horse and Johnson and Merchant took turns riding. They won the very first wild horse race they entered. The rodeo bug had bitten Crosby by this time and from then on, although his New Mexico ranch was dear to him, it became secondary to cowboy competition.[6]

Tex Austin also took the first rodeo abroad. Introduced as the First International Rodeo, held in Wembley Stadium in London, 1924, it offered a total purse of 20,000 pounds sterling. The Programme, which cost One Shilling, had a heap of explaining about rodeo to the Brits, especially since this was the first rodeo in their country and many wild west shows has preceded this rodeo. Much was said about the skill, strength and courage needed to be a cowboy and that rodeo was an insurance against *"any possible development of a race of 'molly-coddles.'"* The literature went on to explain, *"The contestants at a rodeo are not paid employees. They do not work on a salary. They pay their own living expenses plus an entry fee in the various events in which they compete. At the rodeos in Canada, Australia and the United States they must pay all their traveling expenses as well. Their only hope of financial reward lies in their ability to win first, second or third place in the events they enter."*[A28]

NEVER ASSUME

A jackpot roping was held at the San Carlos Agency and Breezy Cox came by car. When the other cowboys saw he had his leg in a cast and was on crutches they assumed he was not going to enter. Not so! He pulled out a wad of money and was willing to bet it all he would win. He borrowed a rope horse, caught his calf on the first throw, hobbled down the rope on one leg and threw and tied his calf with seconds to spare over second place. Someone handed him his crutches, he hobbled over to get his "take," got in his car, and with a wave to everyone he was gone.[A17]

Cheyenne Frontier Days had always had steer roping as an event since its beginning in 1897, but calf roping didn't come to be included until 1920. The entry fee was $10 and the purse was $1,000, with three-day monies of $50, $30 and $20. First place won $400 and a pair of calf-skin chaps, second was awarded $200 and a Navajo blanket and third got $50 and a pair of rawhide bridle reins. Nineteen hands entered that first year, which gave the calf a thirty foot head start. Fred Beeson, of Arkansas City, Kansas, won with a time of 45.3 seconds on three head. Quickly the calf roping became one of the most popular competitions with the most contestants. The payoff kept growing as the entry fees were added to the prize money.[26]

LONGEVITY COUNTS

Ike Rude from Oklahoma went to Cheyenne Frontier Days for the first time in 1923. He entered the calf roping and the steer roping and won second in the calf roping. In 1925 he won the calf roping and got the prestigious Douglas Fairbanks Saddle. He won the calf roping again in 1929. In 1931 and 1936 he won two legs of the Sam Jackson Trophy at Pendleton RoundUp for the All-Around. In 1941 he won the steer roping at Cheyenne and won a stop watch. When he was 62 years old (1956), he won the steer roping again and received the Merritt Trophy, a belt buckle with three diamonds in it. For forty-five years Rude never missed competing at Cheyenne. His last year of roping there was 1968 and he was seventy-four years old.[14] Rude's last calf roping was at the Matador Cowboy Reunion in Channing, Texas, in 1971 at the age of 77.[A26] Rude was quoted as saying about a steer he didn't catch, "The further I went the dimmer he got."

Amye Gamblin was a roper of this day who continued his roping competition for sixty-three years, finally retiring in 1985. His nephew, Junior Turner, wrote about the men of Gamblin's era, beginning in the 1920s, by saying: *"That generation of cowboys was the cream of the crop, the very best that Rodeo or any other sport has ever had to offer. They didn't exactly invent rodeo. What that generation of cowboys did, was*

Postcard titled the "Oldest Cowboy on the Range, "Dad" Hickman, age 72." Look at the mass of rope he has tied to his saddle.

—Photographer unknown. Courtesy of Jim Aplan

take the rawest and most primitive of games, combine them with the showmanship of the Wild West show, laced them together with standards and rules, most of which are still in place today, and hammered out the purest of all sports. They nurtured rodeo through its infancy and eventually created the first organized sports union, the Cowboys' Turtle Association. "A12

The Roosevelt Trophy was introduced in 1923. It was offered by the Roosevelt Hotel in New York City, in honor of Theodore Roosevelt, who had been a cowboy and loved ranchers and everything western. It was to be awarded to the cowboy who won the most points at both the Pendleton RoundUp and Cheyenne Frontier Days. The winner had to be entered in a cow event and a horse riding event. Bronc riding and steer roping gave 120 points for first, second was 90 points, and third was 60 points. Bulldogging netted 100 points, 75 and 50. Wild horse racing paid day points, which were 12 points for first, then 9 and 6 for third.

The first winner was Yakima Canutt who won the bronc riding. He also competed in the bulldogging. Paddy Ryan won it in 1924. Bob Crosby won it in 1925, did not compete for it in 1926, but won it again in 1927. Calf roping was added for the first time to the RoundUp events in 1927. Crosby won it for the third time in 1928. The thirty-one-year-old cowboy roped and tied three big steers in one minute and ⁴/₅ seconds. He won first in the calf roping by tying three calves in 62.4 seconds, and he'd bulldogged one steer in 18 seconds flat. The huge trophy was given to Crosby to keep, and the Roosevelt Trophy was retired.[6, 26]

EQUAL RIGHTS?

Four determined cowgirls, Mabel Strickland, Lorena Trickey, Fox Hastings, and Prairie Rose Henderson, approached the Pendleton RoundUp Committee in 1924, asking if they could compete against the men. The request was turned down.[43] However, in 1925, Strickland, in a steer roping exhibition, set a record of 24 seconds.[44] She was also named the RoundUp Queen for 1927 due to her rodeo expertise and popularity.[13]

Jewel Duncan was raised on a west Texas ranch and her dad was a trail driver. She began roping against men in local rodeos. She became

Group of cowgirls, left to right: Fox Hastings, Dona Cowan, Marie Gibson, Florence Hughes, Tad Lucas, Grace Runyan, Ruth Roach, Rose Smith, Bonnie McCarroll, Vera McGinniss and Mabel Strickland.

—Photographer unknown. Courtesy of Jack Long Collection

the first woman roper at the Pecos Rodeo in 1929. Because of her popularity as a roper she was chosen as the Pecos Queen in 1935.[43]

Cowboys were setting new timed records regularly across the country. According to a December 12, 1925, column in *Billboard* magazine, called "The Corral" by Rowdy Waddy, faster times were happening at Florida rodeos. *"At the Tampa Rodeo Lee Robinson lowered the 'world's calf roping record' to 13¾ seconds, then on opening day of the Elks' Championship Rodeo at St. Petersburg, Herbert Myers lowered the calf roping record again to 12³/₅ seconds, according to arena director, Foghorn Clancy."*[14] Although many of the Florida cowboys are called "crackers," because they use a whip instead of a rope due to the thick underbrush the cattle run in, it is evident plenty of the Sunshine State's cowboys are good rope manipulators.[A1]

Financial difficulties at Calgary in 1919 made it impossible to include rodeo again until 1923.[10] But by 1925 the Calgary Stampede had 104 calf ropers entered, 73 wild cow milkers, 68 saddle bronc riders, 61 steer riders and 53 bareback riders, along with 21 chuckwagon race teams.[9]

The rodeo at Burwell, Nebraska, that began in 1921 progressed year by year. E. Pardee was the winner in the calf roping for 1926 and 1927. In 1928 Richard Merchant won, Jake McClure came in second and E. Pardee won third.[33]

COLLEGE DEGREE IN RODEO

College cowboys began competing in rodeo on campuses in the 1920s. Texas A&M drew a crowd of 1,500 for their rodeo in 1922. By 1927 events included bulldogging, roping, wild cow milking, steer and bronc riding, mounted wrestling and jumping. Colorado A&M followed suit and held a Kow Kollege Karnival to raise money to send their livestock judging team to compete at the International Livestock Show in Chicago in 1922. It was so successful they continued the "Karnival" until 1940.[34]

EARLY HORSE TRAILERING

Timed event cowboys had to be creative about getting their horses to and from rodeos, as rodeos began to spread across the country. The roper and 'doggers horse is so valuable and such a big percentage of a cowboy's chance to place in the money, going to a rodeo without their

To transport your roping horse in 1929 you had to make your own trailer, as did Tom Taylor. Note the saddle across the hood of the car.
—Photograph by Tom Taylor Collection. Courtesy of Tom Taylor, Jr.

horse was not an option. Everett and Skeet Bowman drove from Safford, Arizona, to Cheyenne Frontier Days in 1926 with their horse trailer, the first ever seen on the rodeo circuit, which was made by their older brother, Dick, in a matter of a few hours. It took them the better part of a week to make the trip, some 1,000 miles. The roads weren't top-notch, nor was their equipment. They often had to patch a tire or find a stream to park in, to soak the wooden spokes of their wheels.[40] Sam Garrett and Ed Wright, the rodeo clown, decided to build a horse trailer in 1928, to go to a Red Bluff, California, rodeo. They took Ed's clown mule and Sam's famous performing horse, Yellow Hammer, on the trip. It was reported Yellow Hammer seemed indignant to ride next to the mule to California.[4]

Hugh Bennett and Jake McClure were close friends. *"When we were together we roped day and night—calves, goats, cats—whatever we could find,"* said Bennett. They drove to Calgary Stampede from Plains, Texas, in 1929. *"Jake had a calf horse that weighed about 1,400 pounds and we put him in the back of the pickup. I think we bought every tire between Plains and Calgary,"* laughed Bennett.[A11]

ANIMAL ABUSE? NO WAY!

The Humane Society and the sport of rodeo have always been at odds over the Society's concern about the abuse of animals. The concern, in most instances, is an invalid problem, but it must be addressed. Humane issues became very intense in 1926. The State of Washington formed their Humane Society that year and the president declared, *"Complete abolition of rodeo is our objective!"* Various rodeos had their own general rules regarding animal abuse, such as Prescott Frontier Days Celebration, who posted, *"The management reserves the right to withdraw any contestant's name and entry and refuse to allow his stock used for any reasons, to-wit ... abusing stock."*[10] A *Billboard* article in 1928 entitled, "More Light on the California Rodeo Fight," written by Texas Sherman, said, *"After careful investigation I found that the Humane Society of California and the Los Angeles A.S.C.P.A. are not fighting the rodeo as a sport, but an independent organization, known as the California Anti-Rodeo Cruelty Association is behind it. This society has agents canvassing the State who are paid six cents for each signature received, in which the signers have helped make the bill that may cause*

California to lose the rodeo as a sport. Many who signed say they did not read the petition and did not know that what they signed may do away with rodeo. I also had an interview with the Los Angeles Humane Society, of which William S. Hart, famous western movie star, is a director, and a supporter of rodeo. C. B. Craig, president, got up at the meeting and said, 'The only objection I have to rodeo is that it is too thrilling.'"[A1]

A follow-up article in *Billboard* reported that the Anti-Rodeo Cruelty Association of California had appropriated $25,000 for newspaper advertising and billboards that will adorn all cities in California. San Francisco will be allotted 90 and Los Angeles will receive 60 billboards.[A1] It all came to nothing and California has never ceased rodeo.

A special jackpot steer-tying contest was announced to be held at the 1928 Tucson midwinter rodeo. Teams could enter as many times as they wanted if they could produce the $25 entry fee. Purse money would equal the number of entry fees paid in, which was usually in the $2,000 sum. It would attract the largest number of skilled lariat tosses ever brought together in Arizona. This was in addition to the regular rodeo events that also included team steer-tying, which paid a total purse of $900. Calf roping purse was $600, which would be distributed to the winners, and $900 had been dedicated to bulldogging.[A1]

That same year Eddie McCarty, rodeo manager of the International Exposition and Livestock Show's first rodeo, held in San Antonio, announced the purse would be $9,585. Calf roping purse was $1,500 for best total time on three calves. First paid $350, second paid $275, third was $250 and fourth place paid $175. Day money for six days was $60 for first place, second was $25 and third paid $10. It was also announced in a later column that two of the fastest calf ropers in the country would compete—Jess Perkins of San Antonio, who roped forty-two times and had not missed a loop and was always in the money, and John Bowman, who had not failed to be in the money at any contest he had made the entire season and holds the world's record of eleven seconds flat.[A1]

Although rodeo was making great strides in most places there were still some problems that gave rodeo a "black eye." A letter written by Texas roper, Bob DeForest, was printed in *Billboard* magazine and stated: *"I entered one rodeo that had about 200 head of horses, but not being from that State, they would not let me and my friends have a horse to use in the roping contest. We also made a 200 mile jump to a rodeo but it was called off because they couldn't get enough hands. We got*

Doubleday photo of Oklahoman John Bowman, one of the best steer and calf ropers. He was All-Around Champ in 1936.

—Courtesy of National Cowboy & Western Heritage Museum Collection.

a telegram to go near Houston to a 'sure thing' and when we arrived we discovered it was a 'suitcase outfit.' My dad was a Wild West cowboy and worked with Dr. Carver and Buffalo Bill's first show in the early 1880s and encourages me to follow rodeo, but we need to pull together. My dad said he joined an association started by Richard Ringling in 1912, to keep things in rodeo on the up and up, but it was laughed at. Rodeo's our bread and butter."[A1]

Everett Bowman, the Arizona puncher, bound his calf in a shade under 19 seconds boasted the Phoenix rodeo of 1928. The stands howled their approval as good scores were made. Bob Crosby wrapped his calf in a shade under 20 seconds, but Arthur Beloat, of Buckeye,

Arizona, won the calf tying with a 17³/₅ second tie. After sundown Crosby and Herb Meyers were roping calves in a matched contest to a crowd of over 500. Crosby never missed a toss.[A1]

ROPERS OF THE DAY

FRED LOWRY. Born at Claremore, Oklahoma, Indian Territory, in 1892. His family moved to Lenapah, Oklahoma, around 1900 where the noted 10,000 acre Lowry ranch was developed. He had one sister and three brothers.

He roped his first steer as a professional roper in Dewey, Oklahoma, in 1914. He began his rodeo career, stopped to serve in World War I, then returned to rodeo. He traveled from the west coast to Madison Square Garden with his famous horse, Buster. One of his first trips was to Cheyenne Frontier Days in 1916, where he out-roped one of the biggest and toughest fields of steer ropers ever assembled. He also won the calf roping there in 1921 and won the steer roping again in 1924, '25, '27 and '29. Lowry and his horse, Buster, rode the train to Madison Square Garden, and the cowboy rode with his horse. They used the water dripping off a refrigerated railcar to water the horse and drink. By the time they arrived in New York City Lowry had gotten diphtheria, was hospitalized, and did not get to compete. By the time he got back to Oklahoma he swore he'd never go east of the Mississippi again! And he didn't.

After 1930 Lowry also became a breeder of the Hancock line of Quarterhorses and produced some excellent roping horses. He also taught several up-and-coming cowboys who went on to become champion ropers—Shoat Webster, Everett Shaw, and Clark McEntire. A young fellow wrote Lowry a letter asking to come to his "roping school" and wanted to know how much it cost. Lowry really didn't officially have a school, he was just a good teacher. The response the young man got was "it just costs a lot of hard work."[1, 38, A3]

Everett Shaw came to live with the Lowrys when he was fifteen. He did ranch chores and roped steers day after day. Shoat Webster came to live with Lowry when he was around thirteen years of age. Webster's aunt, Kate, had married Lowry. Both boys learned much from Lowry, but the main thing they learned was how to rope, just like Lowry. It was here, under his tutelage, Shoat and Shaw learned how to catch horns, how to yank their slack rope, how to handle the slack, and how to lay a perfect trip alongside a steer midway between the hock and the hip bone. Lowry explained how to handle his horses, how to roll a steer onto its back, and how to get off. He taught the boys how to go down the rope, fight a steer, string a foreleg and tie. When Shoat left the ranch he was ready.[12, A31]

Monroe Veach, a prominent saddlemaker from Trenton, Missouri, designed a special roping saddle according to Lowry's specifications and called it The Fred Lowry Roper. The Quarterhorse of that era was called "The Bull Dog Type Quarter Horse" and a saddle was needed with a wider tree. Lowry also requested a lower backed cantle, so the rider could get off much quicker. Veach also put a double rawhide cover on the front-half of the tree, which made it heavier, but much harder to break the horn out or break the tree, when tripping a big steer. Some of these saddles were also used by bulldoggers, but they weren't for people who weren't extremely experienced riders because it wasn't easy to stay in the saddle.

Fred Lowry died July 23, 1956, ten days after surgery for cancer, at the Mayo Clinic in Rochester, Minnesota. He was survived by his wife, Kate Chouteau Lowry.

BOB CROSBY. Born in Midland, Texas, February 27, 1897. Shortly after his birth his family moved to Kenna, New Mexico, where he grew up on a ranch. He won his first steer roping contest at the age of 13 in Chelsea, Oklahoma. He was known as a colorful cowboy—full of inconsistencies and contradictions—but he was rough and tough, expected a lot of himself and generally got it. In addition to his roping prowess, he rode broncs until 1928. He competed in Madison Square Garden from 1923 until 1942, except 1929, and won the calf roping in 1923, 1927, and 1928. He won the steer roping at Cheyenne Frontier Days in 1932 and 1936, and won Pendleton RoundUp four times. He won the Roosevelt Trophy three times and it was retired to Crosby in 1928. Never did he and wife, Thelma, go to New York that they weren't treated like royalty by the Roosevelt Hotel.

Crosby went to England in 1924 with Tex Austin and his entourage of cowboys and cowgirls. Richard Merchant and Crosby were pickup men, plus they both competed, using Crosby's horse, Governor. Thelma Crosby and daughter, Roberta, went, too. The trip overseas on the ship was long and Bob was a "scrapper." He was in several fights, which were just part of the restlessness of the cowboys on the voyage. This did not deter Crosby, however, as they returned to Europe with Austin again ten years later.

"If a cowboy wasn't tough enough to survive his own doctoring he had no business being in the arena" was Crosby's saying. He proved how tough he was too many times. A horn ran through his leg at a Willcox, Arizona, steer roping. He poured kerosene on a rag, forced the rag into the injury with a nail and wrapped it up with the rest of the rag, refusing doctors' care. Crosby sustained a broken leg at Prescott, Arizona, in 1930 and it never healed properly. First he refused surgery, then the Phoenix doctor who put it in a cast disappeared on vacation and by the time he returned Crosby's leg was in severe burning pain. Most of the flesh on his heel was gone. Amputation was recommended, but Crosby absolutely refused that idea. He resorted to many of his own remedies which included soaking in hot water with

—Illustration by Gail Gandolfi

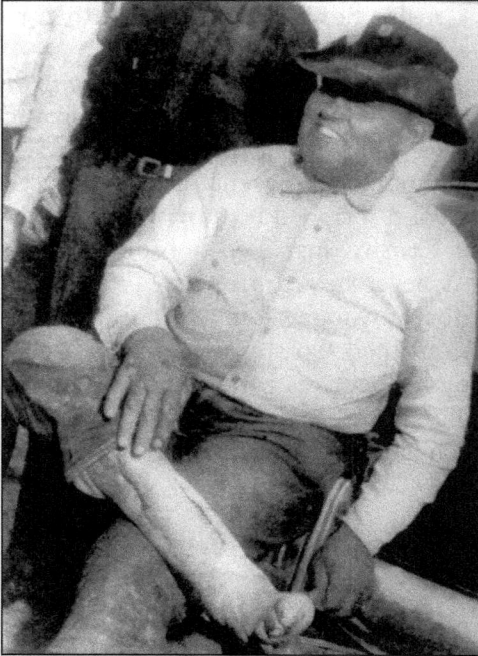

Bob Crosby shows injury that caused him trouble most of his career, BUT never stopped him from competing and winning.
—Photographer unknown.
Courtesy of Jack Long Collection

Epsom salts, putting his leg over hot coals similar to a meat curing method, using fresh manure in which to pack his leg, allowing flies to eat the infected tissue area, and pouring kerosene over the open wound. Nothing worked. Finally Dr. Schrock of Omaha, Nebraska, was consulted. He removed two metatarsal bones, causing Crosby to lose two toes, but in time he healed and had no other problems with it. Crosby took first at Cheyenne Frontier Days the next July in the calf roping. Although he did break his leg again, it healed and he continued to compete in events that did not tax his right leg.[6]

Matched ropings were Crosby's favorite and he competed as often as a worthy adversary could be found. Jake McClure, Carl Arnold, and George and Bert Weir were just a few of those worthy opponents. These competitions went on into the 1940s.

Crosby was a kidder, especially with reporters. He took a *Life* reporter on several rides to inspect the ranch land covering fifteen miles. Crosby and the horses could take it, but the poor New York reporter was so-o-o sore. Another time he took a reporter on a pack trip, spent the night with very meager rations and bedding. The next morning, just over the hill, was the ranch house.[A5]

Crosby was killed in a jeep accident returning to his ranch October 20, 1947. He was fifty years old. A more colorful, tough cowboy with undaunting courage never lived.[32]

CHAPTER FOUR

THE DIRTY THIRTIES

The 1930s were a tough time for many. The Depression had made its deep impression on most everyone across the nation. Having a job and enough money to feed the family was a major concern. The Midwest was plagued by Mother Nature in a way that devastated the farmer and rancher. Drought and wind destroyed the land. The era was dubbed "The Dirty Thirties" because of the horrible dust storms that covered the western part of the country. Top soil was totally blown away and the thought of raising a crop was impossible. Some days the dust was so heavy in the air that a person couldn't see to do their work. Some recall the dust was so thick it was necessary to put a damp rag over their face to keep from breathing in the fine particles that would almost choke off their breath. It was a time when ranchers, farmers, and cowboys, who otherwise were hard workers, industrious and desperate to do a day's work, had to find another way to pass the time. Rodeo flourished and continued to grow in spite of the problems of the day. After all, people have to have something to do and be entertained.

Author Bernard Mason, in a book entitled *Roping*, published in the mid-1930s, said it best: *"All I can say is that I'm infected with roping fever, and it is a hopelessly incurable malady. Not that it is unpleasant in its effect or an affliction of which one would want to be relieved— rather the opposite is the truth of the matter, so deliriously happy is one under its spell."* He went on to say, *"And trying to rope is the way to put it, for no one can rope perfectly—all he can do is to try and keep trying."* Continuing his evaluation he added, *"Now interesting physical effort never hurt anyone, and if exercise is beneficial to the human system, then roping goes down as a bodily tonic par excellence, for no one ever roped without getting a workout. Nothing about roping can be easily picked up. It is a lifetime task."*[15]

Many rodeos were becoming annual affairs by 1930. Steer roping

47

had been banned in most states and calf roping had taken its place in popularity.[38] Jake McClure, a New Mexico rancher, used his "bullet rope" to become the first cowboy to win a leg on the $5,000 Sam Jackson trophy at Pendleton RoundUp, offered by the *Oregon Journal*'s owners, the Jackson family. The term "bullet rope" came from the small speed loop McClure always threw and he threw it like a rock. He put the term "hurry-hurry" into professional roping. Ike Rude won the All-Around title at RoundUp in 1931 with his roping prowess.[13]

Jake McClure used a small speed loop that became known as the "bullet rope."

—Photographer unknown. Courtesy of *Hoofs & Horns* Collection

OLD TIMERS

The Texas Cowboy Reunion and Old Timers Association began as a Stamford community project in 1930. Ninety-eight cowboy contestants took part in the rodeo events, which included calf roping, wild cow milking, steer riding and bronc riding. Only 23 riders signed up to ride steers. Calf roping was the most popular with 59 entries. Joe York of Snyder won first monies on two consecutive days in the calf roping. The second year they honored the old-timers with a special contest. This was a calf roping contest for men who were cowboys before 1895 and were over 55 years of age. It was won by "Uncle Bob" Weatherby of Rotan.[37]

The Rodeo edition of the *Tucson Daily Citizen*, in February 1931, asked William J. "Bill" Clemans, who later became a partner in the World Champion Rodeo Corporation, to pick an "All-American Rodeo team" of cowboys he considered the best of the time. He picked Earl Thode as the greatest living bronc rider; world's best roper was Jake McClure; best bulldogger was Dick Shelton; and Everett Bowman was chosen by Clemans as the champion all-around cowboy.[A28]

North Platte, Nebraska, held their 1931 rodeo with Lou Cogger as stock contractor and John Stryker as the announcer. Roping contest winner was Snooks Jones of Potter River, Oregon, with 104.2 seconds on four head. Jay Snively of Pawhuska, Oklahoma, was the 1932 champion calf roper.[A2]

WHO'S THE TOUGHEST?

It was common knowledge a cowboy was tough. They could endure pain, severe weather, never hesitate to fight when necessary, and the "try" of a cowboy was undying. Junior Turner, a cowboy from Comanche, Oklahoma, wrote the following account: *"Being tough once became a point of contention between two good friends—John Lindsey, who eventually became what many consider the greatest rodeo clown of all time, and Lonnie Rooney, who was truly an all-around cowboy in that he competed and won in all five major events plus being a trick rider and roper. He was also a sometimes Hollywood stunt man and doubled for many early day movie stars, including Mary Pickford. After his rodeo days he became a County Commissioner for Carter County, and served that office with distinction for many years, out of our hometown of Wilson, Oklahoma.*

During the beginning of their careers both John and Lonnie worked on occasions for Red Lyons, who was a stock contractor out of Byers, Texas. One day while the two of them were sitting in a local café, Lonnie announced that he was probably the toughest man alive. This whetted John's interest somewhat and he asked Lonnie how he came to that conclusion. 'Well,' Lonnie explained, 'Indians are given up to be the toughest people in the world and everyone knows that being a cowboy is the toughest occupation there is. So since I am a cowboy and I'm also part Indian, that makes me the toughest man alive.'

John tended to agree with Lonnie but after some recollection said, 'Well, I don't know so much about that. I am an Irishman and Irishmen are as tough as Indians. I am also a cowboy, so I say I am the toughest.'

This sparked an argument that lasted for a spell. They finally agreed that the best way to settle the matter was for each of them to ride a saddle bronc, a bareback horse, a bull, bulldog a steer, and rope and tie a calf— NAKED!

There was a rodeo arena southwest of town where Red Lyons kept some of his bucking stock. That is where they went to determine who was the toughest. John, who later told me the story, said that other than getting a severe sunburn, everything except for the bulldogging went fairly well. The arena hadn't been plowed in quite some time, he said, and was like concrete and full of grass spurs. When he jumped off the horse onto the steer's head and tried to stop it by digging his bare heels in the ground the pain became most unbearable. He said he picked stickers out of his feet the rest of the summer.

I asked John who was determined to be the toughest. He said that question was never resolved. There were no calves at the arena. There was, however, a buffalo cow and her calf, so John and Lonnie tried to pen them, planning to rope the calf. While all this was going, evidently my uncle, Amye Gamblin and Bill Lyons, Red's brother, had slipped up and were watching these two naked cowboys from behind a water tank. As they were trying to pen the buffalo calf they overheard Amye and Bill laughing and became embarrassed about running around naked, so the contest was never finished."[A12]

The Denver National Western Livestock Show and Rodeo included in their 1932 General Rules regarding the protection of ani-

—Illustration by Gail Gandolfi

mals: *"Any contestant who mistreats or in any way enacts cruelty to any animal automatically disqualifies himself in all events, and foregoes any money due him. The manager positively will not permit cruelty of any nature to any animal. It will be the judge's duty to enforce this rule."*[10] Rodeo has, and always will, protect the animal from cruelty, whether it is a calf, a horse, or merely a cowboy's pet dog. Outsiders who are not knowledgeable of the sport are quick to judge, but Denver was farsighted in the decision to include this in their rules.

A TASTE OF WINNING

Junior Turner reminisced about his own early start in rodeo: *"I entered my first rodeo when I was eleven (1933). It was a kid's calf roping at Amarillo, Texas. We got four calves. I missed the first two. I roped the third one, although 'roped' is likely not the proper verb to use. Tangled up would likely be a bit more proper. At any rate, I caught the third calf and for the next seventy-two seconds I was the busiest little guy you ever saw out there in the middle of that arena.*

I placed third, but only because just three calves were caught that day. The next day, I was twenty-six seconds flat and won a day money. All together I won eleven dollars. That was more money than I had ever had before. I thought I would never see another poor day.

When my uncle took me home and told my grandparents what I had done I was so proud I almost burst the buttons off my shirt. My grandfather, probably trying not to appear overly impressed, turned to my grandmother and said, 'Well, we might as well knock this one in the head. He won't ever be worth a darn for anything else. The rodeo bug has done bit him.'"[A12]

EARLY "UNOFFICIAL" FINALS

Madison Square Garden rodeo, the unofficial predecessor of today's National Finals Rodeo, was always one of the most popular rodeos of the day. The calf roping winners in 1933 were Dick Truitt, who had a score of 413.3 seconds on thirteen calves. Second went to E. Pardee with 413.4 seconds on thirteen calves, and third place was Ralph Bennett, with 417.3 seconds on thirteen.[A13]

The Madison Square Garden Official Program for October 1935 had each event described by one of the contestants. The Cowboy's Calf Roping Contest for the Championship of the World Purse, $6,965, was described by Everett Shaw, 1935 Champ [This was a typographical error as the 1935 Champ had not been chosen, it should have read 1934 Champ.]: *"Winning the Cowboy's Calf Roping Contest last year at the Garden was the surprise of my young life. It was the first time I had ever contested in a rodeo event outside of my own home state of Oklahoma. To take the largest amount of day prize money and then the World Championship title was sure some thrill I can tell you.*

Calf roping has been a part of my grind as a cowpuncher on our ranch near Nowata, Oklahoma. We have to do it regularly when we cut out the calves from the herds at roundups, for branding. When a shipment of calves is called for to market as veal, we rope 'em again. So calf roping is second nature to a cowboy.

But I never suspected I was so proficient that I'd beat out all those other old-timers in the World's Greatest Rodeo at the Garden. However, I did it, and am proud of it, and hope to win again this year.

Nearly everything in the rodeo has grown out of the cowboy's work on the cattle ranch. This is particularly true of calf roping.

On the spring roundup it is necessary for the cowboy to ride into the herd which has been gathered together and rope the calves for branding. As each calf is roped, it is dragged up to the branding fire and there receives the mark of ownership.

Cowboy and cowgirl champions of the Rodeo World.
—Photographer unknown. Courtesy of Jack Long Collection

The calf is given a thirty-foot start from the chute under rodeo rules. Then it is up to the roper to catch the animal and tie three of the calf's legs together in as fast a time as possible.

This contest is strictly humane, for the reason that the contestant is not allowed to 'bust' or throw the calf when the animal is caught. The calf is merely stopped. The cowboy then dismounts, runs to the struggling calf, and throws the 'critter,' completing the job of tying as rapidly as he can."[A10]

Hugh Bennett was a take-charge kind of guy. He was right in the "thick of things" when the Cowboy's Turtle Association (CTA) was formed in 1936. He and wife, Josie, kept the very first records, including membership, in the backseat of their car. That year he took a young twenty-three year old roper, Clyde Burk, to Madison Square Garden. Bennett said of Burk, *"For a small man I think he was the greatest roper I've ever seen. He was consistent, and he knew what he was doing and why he was doing it every split second of the way."* In 1938 Burk tied a calf in 11 seconds. He was very particular about his horses. A horse named Bartender took him to three calf roping world titles, 1936, 1938, and 1942.[12]

Tex Austin's entourage unloading in London, 1934. Photo includes Jake McClure, Dogtown Slim Leuschner, Bob Crosby, Dick Griffith and Lucyle Richards.
—Photographer unknown. Courtesy of Jack Long Collection

WOMEN ROPING COMPETITIONS IN RODEO

Cowgirl roping competition became popular by the mid-1930s and several of the major rodeos featured the new event. The Sidney, Iowa, rodeo had over 150 women competing for $6,000 in prizes. Midland, Houston, and Pecos, Texas, plus Pendleton RoundUp all held cowgirl ropings. Jewel Duncan and Isora De Racy teamed up and advertised in *Hoofs & Horns* to do exhibition and competition roping. They worked with Milt Hinkle and Colonel Jim Eskew. It was thought women's calf roping was going to become a regular event, however several strikes by the Cowboy's Turtle Association with various producers caused problems, the most significant toward women was the strike at Fort Worth in 1940.[43]

The main topic of rodeo conversation during the second half of the 1930s was the formation of the Cowboy's Turtle Association. Previously the competing cowboy had little say in the amount of the purses at various rodeos across the country. It was a fact that even though a contestant might get "in the money" at a rodeo, the payoff would be so small he could hardly afford to get to the next competition. By 1936 the cowboys were determined to have their say and be compensated fairly.

When the CTA was first formed, membership was limited to contesting cowboys except for trick riders and ropers. At that time trick riders and ropers had contesting events, paying entry fees; a purse was put up just as the other events. Gradually the number of trick riders and trick ropers willing to travel from rodeo to rodeo to compete dwindled and only a small percentage of rodeos held these two as events, but committees and producers of rodeos began hiring them on a contract basis.[21]

Some of the established rodeos were a bit skeptical of the newly formed Cowboy's Turtle Association. CTA started dictating the rules they expected to be followed at rodeos where their members competed. A letter written in 1937 by Everett Bowman, President of the CTA, to Fred S. McCarger, Secretary of the Rodeo Association of America (RAA—an organization formed in 1929 for rodeo committees, in order to have some semblance of uniformity) requested: *"We the Turtle Association want cowboy judges and flagmen. We want all shows to have their day monies divided 40-30-20-10, as well as final money. If the show does not belong to the RAA we do not guarantee the boys to enter after they get there as we want all shows to belong to the RAA as this is an insurance to the cowboys that the money will be paid."* The letter went on to say: *"We feel that the CTA should not protect a show which is smaller than one hundred dollars day money in each major event."*[A4]

Pendleton RoundUp decided in 1937 and 1938 they could hold a successful rodeo without the Turtles. It wasn't because they disagreed with the Turtles, but having a new organization dictating rules to an all ready well-established rodeo was disturbing. The Pendleton committee knew there were many good cowboys from the Northwest who would participate. In the RoundUp office during 1937 and 1938 a sign read, "No Turtles Allowed." However, by 1939 the Pendleton RoundUp and the CTA had resolved their differences and Turtles headed back to Pendleton. At the 1939 four-day RoundUp the prizes for steer roping and bronc riding were $1,200, with $1,000 for calf roping and bull dogging.[13]

Hugh Bennett lived in Arizona in 1937 and Fred Lowry, the dean of ropers, called and said, *"Bennett, why don't you bring your calf horse, and we'll take old Nig (Lowry's horse) and go to all those ropings up through the Northwest?"* Bennett arrived in Lenapah, Oklahoma, and John McEntire and Everett Shaw decided to go with them. Bennett said, *"We roped steers around there a day or two. We'd get a steer down and practice. Every time we'd get one down for Lowry to practice on, McEntire'd go putting some sand in his eyes, sure made him kick!"*[24]

The All-Around Cowboy standings in 1937 were led by Everett Bowman, number one. Points for the leader were 7,021. Burel Mulkey was second with 5,518 points; Eddie Woods was third with 5,289; followed by Paul Carney, fourth, and Smokey Snyder in fifth place. The top cowboys in the calf roping competition were Everett Bowman, first; Clyde Burk, second; Roy Matthews, third; and Asbury Schell in fourth. Steer decorating was led by Art Lund, then Harry Knight, with Joe Mendes third, and Herman Linder in fourth place. Steer roping was led by Everett Bowman, with Foreman Faulkner in second, Charles Jones, third, and Bill McMackin in fourth place. Team roping was Asbury Schell, followed by Carl Sheppard, John Rhodes, and Breezy Cox sitting in fourth place.[A4]

PROPOSED RULES BY CTA

Hoofs & Horns magazine circulated the proposed rules in January 1938, as requested by CTA.

Rule I. At all shows or rodeos for the year 1938 all entrance fees must be added in each event to prize money.

Rule II. Each rodeo must have as their judges two active cowboy contestants.

Rule III. All members of CTA are not allowed to compete at any amateur rodeo or work an amateur rodeo in any way.

Rule IV. Any cowboy who makes as many as four rodeos in one year shall be classed as a professional, and must have a CTA card before entering at any rodeo contest in 1938.

Rule V. Any member of CTA who leaves a room and board bill of this kind will not be permitted to contest or work at any rodeo until the CTA has been paid in full. They will be subject to a fine also. [CTA was paying room and board bills of competing cowboys who were leaving without paying their bill.]

Rule VI. Instead of CTA giving a 30 day notice to a rodeo that the members of the CTA will work after they get to a rodeo, let each rodeo write to the CTA if they want a guarantee that the members will work after they get there and have it printed on their prize list OK'd by the CTA officials. No member will be allowed to go to any show or rodeo after the CTA officials have passed on their prize lists and judges and raise a fuss. If the contestants are not satisfied with what the officials have done, they should stay away. The officials of the CTA should have plenty of time to see all representatives of the CTA and each representative and president sign his name to the OK.

Rule VII. Any contestant that has contested at any place where the CTA has refused to work, then he shall be fined before he can work again with the members of the CTA. Any time any member of the CTA finds a boy contesting or working on the chutes or with the stock, who has not lived up to the rules of the CTA should report this boy to the management of the rodeo. His entrance fees should be refunded and not allowed to contest or work until he has squared himself with CTA.

Rule VIII. Any cowboy who is paying on a fine should pay not less than $50 down and one quarter of what he wins until his fine has been paid. The first time he refuses or neglects to send in one quarter of what he wins then he is laying himself liable to be put out again and forfeits all he has paid on his fine.[A4]

These rules were reviewed at the RAA Convention in Ogden,

Utah, by RAA representatives and either approved or declined. The results of the Ogden meeting were given in a report by CTA delegates. *"We came to the conclusion that we would not be able to have the RAA delegates accept our requests regarding our appointment of judges and also were advised by nearly all the delegates that while they consider the Turtles the most important part of the contest, they would not stand for all professionals being obliged to be Turtles. It was brought out very forcefully and convincingly, that the cowboy was the greatest sportsman of all and that his whole standing in the eyes of the American public would suffer untold damage if it appeared that contests were no longer open to the world and championships could only be won with a union card."* The report went on to say: *"We therefore settled down and made a compromise, that we feel was fair to all concerned and that certainly placed the Turtles in a very advantageous position, not only as far as the American public is concerned but also in the eyes of the RAA and all rodeo managements.*

We agreed on:

All entrance fees must be added to the purses.

All RAA contests must put up a guarantee for the money prizes they advertise, so that the contestants are sure to get their money after the contest is over.

Only qualified judges will be selected by the various rodeo managements, these judges can be members of the CTA and the list of judges for all RAA shows must be submitted to the RAA Secretary, Fred S. McCargar, at Salinas, California. The Turtles have the right to object through their Officers and Directors to any judge that they don't consider qualified. At the time of such objection cause must be stated in writing and if cause for objection is justified such judge will be removed from the RAA.[A4]

Cowboy's Turtle Association elected the following event representatives in 1938: Calf ropers—Everett Shaw; Bulldoggers—Rusty McGinty; Team Ropers—Johnny Minotto; Bronc Riders—Eddie Curtis; Bull Riders—Hughie Long; Bareback Riders—Paul Carney.[A4]

Hugh Bennett told in his autobiography, *Horseman, Hugh Bennett*: *"In 1938, at Cheyenne one day, I roped an old steer right over the scoreline and got him down. Just as I got to him, he jumped up. I legged him back down and tied him. This lady sitting up there in the stands with Josie, looking through her binoculars, said, 'You can't do that!' Josie said, 'He's all ready done it.' They paid me anyway, but they changed the rules that night. You had to throw him with your horse."*[24]

A MENTOR HELPS A COWBOY GET STARTED

The big money event at Cheyenne Frontier Days at their last rodeo of the 1930s was the steer roping. Dick Truitt collected $1,350.

There was also a new name emerging in the calf roping event—Toots Mansfield.[14] Mansfield was being trained by Juan Salinas of Encinal, Texas. Juan Salinas was a top competitor. He paid Mansfield's entry fees and took a portion of his winnings. He also started him out on a horse called Honey Boy.

Later Mansfield said of Honey Boy, *"I think Honey Boy was one of the best horses I ever rode. He had everything you wanted—speed, calf sense, good break from the box, and a good stop. He could score a calf ten or forty feet. Anybody could rope on him. He would work the same for a green kid as a seasoned pro."*[38]

Juan Salinas' nephew, Ricardo Palacios, spent the last ten years of Juan's life with him and was privileged to hear his uncle tell the stories of his rodeo days until his death at age 94. He said, *"Tio Juan told the story this way. It was about 1937. Juan was roping around the south Texas arenas, and was matched against a young unknown who was reputed to be an excellent calf roper. His name was Toots Mansfield.*

The roping was in Uvalde, Texas. It was a ten calf match, and after it was all over and done, Juan won the match. After the match Toots approached Juan about helping him get into professional rodeo. Juan said that Toots did not have much of a horse, nor equipment, and definitely did not have the money. But Juan noticed, of course, that Toots was an excellent roper, and particularly good at flanking big calves, a Toots trademark.

Tio Juan explained to Toots that he could sponsor him in rodeo, put up the horse, the equipment, the travel expenses, the entry fees, but that the usual deal was a fifty/fifty cut. Toots understood and accepted. This was their relationship for the next four or five years. My mother, Juan's sister, told of Toots coming to the Salinas Ranch near Encinal, Texas, every year in late winter to start training and getting the horses and themselves in shape for a new year on the circuit. Toots stayed at the house with the Salinas for a couple of weeks. When the ropers were ready, they were off on another glorious tour of the nation. I spoke to Toots for the first and last time in 1990. I asked him to nominate Tio Juan for the Hall of Fame in Oklahoma City. He did, and in 1991, I took Tio Juan to the Hall to accept his award."

MORE NEW ORGANIZATIONS

CTA was not the only new organization emerging. Although there had been earlier college-sponsored rodeos, Cal Godshall of Victorville, California, put on a college rodeo in 1939. His daughter, Jeannie was a cowgirl and a college student at the time. Forty-four men and eighteen co-eds from ten California colleges and one Arizona school participated. Professional cowboys attended, including champion Fritz Truan, Burel Mulkey, Andy Jauregui, John Bowman, and Smokey Snyder, as well as several movie stars. It was such a success everyone went home planning more intercollegiate rodeos.[34]

The Southwest Rodeo Association was organized the same year, primarily to permit contestants of the Southwest, where a large number of calf ropers and bulldoggers originate, to accumulate points that would decide the grand champion as well as the champions in various events at the end of the season in their own area. It had been necessary for these southwestern contestants to travel a great distance, either to the Northwest or California, where other associations were primarily represented. Not all cowboys desiring to compete could travel so far, due to employment and family obligations. Requirements for membership were that the rodeos conform to the rules of the CTA by adding entry fees, and paying a purse in each event commensurate to their standard. A member of CTA was placed on the board of directors of the Southwest Rodeo Association and had a voice in the operation of the association.[A4]

The Rodeo Association of America, which was organized in 1929, had completed eleven successful years by the end of the thirties. Their twelfth convention was to be held in Houston, Texas, March 21 and 22, 1940. The champion cowboys of 1939 were to receive their trophies. Their monthly magazine listed the following donors' representatives, the prizes to be given, and the cowboys receiving them; *"Dick Cronin, Advertising Manager of Levi Strauss Company will present $500 cash to Paul Carney, of Galeton, Colorado, World's Champion Cowboy for 1939. Jack Story, Announcer and representative of Montgomery Ward Company, will present $200 to Dick Griffith, Champion Bull Rider; $100 to Hoyt Hefner, Wichita Falls, Texas, second in the bull riding; $75 to Kid Fletcher of Hugo, Colorado, third in Bull Riding. A representative of Keyston Saddle Company will present to Dick Truitt of Stonewall, Oklahoma, Champion Single Roper, a $250 silver mounted saddle. This saddle has been on display at the hotel in Houston for the past month.*

Harry Rowell, Rodeo Stock Contractor and operator of many western rodeos, of Hayward, California, will present $200 to Fritz Truan, of Lancaster, California, Champion Bronc Rider. A representative of Salant and Salant, of New York, makers of Uncle Sam Work Shirts, will present Burel Mulkey, of Isabella, California, former World's Champion Cowboy, $50 for second place in Bronc Riding. Mr. Justin, of H. J. Justin & Sons, Fort Worth, Texas, makers of Justin Boots, will present $100 to Asbury Schell, of Tempe, Arizona, Champion Team Roper. He also will present $50 to John Rhodes, Sombrero Butte, Arizona, second in Team Roping. Harry Taylor of the Plymouth Cordage Company, representing the N. Porter Saddle Company of Tucson and Phoenix, Arizona, will present $100 to Toots Mansfield, of Bandera, Texas, Champion Calf Roper. A representative of West Holliday Company, New York, Chicago and San Francisco, newspaper advertising representatives, will present $50 to Everett Shaw of Stonewall, Oklahoma, second in Calf Roping. A representative of Charles S. Howard Buick Automobile Company, of San Francisco and Los Angeles and owner of famous horses, Seabiscuit and Kayak II will present Ray Mavity, of Helena, Montana, Champion Steer Decorator, with $100 and Frank McDonald, of Maycroft, Canada, second in Steer Decorating, with $50. A representative of the John B. Stetson Company, of Philadelphia, Pennsylvania, makers of Stetson Hats, will present $100 to Harry Hart, of Pocatello, Idaho, Champion Steer Decorator. Roy Ritner, Manager of the Pendleton RoundUp and a Director of the Rodeo Association of America, will represent Hamley & Company, Pendleton, Oregon, makers of saddles and cowboy outfits, and will present to Dick Griffith, of Oakdale, Arizona, $100 for being in twenty-fifth place in the national championship contest in 1939."[A21]

In the same RAA magazine the General Rules of the RAA were listed, including the definition of each event and how it was to be judged and scored. In the roping events the following were defined: Calf Roping, Single Steer Tying, Single Dally Steer Roping, Dally Team Roping and Team Tying.

Calf Roping: Two loops were permitted, rope can be dallied or tied hard, contestant must dismount, go down rope and throw calf with hands and cross and tie any three feet.

Single Steer Tying: To be a qualified, catch rope must be on steer and tied to saddle when roper starts the tie. Two ropes can be used, steer must be roped around horns, over head or half head, or around neck, and loop may include one front foot. Steer must be thrown and three feet crossed and tied. After roper signals, a completed tie horse is then brought toward the steer to give ample slack for judge to determine a fair catch.

Single Dally Steer Roping: Only one throw allowed. Roper must dally to stop steer. No tied ropes allowed. Time taken when horse has been brought to a stop facing steer with rope tight.

Dally Team Roping: Allows each member to carry only one rope. Each team allowed four throws in all. Roper must dally to stop steer. Time is taken when both horses are facing the roped steer in line with tight ropes.

Team Tying: Allows two loops on head and heels. Both ropes must be on the steer when tie is started. Steer must be tied with both feet below the hocks. Steer may be tripped, stretched or tailed down.[A21]

An article in a July 1939 *Hoofs & Horns* issue entitled "Rodeos of Today" had various men in rodeo give their views of the great Western sport as it was conducted in 1939. Cy Taillon, an ace rodeo announcer of that time and for many years, said about roping: *"It is interesting to note the reaction of rodeo fans in different sections of the country. In the South and Southwest, roping seems to command the major interest and from these sections come the game's finest handlers of the hemp such as Everett Bowman, Jake McClure, John Bowman, Breezy Cox, Bob Crosby, Hugh Bennett, John and Tom Rhodes, Juan Salinas, Carl Sheppard, Buck Sorrels and a host of others of equal or near equal caliber. In these sections all roping events command the closest attention and the competition is the keenest to be seen anywhere. While with a few exceptions, calf roping is the only roping event scheduled on the northern shows, invariably you will find the Southwest cowboy entries walking away with the first monies in their pockets."*[A4]

ROPERS OF THE DAY

JAKE McCLURE. Born in Amarillo, Texas, November 2, 1900. His father, Pat, was a rancher in the Panhandle of the state but moved to New Mexico when Jake was just a little guy. Just two years old, Jake started carrying a rope, and by the age of five he was dangerous with all the animals on the ranch—cats, dogs, goats, chickens, calves, and even other children. He didn't finish grade school, but went to work on ranches and was known for his ability to break and train good roping horses. He began rodeoing in the early 1920s, but being caught by an occasional promoter known to run off with the money, he did not rodeo full time until 1928.[12]

McClure stayed in excellent condition, never smoked, and only drank on rare occasions. He always wore a tie, whether he was competing or working on a ranch, and was always neatly groomed. Breezy Cox said, *"McClure wore the tie so that if he missed roping a calf he could hang himself."* He won the calf roping at Cheyenne in 1930 and the steer roping in 1933. He won the calf roping again in 1934 by roping three calves with an average of 19.4 seconds. At Denver National in 1933 he averaged 16.2 seconds on four head of spirited Hereford calves. At Billings, Montana, he roped four head in an average 14.2 seconds and was paid off with 620 silver dollars.

He married Catheryn Mathews in 1933 and bought a ranch west of Lovington, New Mexico. They went to England with Tex Austin in 1934. Legs, his good roping horse, went, too. On the trip over, Legs ate too much and with no opportunity for exercise was in bad shape once they arrived. It took awhile before he could be used for roping. Unfortunately, shortly after the rodeo commenced, the English Humane Society took such a bad view of roping, it was eliminated and McClure didn't win a dime. It took practically all he had to get him, his wife, and Legs back to the United States.

McClure was determined to win back the money he'd spent getting back from England and hit the rodeo trail with a vengeance. Will Rogers came to see McClure rope after he heard he had won the calf roping with a time of 15 seconds flat. He told McClure he would pay him one hundred dollars for every calf he could rope consecutively in 15 seconds. McClure won $700. The eighth attempt ended the challenge when, as he jumped off his horse, he nearly severed his finger when it got caught between the rope and the silver plating covering the saddle horn. A quick, efficient medical crew saved his finger.

Tragedy struck the roper when he lost both his good roping horses, Legs and Silver, the same week in 1937. Silver was given the Prince of Wales Rope Horse Trophy at Calgary Stampede in 1931. Legs died suddenly while grazing and Silver was hit by a car. McClure was devastated. He continued to rope, but it was never the same. His last roping check was in 1939 at San Francisco's World Fair Rodeo. On July 3, 1940, McClure roped a steer on his ranch, the steer cut back and the rope jerked the horse down on top of the cowboy. He never regained consciousness and died six days later at Lovington, New Mexico.[12]

In 1955 Jake McClure was the first inductee recognized by the National Cowboy & Western Heritage Center Hall of Fame. The museum didn't actually open until ten years later.

EVERETT BOWMAN. Born in 1899 in Hope, New Mexico, of Irish and Dutch extraction. His father ran an "all-purpose" store found in every small western town and had a ranch about twenty miles from town. Although Everett leaned heavily toward being a cowboy, his father was determined he would follow in his footsteps and be a merchant. Mr. Bowman had no use for the cowboys who would come in his store with their meager wages and buy "beans and fixin's."

At fifteen years of age Everett ran away from home and headed to Arizona by any means he could find. He got a job on the Double Circle Ranch as a horse wrangler. He got fired for sleeping too much and getting lost one time too many when going to find stock. He then worked at the Three C outfit breaking horses and learned to rope. His first big rodeo was Salt Lake City in 1924 where he entered the bulldogging. He really didn't know how to bulldog and came out looking like raw beefsteak. His second rodeo was Oklahoma City, but it took hocking his saddle to get enough money to get there. The last day of the rodeo he won some day money bulldogging.

He always entered the calf roping and the bulldogging, but had been known to work every event. He won the All Around Cowboy World Championship in 1935 and 1937. He also held the Champion Bulldogging title in 1930, 1933, 1935 and 1938, and was World Champion Calf Roper in 1929, 1935 and 1937, and Champion Steer Roper in 1937. This versatile cowboy became the first president of the newly formed Cowboy's Turtle Association in 1936. His last rodeo was Madison Square Garden in 1943. During his career he won 18 buckles, four saddles, eight loving cups, and every event is represented in these prizes. He was six feet two inches and weighed around 200 pounds.

He was killed October 25, 1971, at age 72, in a Cessna 172 airplane accident flying between Boulder City, Nevada, and his Wickenburg, Arizona, home. He was alone and had been visiting his son, Roger, and family. He was reported missing on Monday but the crash site was not found until Wednesday.

RICHARD MERCHANT. Born in Eddy County, New Mexico, on July 9, 1896, and grew up on his father's ranch near Carlsbad. Always

Everett Bowman, first president of the Cowboy's Turtle Association.
—Photo by Devere Helfrich, 1937.
Courtesy of National Cowboy & Western Heritage Museum Collection

running away, he quit school at age fourteen. His father wanted him to get more schooling and made a deal with him that he would get him a job on the H Slash Ranch if he would continue his schooling, which he did for several years.

He worked on other ranches and went into the military for World War I. He said, *"When I began rodeoing they were not highly praised and fellows who worked the shows were called 'carnival boys.' There was a law in New Mexico against roping cattle under time so we roped goats. We had a bunch of practice goats."*

His first win was for $500 in Midland, Texas. In 1923 he won the calf roping in Madison Square Garden and pocketed $1,500. He won the Calgary Stampede calf roping for 1927, 1928, and 1930. He won Prescott, Arizona, roping in 1926 and 1933. He won many other ropings across the country—Salinas, Washington, Philadelphia, Deadwood, Cheyenne and Reno. He was named RAA 1932 World's Champion Calf Roper and in 1935 he won the RAA World Champion Steer Roping. He was injured at Pendleton RoundUp in 1936 roping steers, which ended his competitive years. However, he continued in the rodeo arena as arena director and working with roping stock.[A11]

SPECIAL HORSES

SONNY JIM. A thoroughbred colt that nobody seemed to want. Billy Wilkinson bought him from a horse breeder for $35. The breeder told Billy to see if he could do anything with him; if he couldn't, bring him back. Billy trained him to be a first-class cow horse. He then sold him to his brother, Jim, who used him for calf roping. The minute the barrier was down, the horse was off, taking the shortest route to the calf, giving his rider a clear throw. Jim threw his loop, sliding to a dusty stop. Sonny Jim began to back away, keeping the rope taunt. The minute Jim threw his hands in the air signifying his tie was complete, the applause was deafening. Not just for Jim, but also for Sonny Jim. You see, Jim Wilkinson rides Sonny Jim with no bridle—no bit—no reins to guide him. This special horse knew what was needed to be done, and did it with ease and sureness. A special one, indeed.[A4]

STREAK. Owned by Dick Truitt, of Stonewall, Oklahoma, Streak was killed in a highway accident in September 1939, a few miles out of

Woodward, Oklahoma. Truitt and Bob Crosby were enroute to the rodeo at Pendleton, Oregon. The trailer carrying Streak and Crosby's horse broke loose and went across the ditch, breaking Streak's neck and his back.

Streak had carried more cowboys who won roping championships than any other horse in the world, at that time. Truitt had bought Streak from Crosby three years before, after he had sustained a broken jaw in a similar wreck. Broken jaw and sore body Streak went into the arena with Truitt, plus numerous other ropers, winning events at Cheyenne, Pendleton, Woodward, and many other major rodeos. Truitt won the 1939 Steer Roping Championship. Streak was buried near the chutes of the Woodward rodeo grounds.[A4]

CHAPTER FIVE

THE FORTIES—WAR & RATIONING

World War II had shaken the world by the early 1940s and the unrest had sent many Americans to fight for our country. Cowboys were no exception. Many cowboys were the first in their communities to serve our country. A cowboy's patriotism has always run high. Everett Bowman, president of the Turtles, during the 1942 Cheyenne Frontier Days, was concerned that the rubber shortage caused by World War II might curtail the cowboys' travel in the use of cars and horse trailers, and cause a shutdown of rodeos. The ropers, however, were more worried by the depleted supply of manila ropes.[14]

Another dilemma continued to thwart rodeo back home. They continued to fight the war to get competing cowboys and rodeo the media coverage they deserved. A *Western Horseman* article, "Modern Cowboy Contestants" in the 1939 July/August issue by Bruce Clinton deplored the lack of coverage of rodeo by sportswriters. *"If all athletes had to pay entrance fees such as rodeo contestants have to pay—which is often as much as fifty dollars in the roping events—I am sure there would be lots fewer sporting events held in the country,"* he commented.[10]

The Tucson rodeo had 191 contesting Turtle members in 1941, and their entry fees totaling $5,040 was added to the purse provided by the Tucson committee. Jess Goodspeed copped the calf roping prize with a three-day total of $57^2/_5$ seconds, with Clay Carr, Buck Goodspeed and Clyde Burk placing in 2nd, 3rd and 4th place. The Salt Lake City rodeo called Covered Wagon Days had stock furnished by Leo Cremer. Fast Brahma calves were used in the calf roping. Carl Shepherd took final money when he made his tie in 15 seconds flat.[A4]

Once in a while it takes a complete flop to make rodeo committees realize how important it is to have a well run rodeo to keep the spectators interested and in their seats. Louisiana State University, at Baton Rouge, held a rodeo that turned out to be a "stinker." It left a bad taste in the mouth of all who attended who were familiar with the professionalism of an RAA-run rodeo. This rodeo certainly was not! The "movers and shakers" made a beeline to Colorado Springs to see a rodeo produced by Leo Cremer, a well-known top-rated rodeo producer. After watching the superbly executed event by Cremer, the officials of LSU signed a contract with Cremer to produce the 1940 rodeo in Baton Rouge. A coliseum on the campus holding 8,500 spectators was picked as the site. Four major events, with a purse of $900, plus added entry fees, enticed the best cowboys to attend. Some of the best times in calf roping were made and tied with a 15$^2/_5$ seconds run by Amye Gamblin and Jess Goodspeed. Clyde Burk wrapped his veal in 15$^3/_5$ seconds, while Buck Echols lowered all show marks with a fast 14$^8/_{10}$ seconds. They used 260 pound Brahma calves and the winners were Clyde Burk, Buck Echols, Buck Goodspeed, and Leo Brannan.[A4]

Cowboys waiting for the rodeo to begin, left to right, Front row:. Everett Shaw, Hughie Long, Dick Truitt, Clyde Burk, Shorty Hill, Horbart Flowers, Hershall, Peavine Slim. Back row, left to right: Joe Orr, Leo Murray, Lynn Huskey, Herb Myers, Lonnie Rooney, Jim Whiteman, "Heavy" Henson, Pete Adams, Barton Carter.

—Photographer unknown. Courtesy of Jack Long Collection

NO CALF ROPING—NO TURTLES!

The National Western Livestock Show & Rodeo in Denver had not had calf roping on their program until the Cowboy's Turtle Association asked them to add it to their January 1941 rodeo. Denver officials said "No." The CTA Board of Directors took a vote as to whether or not they (the CTA members) should work the Denver show. The vote was five to two NOT to work it, unless calf roping was added. When the Denver representatives were advised of this decision, they renegotiated and calf roping was added to the program. As of 1941 the National Western became an accredited CTA rodeo, reported Bill Clemans, secretary of the CTA.[A4]

MATCHED ROPINGS

Matched ropings were quite popular during the forties. Carl Arnold and Bob Crosby had a contest at Carlsbad, New Mexico, on May 4, 1941, with a purse of $2,000. Each roper put up $1,000, but many spectators attended and many side bets were made on the match. Crosby had also done some side betting on the match. Arnold held the world's record in steer roping at the time—16 seconds flat. Steer roping had been taboo in New Mexico for twenty-five years, so the fans were thrilled to have the opportunity to witness these great ropers on their home turf. The grandstand filled to capacity, and then some.

Arnold and Crosby were to rope twelve big, wild, Mexican steers each. In steer roping the roper drops a loop over the animal's head or horns, let the rope trail down the steer's side and around its hind quarters. The speed of the horse causes the rope to trip and throw the steer violently enough to stun it momentarily. At least that is the aim of the roper. If he succeeds, the roper can tie the steer's three legs before the steer can offer much resistance.

Crosby had a serious injury to his leg. His bad leg was encased in his boot and a brace that he and the blacksmith had contrived. It would be necessary for him to hop, hobble—whatever it took—to tie each of his steers. Crosby rode June Bug, and Arnold rode Big Red. When all twenty-four steers were roped and the scores were totaled, Crosby had 575.8 seconds and Arnold had 579.6 seconds. Crosby had won by a hair over three seconds!

Pasture roping, a common sport during the 1940s era. Note the timer on horseback.
—Photograph by Van Nocker. Courtesy of Imogene Veach Beals

REMATCH

Crosby and Arnold had a repeat match at Roswell, New Mexico, on June 29, almost two months later. Another twelve steers each, were to be roped. On his eighth head, Crosby threw his rope, but his horse went down and so did Bob. He didn't get up. Rumors went flying through the grandstand that Crosby had broken his neck. He was carried out of the arena on a stretcher. At the hospital the doctor's diagnosis was that he had a severe concussion. Arnold won by default, not the way he had hoped to win the match.[6]

NEW IDEAS & INVENTIONS

New inventions were tested and tried from time to time in rodeo, just as in other sports and businesses, across our country. Some worked and some did not. An article in *Hoofs & Horns* March 1940 issue entitled "A Real Steer Starter" stated, "*Rodeos throughout the country are finding the new Special Rodeo Wasp Model Kow-Kicker the original electric prod, a big help in starting each event in a sure-fire man-*

ner. By its proper use, the Kow-Kicker starts the animals out of the chute in a thrilling manner that's sure to please the spectators. Its automatic switch and convenient length safeguard both the operator and the animal from any injury. Kow-Kicker is unique in construction and performance. It delivers a high voltage shock at safe low amperage instantly at the touch of the automatic switch, and can be relied upon for long performance at exceptionally low battery cost."[A4] This was a great innovation in its day and considered to be an improvement in the event. All steers would begin with the same response to the newly devised prod, giving competitors a more even, fair start.

STANDARDIZED RODEO, FINALLY

Hoofs & Horns was the primary magazine to publish rodeo related information in the early 1940s. An article in the July 1941 issue gave comments from various people in the world of rodeo about the development of the sport. An excerpt from that issue explained "*During the past few years Rodeo has developed from the old-time roping and riding contests into well regulated performances with standardized rules to make for fairness to contestants, stock and producers. The following are presented from various phases of Rodeo, each one written by someone well qualified to speak on his particular phase.*" L. B. Sylvester, president emeritus of the Rodeo Association of America said, in part: "*The spirit of 'contest' was born and bred in the old 'gang' long before we ever heard of organized rodeo. Sundays were horse races, calf ropings and bulldoggin,' and very often horse races with neighboring ranches—. I pay my respects to President Hoffmann's recent letter voicing the necessity for cooperation, understanding, bigness of soul, and greatness of heart and aim of all those connected with the SPORT.*" Fred S. McCarger, secretary of the Salinas, California, rodeo, made reference to the various rodeos that were part of the RAA: "*No member has failed to pay contestants; they have unhesitatingly enforced the rules for protection of stock; have secured dependable and efficient judging of rodeo events; eliminated unfair tactics or methods of competition; have contests open to all who want to participate, and endeavor to prevent conflict of dates. The public has shown their approval and commendation of those efforts by ever increasing attendance and their enthusiastic interest in this community undertaking.*"

The Cowboy's Turtle Association was represented by Bill Clemans, secretary-treasurer: *"The CTA was originally formed as a protection for the cowboys against, what the cowboys considered at the time, unjust conditions in rodeo. Now as a full-fledged organization of approximately 1,500 members the CTA can look back over the past with few regrets."*

Richard Merchant, of Tucson, Arizona, World Champion Calf Roper in 1932 and World Champion Steer Roper in 1935, and still a contestant and an arena director: *"I began contesting in 1921 and there were no rodeo organizations, we didn't travel by car, we traveled by rail in groups, we were friends because of the way we traveled, and we could all win some money and we didn't pay much attention to rules. When autos and horse trailers came in to use things changed. More cowboys—more competition—some would cheat to win. Some producers put up a flat fee for a purse, and did not include entry fees. This also caused the audience to watch very poor talent. The cowboys are a real bunch of sportsmen and didn't really want to go in to any union as it didn't seem to fit their boots, but finally in self-defense they formed the CTA. Yes, I'd say the CTA and RAA have really helped the contestants. You can enter the calf roping contest, and don't have any worries about the judges, timers, etc., as they have all been carefully selected for their honesty and effi-*

World Champions for 1942, taken at Madison Square Garden. Left to right: Hank Mills, bareback bronc riding; James Kenney and Toots Mansfield (tied for calf roping title); Brig. Gen. John Reed Kilpatrick, president of Madison Square Garden Corporation; Jerry Ambler, saddle bronc riding; Irby Mundy, wild cow milking; Jack Favor, steer wrestling; and Dick Griffith, bull riding.

—Photographer unknown. Courtesy of Jack Long Collection

ciency. You can win if you beat about one hundred top ropers. If you do, you will know you had plenty of luck, but you done'er honest."[A4]

The RAA reported the biggest rodeos in the country, in 1942, according to the amount of money paid to the contestants per event were:

1. Los Angeles Coliseum Rodeo, 1 performance
2. Cheyenne Frontier Days, 5 performances
3. San Bernardino (CA) National Rodeo, 2 performances
4. Salinas (CA) Rodeo, 4 performances
5. Madison Square Garden, NY, 26 performances
6. Fiesta de los Vaqueros, Tucson, 3 performances
7. Iowa Championship Rodeo, Sidney, 4 performances
8. Reno Rodeo, 3 performances
9. Klamath Falls, Oregon, Rodeo, 3 performances
10. (tie)Pendleton RoundUp, 4 performances and Lewiston (ID) Rodeo, 3 performances.[A4]

World Championship Rodeo, run by Everett Colborn, and the Gene Autry Rodeo merged in 1942. Due to a shortage of gasoline, Colborn made arrangements for the contestants' mounts to be hauled on the Rodeo Train from Dublin, Texas, to Madison Square Garden. Allowing contestants' horses to ride the train had not been done before, only the rodeo stock owned by Colborn was hauled in earlier years. Just two weeks prior to Madison Square Garden Rodeo, a "freeze" was issued from Washington, D.C., on baggage cars and horse cars. However, some quick negotiating was done and the mounts were shipped by old-style cattle cars. The roping horses were a little bruised but did arrive by rodeo time.[A4]

EVERY MAN

The majority of cowboys who found the sport of roping a challenge were primarily ranchers or they worked on ranches and did not, or were unable to, pursue the sport full time. To these cowboys it was a weekend or occasional competition. The ropers who did this were the "every man" of the rodeo. Tom Taylor was such a man. He was raised a cowboy. The first rodeo he ever competed in was 1923, when

Tom Taylor on roping horse, 1928.
—Photographer unknown. Courtesy of Tom Taylor, Jr.

he was sixteen. In the late 1920s, when he was working on a ranch in New Mexico, he rode seventy miles to compete in a rodeo somewhere in New Mexico, and won the calf roping. That is all it took. From then on he competed as often as he could. During the next decade Taylor competed in bronc riding, goat tying, calf roping, and an occasional wild cow milking or wild mare race. He even competed in a coyote roping contest in Oklahoma. He was a good hand and enjoyed the competition. He joined the Cowboy's Turtle Association (number 162).

Articles were written in local newspapers about the results in rodeos in small towns in Texas—Rock Springs, Kerrville, Mertzon—and in New Mexico, at Magdalena, often mentioning Taylor's name as winning here and there. He even had several matched ropings. Buff Douthitt, Rodeo Historical Society Hall of Famer, knew Tom Taylor well and said, *"I remember one year we roomed together at Cheyenne. He got along well with everyone."*

Taylor knew he was good enough as a calf roper and went to Madison Square Garden in 1944 to compete against Webster, Mansfield, Rude, Wharton, Everett Bowman, Douthitt—all the "tuffs." Ray Wharton remembered, *Tom and I drove and pulled a trailer to New York and Boston. Tom didn't travel away too far. He ranched near Del Rio and had a bunch of cows.* Laughingly, he added, *"He was a heck of a poker player."*

In the 1945 Madison Square Garden event he drew twelve calves over his month-long stay in New York City. He won day money with a first, two seconds and a third place. He returned to "the Big Apple" in 1947 and 1948 to compete again. Taylor's wife kept records of all his competitions. One of his last ropings was a matched roping against Toots Mansfield at Kerrville, Texas, during a Junior Rodeo. Jack Hoggett and Jim Bob Altizer were matched as juniors in a roping, and Taylor and Mansfield were invited as seniors. Taylor was winning, up until the last calf, which kicked like crazy. Mansfield won. Although Taylor died in 1986 in Del Rio, his son, Tom Taylor, of Georgetown, Texas, has kept all the clippings and papers on which his mother used to keep scores. She also kept the scores of all those he competed against. These mementos and his trophy saddles are the legacy of a man who loved to rope and compete. He was unable to do it full time, due to family responsibilities and the ranch, and eventually in the early 1950s gave it up completely. This is the story of most of the roping competitors of any era—our "every man."

The Cowboy's Turtle Association held meetings during rodeos in 1945 at Madison Square Garden, Houston and Fort Worth. The CTA had been in effect for nine years, and it was decided to change the name to Rodeo Cowboys Association (RCA). The Cowboy's Turtle Association name was confusing to many, and the name had been abused on occasion. The word *Turtle* had no real connection with rodeo. A second major accomplishment was the establishment of national headquarters for the RCA in the Sinclair Building in Fort Worth. Earl Lindsey was retained as business manager, Toots Mansfield became the first RCA president. Fanny Jones (Lovelady), secretary-treasurer, who had replaced Josie Bennett, Hugh Bennett's wife in 1942, resigned. She had worked out of her home in Phoenix and did not feel she could relocate to Fort Worth.[10]

The Goals of the RCA were very much the same as the goals of the CTA.

Toots Mansfield of Bandera, Texas, was mentored by Juan Salinas in his early days of competition. It paid off for everyone.

—Photographer unknown. Courtesy of Jack Long Collection

1. Organize for the mutual protection and benefit of professional rodeo contestants.
   a. To insure a just amount of prize money.
   b. To require that all entrance fees be added to prize money.
   c. To secure competent, honest judges and officials.
2. To raise standards of cowboy contests to rank among top American sports.
3. To cooperate with management of all rodeos where members contest.
4. To protect members against unfairness on the part of any rodeo management.
5. To have honest advertising by rodeo committees.
6. To work for the betterment of conditions and of the rules governing rodeo events.
7. To establish a central place of registration for the rodeos, names of contestants, the prize money, etc.[10]

CALF ROPING ONE OF MAIN EVENTS

Calf roping had become a major event in rodeo and in many places had replaced steer roping contests that had been so popular in earlier years. Steer roping came to be frowned upon in many states. The calf roping competition was fast moving; however, no world record time could be established because every arena had different working conditions, and standardization was impossible. Ten or eleven seconds in which to tie a calf, by 1940s, was considered a record time. The calf roping rules were flexible but it was always a timed event requiring three timekeepers, a tie or field judge, and a deadline referee. The calves used were from four to eight months old, weighing around two hundred and fifty pounds. Common breeds used were cross-bred Brahmas, Whiteface, Black Angus, or Mexican Longhorns, which are quick on their feet. The saddle used by a roper is much lighter than a ranch cowboy's saddle. His rope varies in length, depending on the speed of his horse. The average length of the rope in the 1930s was twenty-five feet, but it has been reduced to twenty or twenty-one feet due to faster horses.[2]

Ropers were "legging" a calf to get him down in this era. The cowboy would pick up one front leg and lift it until the calf fell over. Toots

1945 World Champions, left to right: Toots Mansfield, calf roping; Homer Pettigrew, steer wrestling; Everett Colborn, Managing Director; Bud Linderman, bareback bronc riding; Gen. John Reed Kilpatrick, President of Madison Square Garden Corporation; G. K. Lewallen, bull riding; Roy Rogers, guest star; Shoat Webster, wild cow milking; Ned Irish, Executive Vice President of Madison Square Garden; Bart Clennon, saddle bronc riding.

—Photographer unknown. Courtesy of Jack Long Collection

Mansfield of Bandera, Texas, was the first roper to experiment with "flanking" a calf, which was actually picking the calf up and laying it on the ground. It is said this change revolutionized calf roping and by the end of the 1950s most calf ropers were using this technique unless the calf was extremely big or difficult. By the 1970s legging was obsolete.[A11]

A ropers' show was held at Ozona, Texas, by Joe Davidson on his ranch. On December 14 and 15, 1946, he had 131 ropers, and the purse was the entrance fees, which totaled $5,980. Sonny Edwards and Dan

Jiggs Burk and brothers Clyde and Dee often won 1st, 2nd and 3rd in roping contests.

—Photograph by John Stryker. Courtesy of The Stryker Collection.
Special Collections. Dunagan Library, University of Texas of the Permian Basin, Odessa, Texas

Taylor tied for top honors with 12.6 the first day. Troy Fort took third and Tom Powers was fourth. Toots Mansfield beat everyone the second day with a tie of 11.7 seconds. A free barbeque was offered, free feed for the horses, and a free place to bunk for all the competitors. He also gave the winners of each event a fine Quarter Horse. Not a bad deal!

Ike Rude was a contestant and he wanted to win one of the colts. When the contest was over, Rude was a winner. He had picked out a colt he really wanted, but the winners drew numbers out of a hat for their turn to pick, and Rude pulled the fourth turn. Rude held his breath until it was his time to choose, hoping no one else would select the colt he admired. When it came time for Rude to pick, the colt of his choice was still there. *Rodeo Fans of America* magazine reported *"He was as jubilant as a four year old kid with his first Christmas toy."*[A35]

Dewey (Oklahoma) Roundup was always a favorite rodeo of the cowboys. Everett Shaw beat Ike Rude in a ten steer match in 1945 at Dewey. It was called "a perfect roping," with no errors on Shaw's part. He never missed a loop, never missed a trip, and never missed a fall. Later when wife, Nell, was writing to Bob Crosby she asked Shaw, a quiet man, if he wanted to write anything. He thought a while then said yes, he would. He wrote on the bottom of the letter, *"Ten steers, ten loops, ten trips, ten falls. Shaw."*[A34]

Dick Truitt, of Stonewall, Oklahoma, won both the steer roping and bulldogging averages at Dewey in 1946. He got two firsts and a second and a third in four go-rounds in the "doggin," won two firsts and a third day money in the three steer roping programs, and one third money in the calf roping. Bobby Vincent's report in the *Ranchman Magazine* said, *"He got out in time to beat Buck Goodspeed some five seconds on three 950 pound steers. Buck was in second place until the finals with 73.2 seconds, Ike 'Jitney' Rude was third with 77.4 and Jiggs Burk was fourth with 82.2 and all those times are the number of seconds it took to tie three head of big, stout steers."*[A15]

Toots Mansfield encouraged Buddy Neal to go to the 1947 Tucson rodeo. Steer tying was one of the events and it just so happened that Mansfield was teaching Neal "steer bustin'." A better teacher for that event would be tough to find. The committee had never had this event before, nor since, and Neal won first place with a total two-head time of 78.2 seconds. He won $1,250. Mansfield was second with 78.8 seconds. Teacher and student both went to the head of the class![38]

The Merced, California, rodeo spectators were just leaving the stands when it was announced that Clay Carr, on his horse, Charlie, would rope against Stan Gomez, riding Rusty. Many of the spectators returned to their seats. They knew that the main attraction was that Carr would be roping without a bridle on his horse. Carr, who had been in the rodeo business since 1925, when he was sixteen, won the match. Anyone who knew him knew he liked to be under pressure.[A11]

WHAT'S THE SCORE??

When watching rodeos today we are accustomed to watching the seconds on the scoreboard during the timed events, but that has not always been the case. A Cow Palace rodeo fan wrote a letter to *Hoofs & Horns* in 1948 saying, *"What's the Score??? I know of no other sport where so much depends on the stopwatch, and when I look around and see so many wives checking the accuracy of the timekeeper's thumb, then it is clear to me that in at least the timed events the fans will know— What's the Score? However, from the fans' standpoint there should be something done to throw a little light on the 'judged' events. When I go to a basketball, baseball or football game, or a prize fight, I know the score. There is a scoreboard or something to keep the public informed. When I go to a rodeo I have to hear the winners an hour or so after the contest, or wait until the next day and buy a paper to find out the scores.*

In conclusion, I would hope that there can be a better understanding between the public and the contestants, a whole lot more appreciation of the guts of these boys, and a lot bigger crowd at all the rodeos if the promoters will only let the fans know 'What's the Score?!?'"[A4]

Young Shoat Webster won the all-around title over veteran Bud Linderman at the 1949 Pendleton RoundUp. Webster won first in both the steer roping and the bulldogging, and Linderman, also with two firsts, won in bareback and saddle bronc events.[13]

NO BUGS!

Bud Gilliland and Barney Willis left Yuma, Arizona, headed to the Tucson rodeo in 1949 and were pulling their horse, Bugs, in a trailer. Near Gila Bend a car passed them and shouted to them that the trailer door was open. *"I'll slow down real easy like,"* said Willis, *"so's not to throw old Bugs out."* When they stopped Bugs was not in the trailer. He must have fallen out while they cruised along about 70 miles per hour. They went back and looked alongside the road for him. No Bugs! Feeling pretty low, they notified the sheriff at Gila Bend of their plight and went on to the Tucson rodeo. On their return to Yuma they stopped in Gila Bend, and found that the sheriff had located Bugs in the desert and had him waiting for them, no worse for wear.[38]

COLLEGE RODEO, RAH! RAH!

The National Intercollegiate Rodeo Association was well on its way. Representatives from twelve schools from four states met in November 1948 to elect officers for NIRA. In January 1949 the new representatives met in Dallas, battling a snow storm to get there, and in two days they had created the official organization. Cecil Jones was the 1949 Invitational Championship Rodeo secretary, with the first

Madison Square Garden Grand Entry, always colorful and impressive. The Madison Square Garden rodeo was the unofficial predecessor of the National Finals Rodeo.
—Photograph by Alexander Archer. Courtesy of Tom Taylor, Jr.

NIRA Championship Rodeo held at the Cow Palace in San Francisco. Two familiar names at that first finals were Harley May and Tom Hadley.[34]

Foghorn Clancy's book, *Rodeo Rules & History, 1948 & 1949*, reported the calf roping rules were:

1. Roper must not start before starter's flag drops, penalty for breaking the starting barrier is ten seconds.
2. Roper must make catch that will hold calf until he gets to him, fine for roper jerking down or busting calf with lariat in making the catch, or roper's horse dragging calf for any distance more than three feet, is left to the discretion of the judges.
3. Roper must throw calf by hand, if calf has fallen down when roper gets to calf he must allow calf to regain feet and then throw by hand, roper may cross any three feet and tie, tie must hold until after judge has passed upon same.
4. Each roper is allowed two loops and failing to catch with either must retire from the arena and will be given "no time."[32]

COWGIRL ROPERS

The "grass roots" of rodeo are all the small rodeos scattered across the nation. At these rodeos there are always local cowboys testing their mettle, as well as some of the fairer sex who like to get in on the action. Ramona Merritt, daughter of 1942 World Champion King Merritt learned how to rope from her older siblings and by ten years of age was roping and riding like the best. At the 1949 King Merritt Annual Steer Roping in Laramie, Wyoming, Ramona roped, tripped and tied a big steer as exhibition. She was also a calf roper and participated in team tying. Since the men didn't allow her to compete, she had to be satisfied with exhibitions. She rode her dad's famous horse, Powder Horn, which he purchased from Mrs. Crosby, shortly after Bob Crosby was killed. Later she became a jockey and rode at tracks all over Wyoming, Colorado, Nebraska, and Kansas.[A37]

Another good roper from this area was Maybelle Abernathy Wilson of Mead, Colorado. Her dad started her riding career when she was so young she had to climb up the horse's leg and grab the mane to get on him. Eventually she, and her sisters, helped her dad and mother with all the ranch chores, which included roping, on their home place near Marshall, Colorado.

Maybelle met Don Wilson, a roughstock rider. They married and spent their life in rodeo. They would eke out enough money to go to the rodeo, pay their entrance fees for Don to ride and Maybelle to rope. She was a good enough roper that on occasion if men knew she was entered in the roping they withdrew. Both Don and Maybelle helped Earl Anderson, an early day stock contractor, of Grover, Colorado, with the rodeos he held by working as part of his crew.[54] When they retired from rodeo competition they provided roping calves and steers to various stock contractors, including Walt Alsbaugh. Maybelle drove a semi-truck loaded with cattle to rodeos across the west until 1980. She admitted, *"I finally 'road foundered'! I had about all those white and yellow lines I could stand."* Although Maybelle and Don raised cattle for their livelihood, they also put on many ropings and were the first to bring Corriente cattle to the north central area of Colorado.

These hardy women mentioned learned their craft by working on the ranch and by their strong work ethics. Maybelle will be the first to tell you she loved every minute of it.[A36]

ROPERS OF THE DAY

EVERETT SHAW. Born on Hogshooter Creek, between Nowata and Bartlesville, Oklahoma, on June 7, 1908. Raised a cowboy, the youngster began competing in nearby rodeos in the early 1920s. He was primarily known as a steer roper, however, he won the Madison Square Garden calf roping event in 1934, 1936, and 1939. The New York event demanded ropers not "jerk down" a calf. Shaw was also very involved in the forming of the Cowboy's Turtle Association. His signature is the very first one on the petition signed in October 1936, and he held many offices with the organization. His horse, Posey, was an excellent calf roping horse and was said to have won every indoor calf roping event in which he was entered. Shaw won the World Champion Steer Roping title in 1945, 1946, 1948, 1951, 1959, and 1962. His steer roping horse, Peanuts, was in the Trail of Great Cow Ponies.

Everett Shaw died after heart surgery on November 20, 1979. The National Cowboy & Western Heritage Center changed the requirement that an honoree must be deceased for five years before consideration, and honored him in 1980.

TOOTS MANSFIELD. Born in Bandera, Texas, May 15, 1914. His father ranched but died when Toots was only four years old. He helped his mother with the ranch when he was old enough. He went to work for his uncle, Ed Mansfield, and began roping. Later he went to work for Juan Salinas at Encinal. Mansfield was tall, fair-haired, blue-eyed, and had large hands. He roped well but the ground work was where he excelled. He could approach a calf from either side. Salinas took Toots and Royce Sewalt to rodeos and paid their entry fees. Toots roped for Salinas for four years on a percentage basis. He rode a horse named Honey Boy, which Toots thought was the perfect roping horse—he had speed, calf sense, a good break from the box, and a good stop.

Mansfield was Calf Roping Champion of the World for three consecutive years—1939, 1940, and 1941, then again in 1943, 1945, 1948, and 1950. He won the calf roping at Madison Square Garden rodeo seven times, Pendleton RoundUp three times, Cheyenne Frontier Days three times and Fort Worth four times. In 1948 he was All-Around runner-up to Gerald Roberts, missing the title by $397.[45]

Toots Mansfield roping at Clovis, New Mexico, September 1, 1947. He was the winner of the biggest prize ever offered at that time, $11,500 plus one-third of the gate, a total of $19,800.
—Photographer unknown. Courtesy of James and Jancy Jester Collection

The talented roper also competed in steer roping and team roping. He was the first president for the Rodeo Cowboys Association, from 1945 through 1951. He also began the first official rodeo school in his home town of Big Spring, Texas. The school began in 1958 and lasted until 1964. It has been said he roped well, but was an expert on ground work. He was one of the first cowboys to flank calves, when most cowboys were legging their calves. He seldom got into trouble when roping and could approach a calf from the right or the left side. Willard Porter, long time writer of rodeo with a special interest in roping, said of Mansfield, *"A master at ground work, a student of the business of getting to his calf, never seemed to be in a hurry to the casual spectator. Of course he was in a hurry—a big hurry! He did it by extraordinary consistency and just enough speed so that he seldom made a bobble."*[38]

He died December 16, 1998, in a hospital in El Paso, Texas. He was 84. He was survived by his wife Mary Nell, daughter Deane, son-in-law Harold Kelley, and grandson Paddy Bryne Kelley.

GENE RAMBO. Born in San Miguel, California, on June 12, 1920. His dad was a foreman of the Wayland Cattle Ranch in Stone Canyon, Monterey County. He was a good bronc rider and broke many horses, and taught Gene to follow in his footsteps. Gene was breaking horses at the early age of seven. His versatility as a cowboy was unique as he was just as capable of winning a roping event as he was at winning a rough stock competition. He grew to 5'10", weighed in at 180 pounds, and kept himself in perfect shape.

Rambo was a good high school athlete but left after his sophomore year and turned to rodeo. His first win was at Prescott, Arizona, in 1938, placing in the bronc riding. John Schneider, an all around cowboy taught him to ride bulls and bareback broncs. He won most of his money in the roping events on a good horse named Nita. One of his fastest times in calf roping was 11.2 seconds at Salt Lake City in 1945.

Rambo won first in the bareback bronc competition at the Cow Palace in 1948. He also won third in saddle bronc riding and fourth in calf roping. He became the International Rodeo Association's All-Around World Champion for 1948, and had all ready held that honor two years earlier (1946). What made the 1948 win so sweet is that Rambo had broken his ankle early in the year and did not get back to competing until May. By Cheyenne Frontier Days he was hitting his stride and beat Toots Mansfield in the calf roping event by two-tenths

It was no wonder Gene Rambo became an All-Around Champ. He was one of the most versatile cowboys of his era.

—Photograph by Lucille Stewart at Cow Palace Rodeo, 1949.
Courtesy of *Hoofs & Horns* Collection

of a second, tying three calves in 47.2 seconds. He traveled more than 30,000 miles and entered more than 30 rodeos to win the 1948 Championship.

His ability to ride broncs was not to be ignored. He successfully rode PDQ, owned by Bob Barmby, Rowell's Scene Shifter and Major Lou, Verne Elliott's Ham What Am, Jauregui's Will James, and Kelsey's Snake. He said his toughest ride was on Fox, a Doc Sorenson horse, at Ogden, Utah, that had not been ridden in two years.

Don McMillan, life-long friend of Rambo, told that at the Salt Lake City rodeo in 1947 during a bronc ride, the horse ran head-on into the fence, leaving Rambo hanging on the top. The horse bounced back, dead from the impact. Rambo was shirtless, bruised, and had a deep gash in the palm of his hand. In spite of the injuries he competed in three events that afternoon and three that evening. Then he sat around until 2 A.M. to be paid, loaded his horse and drove 480 miles to Cheyenne. McMillan said, *"I was with him during all of this and it liked to wore me out just watching him."*[A4]

Rambo won the all-around title at Pendleton RoundUp in 1944. In 1969 he said, *"When I started calf roping fifteen to sixteen seconds was good enough to win. When I quit, it was down to eleven seconds. I had to get better or get out!"*[13]

Later he team roped with his son-in-law, Jim Rodriguez, Jr. Rodriguez won the Team Roping World Champion title in 1959, 1960, and 1962 with Rambo as his heeler.

Gene Rambo died of a gunshot wound while on a squirrel hunt near his ranch at Parkfield, California, on February 21, 1988.

BUFF DOUTHITT. Born in southeast New Mexico Douthitt learned to rope early and at age eight was a working hand on the ranch. Bob Crosby invited the youngster to come and spend a winter with him and every time Crosby roped, so did Douthitt. World Champion Crosby took his protégé to Cheyenne Frontier Days when the young cowboy was only fourteen. In 1939 they went to Madison Square Garden and Douthitt entered his first competition there, riding Crosby's horse.

Except for the years spent in the military Douthitt continued to make money roping. One year at the New York rodeo, a modeling agency representative approached the roper and he began a very lucrative career with the Harkrider Modeling Agency, which represented men's clothing, not just in the United States but Europe as well, and

Buff Douthitt was a calf roping competitor who also had an amazing balancing act on a loose rope. He continues his competitive roping career to this day.

—Photographer unknown. Courtesy of Buff Douthitt.

he began modeling in France and Italy. Douthitt became the first "Mr. Lee Rider" for the R. D. Lee Company, and he was a spokesperson for the jeans. He would attend events and rope across the United States, especially playing to children. During this time Douthitt was not only competing in roping events, he also learned to trick rope. He found he had a talent that was quite unique. He could walk a loose rope, in cowboy boots, and spin two or three ropes simultaneously while on the rope, sometimes as high as one hundred feet in the air. Junior Meek, well-known bullfighter of the fifties and sixties said, *"It was a hell of an act. In all my rodeo days I never saw another act like it."*

Douthitt married and had two children and the family traveled with him from rodeo to rodeo. Out of necessity, and ingenuity, Douthitt designed and built a trailer to not only carry his roping horses, but for the family to live in. The trailer was so utilitarian, he had offers to sell at every rodeo. He eventually got into the manufacturing of custom trailers. In time he changed his manufacturing plants from building trailers to building modular homes. He sold thousands under military contracts to third-world countries in need of housing. Eventually they tired of the hectic pace and he sold the lucrative business and moved to Santa Fe, New Mexico, where he got involved in the movie business, supplying tack wagons and a stage coach to various film companies on location in the New Mexico area. He even became an actor in an Italian western when the creative director saw him working cattle horseback. Throughout all his endeavors Douthitt continued to rope competitively. He won the calf roping event at Madison Square Garden in 1946. Fifty years later, in 1996 he won the United States Team Roping championship.

CLYDE BURK. Born June 14, 1913, on a tenant farm near Comanche, Oklahoma, the oldest of five children. He was one-quarter Choctaw Indian, 5'8½" tall, and weighed 140 to 155 pounds. His mother died when he was sixteen and his dad died when Clyde was nineteen. He managed to keep his brothers and sisters together until all were raised and able to go out on their own.

Burk was well coordinated mentally and physically. In roping he had the ability to change directions if he saw the calf change. Hugh Bennett took him to Madison Square Garden when he was 23 years old. He won the World Champion Calf Roping titles in 1936, 1938, 1942, and 1944. He had two horses, Bartender, which he rode to win the first three titles, and Baldy, which he bought from Ike Rude for

Clyde Burk on Baldy, who had an amazing stop. Baldy started his career with Ike Rude, who sold him to Burk. When Burk died his widow sold him to Troy Fort.

—Photograph by John Stryker. Courtesy of The Stryker Collection, Special Collections, Dunagan Library, University of Texas of the Permian Basin, Odessa, TX

$2,500 in 1942. That was a whole lot of money in those days. The very next day he won a go-round at Denver on him and proved the purchase was a good one. Burk was killed while hazing for a bulldogger, when the steer cut under his horse's neck, upending him, and throwing Burk. He died in Saint Lukes Hospital in Denver later that evening in 1945.[12]

TROY FORT. Born December 8, 1917, near Lovington, New Mexico to Mr. and Mrs. Claudie Fort. At fifteen years of age Troy entered a goat roping at Seagraves, Texas, on a borrowed horse. He won only part of the roping and decided to practice more. Jake McClure, well known rodeo cowboy, worked for Claudie and spent hours drilling Troy on how to get down, get next to the calf, and get him on the ground. This eventually became the best part of Fort's roping ability. Fort won the calf roping on a horse named Smarty, trained by McClure. Clyde Burk's roping horse, Baldy, fit Fort perfectly and he was often mounted on him. He matched Fort against Royce Sewalt at Midland, Texas, in 1943, and Fort won riding Baldy. Several other matched ropings on Baldy in less than 30 days, including one match against Toots Mansfield, earned Fort more than $3,600. Fort was World Champion Calf Roper in 1947 and 1949 and twice runner-up for the title. He never flanked more than three calves during this entire time. He legged his calves to the ground by using their right foreleg for leverage.[A20]

GOOD ROPING HORSES

DRIFTER. Hughie Long bought a chestnut stud colt from Dr. Vern Scott of Stephenville, Texas, in 1939 after George Glasscock loaned him $150 to buy the colt. Drifter's dad, Band Time, was a thoroughbred that sired many good short running horses. When he was delivered to Long a few months later, he was gelded.

By 1942 Long became a mounted guard for the Blue Bonnet Ordnance Plant at McGregor, Texas. When he was not working he and other good cowboys employed there held rodeos or did a lot of roping at the plant. When Long joined the service, he was sent to Kansas, and Drifter stayed home. After basic training Long was sent to Brownwood, Texas, and on weekend passes he'd drive to Cresson, where he and Drifter would rope all weekend. In 1945 Everett Shaw was on his way to being a success as a roper and came to try out Drifter. Shaw was a big man, and although Drifter was not a large horse, 14.2 hands, Shaw said, *"He's the best young horse I ever sat on,"* and with that he wrote out a check for $1,000 to Long. Shaw saw he was a top-notch horse, and also did well in indoor arenas, which not every good roping horse could. They missed winning the calf roping at Madison Square Garden by a fraction of a second in 1946. In 1947 at Cheyenne Bill Wilkinson of Lander, Wyoming, was impressed with Drifter's speed and ability and made a deal with Shaw to buy him for $2,000. Wilkinson and his two sons and his brother all used Drifter and in just a few months he had made their money back.[A7]

BALDY. Born on the John Dawson ranch near Nowata, Oklahoma, in 1932, he was sold to King Merritt. He was later bought by Ronald Mason of Nowata, Oklahoma. Ike Rude then bought him from Mason for $400 in 1936.

Rude trained the horse to rope in the tied team roping in Tucson on a 90-foot score, and lay the groundwork for the "dying stop" which he kept all his life. When traveling from Winnipeg, Canada, to Burwell, Nebraska, the trailer caught fire from a recklessly thrown cigarette, and Baldy was burned badly. The first veterinarian suggested putting him down, but Rude took him to other doctors, and finally to Dr. Darrell Trump of Utica, Nebraska, who knew he could cure him. For eight months Baldy stayed in a screened-in stall, so no flies could get to him and cause infection. When he began to heal and get healthy, he was ridden fifteen miles a day for exercise. When he returned to the rodeo arena, he worked so hard it was as though he was trying to make up for lost time. He made money for Ike and every other roper who rode him for the next six years.

Rude eventually sold him to Clyde Burk for $2,500. Rude knew Burk would treat him well. Burk and Baldy won the world title in 1944. Baldy's reputation also grew bigger in matched ropings against Toots Mansfield. When Burk was killed in a freak accident while hazing for a bulldogger, Mrs. Burk kept the horse until he was sold to Troy Fort, who again won the world title in 1947, and a new record in earnings, $18,482. They repeated their title win in 1949 and just lost by $581 to Don McLaughlin in 1951. He made lots of money for his riders, but he wasn't an easy horse to ride. He ran with his head high and back in the rider's lap. He stopped with such force he was known to throw a cowboy to the ground once in a while. His admirers were justly proud of his quick stop. When his rider roped a calf and would pull the loop tight, Baldy would dig all four hooves into the ground and stop in short notice. When he began having heart problems, in 1952, Fort retired him. In 1961 Fort reluctantly had him put down as his quality of life had greatly deteriorated. He was buried in front of the Lovington, New Mexico, rodeo arena where a monument was placed.[38, A4, A11] At a Rodeo Historical Luncheon on December 10, 1970, Baldy was honored as a Great Cow Pony, with a plaque unveiled by Kathryn Burk, widow of Clyde Burk.[A28]

THE PROGENY OF OKLAHOMA STAR. This great, blood-bay, named Oklahoma Star, was a bulldog-type Quarter Horse stallion, which was foaled near Guthrie, Oklahoma. He was owned by Ronald Mason, a Nowata, Oklahoma, rancher who was quoted as saying, *"When I started out to produce roping horses I started looking for a horse that had three things; first was speed, second was good conformation, and third and last, but by all means not least, sense."* This statement was in an article entitled "They Carry the Champions," written by Bobby Vincent, in a column called "The Oklahoma Herdsman" in *Ranchman* magazine.

Since that time Oklahoma Star stamped his likeness on so many outstanding rodeo mounts that it is believed any careful analysis will show that more money has been won on the sons and daughters of this great old horse than on the progeny of any other stallion. Boys like Jess and Buck Goodspeed, Everett Bowman, Hugh Bennett, Bob Crosby, Fred Lowry, Ike Rude, Herb Meyers, Floyd Gale, John Bowman, Jim and Hub Whiteman, Foreman Faulkner, Bill Eaton, and many others own and rope off colts sired by Oklahoma Star. Some of these boys own three or four of his colts. The article went on to say, *"Ask any of them what they think of them and consider the fact that many colts by old Star are being bought these days as weanlings, and at fancy prices by many of our leading cowboys and you'll agree that, as the sayin' goes, Oklahoma Star 'has sumthin.'"*[A4]

COWBOY. His sire was Driftwood, also known as Speedy, by Miller Boy. As a nine year old, in 1946, Asbury Schell bought Cowboy from Abe Graham of Chandler, Arizona, for $3,500. He stood 14.3 hands and weighed 1,035 pounds. He soon had earned Schell more money than was paid for him. Speedy, also known as Driftwood, had a spectacular career on the race track, but Schell turned him into a rodeo horse. He was used in bulldogging, hazing, calf roping, steer jerking and team tying.

Buckshot Sorrells and Homer Pettigrew took Cowboy to Madison Square Garden for their chores of roping and bulldogging. He was eleven years old before anyone tried to train him to rodeo. Asbury said Cowboy's best lick was to put a roper within heeling distance of a steer. In 1947, in a four-steer-average team roping at Salinas, California, Asbury on Cowboy and John Rhodes won two go-rounds, placed third in another, and ended up in top spot in the finals. Over a long score they averaged 17 seconds on four head. At Great Falls, Montana, he roped a calf off Cowboy in twelve flat. He had roped several in 13 seconds, but never in 12. The classy looking bay gelding had a career on the track as a racehorse, then switched to one of the best all-around horses in the rodeo arena. Quite a versatile mount.[A14]

CHAPTER SIX

TOO MUCH WASN'T HALF ENOUGH

Rodeo was on a whirlwind roll by the 1950s, which has been called "The Golden Age of Rodeo." Small towns and large cities were holding annual rodeos and there was an abundance of competitors. If ropers couldn't find a rodeo nearby there was always a jackpot roping or just a group of cowboys roping calves in someone's corral every night of the week. *"Too much wasn't half enough,"* according to avid ropers.

The big war, World War II, was over. Financially the country was in much better shape. Professional rodeo had spent over twenty years working at improving the sport and cowboys who could compete and could get "in the money," at a rodeo now and then, wouldn't hesitate to travel from one end of the country to the other to compete. Ellensburg, Washington, to Fort Worth, Texas, to Madison Square Garden, New York, to Salinas, California, to rodeo was not a big deal to a rodeo cowboy.

JACKPOTS & MATCHES GALORE

The trend for jackpot and matched ropings continued through the 1950s. At Wetumka, Oklahoma, Jess Goodspeed snagged and tied ten calves with an average time of 15.5 seconds per calf, and $^5/_{10}$ths of a second behind him was Everett Shaw. At the Saddle and Bridle Club in Colby, Kansas, Walter Alsbaugh roped and tied a calf in 12.03 seconds. In a jackpot contest J. D. Holleyman, of San Angelo, Texas, snared and wrapped up his veal in 10.5 seconds. Walter Poage, of Hobbs, New Mexico, in a four-state contest, did the job in 9.5 seconds.[A4]

In an article by Willard Porter about steer bustin' he wrote, *"There may be flashier performers in rodeo, but for my money the real salty dogs of the business are the steer ropers. Spot-looping a 900 pound steer from a galloping horse, tripping it and trussing it on the ground, takes more than showmanship, and the men who do it for a living are tougher than coyote gristle.*"[A29] Ike Rude set an arena record at Pendleton RoundUp in 1931 for steer roping with 17²/₅ seconds. Twenty years later, in 1951, Shoat Webster set a new steer roping record with a time of 17 seconds flat. That was also the year that Webster won the third leg of the Samuel Jackson Trophy, and took it home to Lenapah, Oklahoma. This trophy had four other contenders with two wins each in the twenty-one years it had been challenging competitors. Those hopeful ropers were Everett Bowman, Everett Shaw, Bill McMackin and Ike Rude. Webster claimed his fourth All-Around title at the RoundUp in 1952.[13]

Cowboy-raised Ben Johnson, Jr. grew up in northeast Oklahoma, under the roping tutelage of his dad, Ben Sr. He "struck it rich" when the movie industry hired him as an actor. But Johnson had to "satisfy an itch." Regardless of the money he made in movies, he loved to rope. In 1953 he took a leave of absence from Hollywood and spent the year on the rodeo road. He became the World Champion Team Roper in 1953 by winning more than any of his competition, $5,858. At the Pendleton RoundUp in 1950 he set an arena record by roping a calf in 12.5 seconds. His fastest steer roping time, 16 seconds, was in Vinita, Oklahoma.[12]

Shoat Webster on his famous steer roping horse, Milligans Roany at the National Finals Steer Roping, Pawhuska, OK.

—Photograph by and courtesy of Ferrell Butler

Toots Mansfield was matched with J. D. Holleyman, in a ten Brahma calf match, at Leveland, Texas, in the spring of 1953. Mansfield won with 204.4 seconds to Holleyman's 247.1 time. A second match was held with Mansfield against Shoat Webster, at Big Spring, Texas, that spring. Webster won with 189.4 seconds on ten calves to Mansfield's 230 seconds.[A4]

Willard Porter's column "Ropers & Doggers," in the *Rodeo Sports News*, on February 15, 1954, reported on several matched ropings held in Texas and New Mexico. Don McLaughlin held one in December 1953, which George Epperson won, with Sonny Davis, Buddy Groff and Ray Wharton winning the next three spots. The next day Jim Bob Altizer and Sonny Davis were matched on twelve head. Jim Bob won with 162.4 seconds on twelve, to Davis' 250.3 time. Davis' New Mexico backers re-matched this affair. Jim Bob won again with an average of 13.1 on 24 calves. Ray Wharton and Don McLaughlin were matched and McLaughlin won the close match with a score of 173.1 seconds compared to Wharton's 176.3. A match between Troy Fort and Jimmy Cooper was held in Monument, New Mexico, in December with Cooper winning by 1.2 seconds. Once the big rodeos started the new season most of the matched ropings were put on hold.[A11]

STILL GETS THE JOB DONE

The loss of his left arm seventeen years earlier did not deter John Wheatley, of Turlock, California, from being a rancher and a rodeo contestant. He and partner George Garfield won team ropings at various rodeos, and he also placed in calf roping. When roping, Wheatley holds the reins in his teeth, so his mounts have to have a good mouth, but he trains his own roping horses. With just one arm he can shoe horses, make his bosals, and ties the hondas in his ropes.[A22]

The Roping Fiesta was introduced to the San Angelo Stock Show and Rodeo program in 1954. It was roping, tripping and tying steers. That first year Toots Mansfield won the pot after five rounds with 114.9 seconds and took home $1,598. Shoat Webster was second with 121.2 seconds. The following year Webster took home the money, which had increased to $2,246, with a time of 113.9. Don McLaughlin was second with 115.4, and Clark McEntire was third.[29]

Shoat Webster and Clark McEntire got together for a matched calf and steer roping at Copan, Oklahoma, on May 15, 1955. They would each rope six calves and five steers. Webster's total on six calves was 111.4 seconds. McEntire's total was 92.4. On five steers, Webster had 152.8 seconds and McEntire totaled 129.4. They added both totals together and Clark McEntire won with 221.8 seconds against Webster's

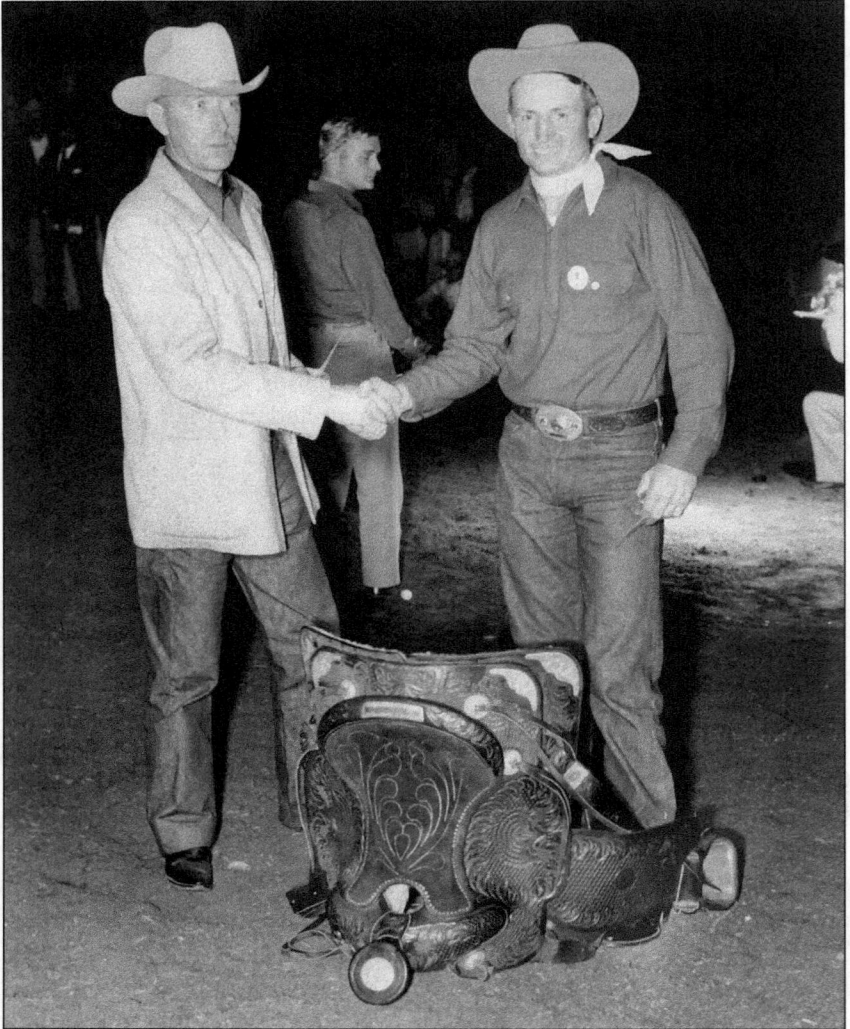

Jerry Armstrong presenting Chuck Sheppard with the calf roping saddle at Cow Palace, 1951.
—Photographer unknown. Courtesy of *Hoofs & Horns* Collection

"Buckshot" Sorrels and "Ma" Hopkins, editor of Hoofs & Horns. *Sorrels, who won the Team Roping World title in 1950, had just won the team roping at Cow Palace, 1951.*

—Photographer unknown. Courtesy of *Hoofs & Horns*

264.2 seconds. A jackpot roping held after the matched roping ended saw Webster and McEntire continue to participate. Webster split first and second with Bud Beason with a time of 11.2, McEntire was third, with 12 seconds, and Royce Sewalt took fourth with 12.1 seconds. Ropers can never get enough roping![A3]

The Ben Johnson, Sr., Memorial Steer Roping had more than 10,000 spectators at the second annual event in 1955. Fifteen steer ropers paid $500 each to rope five steers. Shoat Webster was first with 113.4 seconds, Clark McEntire was second with 121.3, and Everett Shaw was third with a time of 141.4.

The annual King Merritt Memorial Steer Roping's eighth event at Laramie, Wyoming, found Shoat Webster first on five steers with a time of 116.9. Second was Carl Arnold with 121.1 seconds, third was Everett Shaw with 130.1, and fourth was Cotton Lee with 132.9.[A3]

By 1956 the automatic barrier was requested by RCA to be used in all rodeos with a purse of $1,000 or more in each timed event. It was the hope of the organization that by 1957 every rodeo committee and stock contractor would recognize the value of the automatics and they would be used at all rodeos. No specific brand was recommended.[A11]

WATCH OUT!

They say accidents happen in threes. Shoat Webster was heading home to Lenapah, Oklahoma, from Cheyenne Frontier Days and near Grafton, Nebraska, his shotgun trailer broke loose from his car, hurtled into a field, and hit a big Chinese Elm tree, killing both his good steer roping horses, Popcorn and Roany. Webster had just won the Steer Roping the day before. The horses were buried on the Webster ranch.[A11] Popcorn was of Joe Hancock breeding. Webster and Popcorn worked together from 1949 through 1951 and won the Sam Jackson Trophy by winning the All-Around at Pendleton three years in a row.[38]

The second accident happened just about a week later. Clark McEntire and Everett Shaw, coming home to Oklahoma from the Pinedale, Wyoming, Steer Roping, dumped their horses from their trailer near Laramie. Shaw's well-known horse, Peanuts, was shaken up and spent a week at Fort Collins, Colorado, recuperating before returning home. McEntire's horse was not injured but his Chevrolet station wagon was totaled.[A3]

The third accident in this medley happened just about a year later when Shoat Webster was headed to Laramie, Wyoming, for the Steer

Shoat Webster, Toots Mansfield holding his grandchild, and Shirley Webster at a Rodeo Historical Society gathering.

—Photograph by Imogene Veach Beals

B. J. Pierce wins calf roping saddle at the Cow Palace, 1952.
—Photographer unknown. Courtesy of *Hoofs & Horns*

Roping. It was Friday the 13th and at almost the same spot where he lost his two horses the previous year, he spilled his grey steer roping horse out on the pavement when the one-horse trailer gate flew open. The horse, Old Grey, was not hurt badly, only skinned a knee, an ankle, his hip and hock, but a little doctoring and he was O.K.

Peanuts was a bay gelding by Roan Hancock, and out of a dun Triangle Quarter mare. Everett Shaw trained him and roped on him for sixteen years. Shaw's wife, Nell, said, *"I think Peanuts was the smartest horse I ever saw. Our daughter, Mary Sue, was four and she followed Everett everywhere. Peanuts did not like anyone messing with his ears and wouldn't let anyone brush them. One day Everett took Mary Sue out in the yard, and suddenly missed her. When he found her she had a bridle around Peanuts neck and he was standing as still as he could, and she had a hold of his ear, trying to put the bridle on."*[38]

1956 Rodeo Cowboys Association Champions. Left to right: Ray Wharton, calf roping; Harley May, steer wrestling; Jim Shoulders, bull riding, bareback bronc riding and All-Around; Deb Copenhaver, saddle bronc; and Dale Smith, team roper.
—Photograph by Devere Helfrich. Courtesy of
National Cowboy & Western Heritage Museum

RODEO COMES TO TELEVISION

Pendleton RoundUp was abuzz on the final day in 1957, with five cowboys who were in contention for the All-Around title holder. CBS-TV was there to film the RoundUp's first TV exposure. Clark McEntire repeated his win there ten years earlier (1947) and claimed the title.[13] The headline of the *Rodeo Sports News* was "38 Million See Pendleton Rodeo on TV." The Neilson rating figures of the telecast were sent to RCA with a note from CBS, *"We had a hit."* The program was opposite a favorite of the day, *The Perry Como Show*, plus there was fine weather and only 49% of all TV sets were turned on during that hour, but a strong 41.6% were watching the rodeo action.[A11]

A major change in the RCA during 1957 were the meetings of the Board of Directors at six different locations in the country, usually in conjunction with an RCA rodeo, to discuss new ideas, ways to improve the organization, and to encourage hearing from the general membership. The membership was truly getting more voice in the twenty-one year old organization than it had ever had in the past. A rule that was questioned by the membership was the "No Trading Out" rule which was put into effect in January 1957. Previously RCA had allowed contestants to trade position after stock or position had been drawn, allowing the cowboys to arrange their schedule to enter several rodeos at the same time. The practice had grown, and abused in some cases, to the extent that the question had been asked, "Is it detrimental to rodeo?" After much discussion and several meetings over a long period of time, it was determined that the rule was detrimental. It was brought to the Board's attention that the paying customers are the ones who make rodeo happen. They expect to see their favorites *compete*, not to hear about them trading for a better draw. The vote was overwhelmingly in favor of "No Trading Out." Several abstained from voting, but no one voted "no." It was determined to continue the rule in 1958, although there was a good bit of controversy to it.

Another highly scrutinized subject was the "Permit System" which would allow nonmembers of RCA to contest until they won

1957 Rodeo Cowboys Association Champs: left to right: Alvin Nelson, saddle bronc riding; Duane Howard, runner-up to the All-Around Champion; Willard Combs, steer wrestling; Jim Shoulders, All-Around and bull riding; Don McLaughlin, calf roping; Dale Smith, team roping.
—Photograph by Devere Helfrich. Courtesy of National Cowboy & Western Heritage Museum

$1,000 at an approved rodeo. Then the permit holder must become a full-fledged member or could no longer work RCA approved rodeos.[A11]

From time to time the fans of a sport get forgotten when new rules and ideas are put into play. The Board of RCA recognized that the spectators at a rodeo were an important part of the success of the sport. Without spectators, rodeos could not be held. Producers began realizing that keeping the fans informed about scores and times, as they happened, was important, but the method of how to keep them "in the know" was still being developed. Often they were only aware if and when the announcer told them which cowboy had won an event for that performance. In addition to the announcer, the scoreboard was beginning to hold the answers. Rodeo scoreboards were just beginning to be used at a few rodeos.[A11]

SCHOOL BELLS TOLL

A tiny ad (1x4 inches) appeared in the *Rodeo Sports News* on September 1, 1958: *Toots Mansfield's Fall Roping School, October 20th through November 15, 1958. For full information and reservations 100 So. Virginia—Phone AM4-5991—Big Spring, Texas.*[A11] Mansfield also advertised in the popular *Hoofs & Horns* magazine.[10] This was the very first official school in rodeo. Competitive arena calf roping was much different than what a ranch cowboy does at branding because of the time element Mansfield explained, *"In calf roping a fourteen second tie is pretty fair time, but it can happen in less. To tie one in that time a roper is doing a lot of things right, and has practiced and worked at it."* He explained to his students that practice makes consistency. He also pointed out, however, you can practice wrong methods and build up bad habits. At Mansfield's school he left the stopwatch at home and worked on "right," not rapid.[5]

Manfield always defined what the roper's responsibility was, and the horse's responsibility, too. The roper needs to know how to put on and adjust all the necessary tack required, ride well enough to get to the calf, rope well enough to catch it, dismount and get to the calf, throw the calf, and tie it securely. The horse must be fast enough to catch a calf, and be big enough to hold it, to be quiet in the box, have fast-breaking speed, know how to rate the calf, have a good square stop, and know how to work the rope.

He continued by saying a beginner roper needed to learn on an experienced horse. He also felt the horse should have the right temperament and disposition. The horse should have the will to learn and do what is expected and required of him.

A horse should be at least five years old, because no matter how big they are, younger horses are still forming and developing. Usable muscling is desirable—not beefy, but long strong muscles that pull down into the knee and hock. Legs with a little width between them help to brace and hold when the calf hits the end of the rope. Short cannons, strong pasterns, and good feet are important. Good withers hold the saddle in place, depth and heart-girth tend to give your horse more durability and lung capacity. Low head carriage is desirable, as he is down watching the calf, and has his head out of the way of the sight of the roper, allowing more room to swing a loop.

Mansfield also liked to use calves that averaged 200 pounds for his school. He never worked one calf too long. He would leg, flank or tie one a few times, then release him for another. He knew good feed, water, and salt blocks would keep roping stock working longer.

The World Champ's recommendation was a full double-rigged saddle, to get as much "horse" between the two cinches. The roping fork is pretty slick, swells offer resistance to quick dismounts. Roping stirrups should be wide, with a slightly deeper drop from the stirrup leather to the stirrup tread, to prevent an upturned toe from hanging in the stirrup. Ropers need a stout saddle with a low rolled cantle and well-made wide cinches, kept in good repair.

Ropes should be Plymouth silk manila, and a roper should carry some 33 strand and some 36 strand, the smaller to be used if it is an indoor arena or there is little or no wind. Most ready-made ropes are usually thirty feet. But Mansfield preferred twenty-five feet of raw rope, then put in the Honda and horn knots.

A rope can is a must. Regardless whether the weather is hot or cold, rain or shine, the ropes stay in the same condition when kept in a rope can. Mansfield carried one big coil and two smaller ones.

He advised using a good pair of skid boots for the horse, to keep fetlocks from burning. Put them snug so they don't feel floppy. Have a neck rope and a tie down. Make sure they don't slip. The roping rein should be single fastened to both sides of the fit and short enough that you have a little control over your horse while you have your rope carried in your rein hand. Short rein keeps the horse from getting his front leg caught in it if it comes over his head on your dismount. A bit should be as easy as you can use.[5]

Martin Fryar of Big Spring, Texas, was a young man at the time of Mansfield's roping school. He recalled, *"It was a big deal, it lasted about 30 days and cost around $300. I couldn't afford to go to the school, but I often sat, under the arbor that was beside the arena, and watched the fifteen or so guys that signed up as they roped each day. Toots worked 'em real hard. Those guys all had sore hands. They would train on catching a calf for half a day, then train on tying a calf for the other half a day."*

RENT A HORSE

It has always been the cowboy way to lend a helping hand, even to his fiercest competitor. Borrowing a horse or using someone else's horse was not unusual in roping competition. A cowboy's generosity can sometimes make you wonder why he is so willing to share. It became a custom, however, when loaning a horse for roping or steer wrestling, to expect part of the winnings if the borrower got "in the money." Some cowboys didn't even compete but loaned their well-trained horse out to enough competitors to make a fair living.

Willard Combs' steer wrestling horse, Baby Doll, netted him $75,000 in 1957. Some "renters" made as much as $20,000 a month in the 1950s, but don't think the horse is overworked. Keep in mind a steer wrestler rides his mount about two seconds before he reaches for the steer. A roper may expect his horse to last a few seconds longer and then assist its rider as the roped steer or calf is being tied, but we are only talking about a few seconds.[10]

The 1958 Team Roping World Championship was won by a slim margin of $13. Ted Ashworth of Phoenix, Arizona, with $5,363, won over Dale Smith of Chandler, Arizona, who ended the year with $5,350.[A11] The first RCA National Finals Team Roping and Steer Roping Championships were held in Clayton, New Mexico, in 1959, in the coldest weather anyone had ever experienced in a competitive outdoor arena. First day temperature was 22 degrees, but the roping was hot! Everett Shaw won the Steer Roping and Jim Rodriguez, Jr., with heeler Gene Rambo, won the Team Roping.[38]

ELECTRONIC RODEO?

Headlines in the May 1959 *Rodeo Sports News* were "Electronics May Revolutionize Rodeo Timing." Two electronic technicians, E. L. Sutherland and Jim Wooldgridge of Grand Junction, Colorado, developed an invention using an electronic eye instead of a barrier rope. As the calf or steer trips the barrier, the eye goes off. If the horse reaches it before the calf or steer trips it, a signal flashes on the control panel. The ten-second penalty is immediately visible not only to the person watching the control panel but also to the spectators by way of the scoreboard clock. The clock begins when the animal trips the flag. To stop the clock in the timed events, the field judge carries a remote control unit that works by gravity. The flag judge need not be concerned as there are no moving parts or switches.[A11]

THE FIRST FINALS

The very first National Finals Rodeo was held in Dallas, Texas, in 1959. Preparations for the new annual "finale" to the sport of rodeo unfolded slowly as the year progressed. Two months before the December event, President Dwight D. Eisenhower was presented with a golden National Finals Rodeo ticket. The presentation was made by All-Around Cowboy Jim Shoulders; RCA president Harley May, and National Finals Manager John Van Cronkhite. Olin Young of Lovington, New Mexico, roped ten calves faster at the finals than anyone, and ended the year in fourth place, with winnings of $17,732. Jim Bob Altizer ran away with the Calf Roping World Championship with a total of $24,728 in total earnings, $6,000 more than his nearest competitor, Dale Smith.

The Team Roping and Steer Roping part of the "World Series of Rodeo," as it was touted in the *Rodeo Sports News*, was to be held in Clayton, New Mexico, on November 13 and 14. The National Finals Commission members of the roping committee who chose where and when to hold it, at their Tulsa, Oklahoma, meeting were: John Van Cronkhite, overall producer of the NFR; Bill Harlan, citizen of Clayton and a team roper; Dale Smith, Team Roping director for the RCA; and Clark McEntire, Steer Roping Director. Carl Arnold was

Jim Snively, Steer Roping 1956 Champion, from Pawhuska, OK.
—Photograph by John Stryker. Courtesy of The Stryker Collection,
Special Collections, Dunagan Library, University of Texas
of the Permian Basin, Odessa, Texas

chosen to be Arena Director, with Chuck Sheppard and Joe Crow, Jr., as the flaggers. It was decided to have six go-rounds in each event. In team roping there were two kinds of team roping—tied team roping and dally team roping, therefore, it was decided to have three go-rounds of each. The Steer Roping World Champion was Everett Shaw of Stonewall, Oklahoma, who won $924 during the Finals. His total earnings that year were $5,155. Shaw had won the title a total of five times since 1929. Steer roper Jim Snively of Pawhuska, Oklahoma, won the Finals Steer Roping average by leading more than fifteen seconds. His Finals payoff was $1,493. Eighteen-year-old Jim Rodriguez, Jr., won the Team Roping Championship with his partner, Gene Rambo. He was the youngest cowboy to become a world champion. Their Finals winnings totaled $965 each, adding to Rodriguez's earlier winnings for the year to give a final tally of $6,185. He ended up qualifying to go to the National Finals eighteen times. Sounds like "eighteen" might have been his lucky number.[A11]

Dale Smith was the first cowboy to qualify in three events the same year at the first National Finals Rodeo in 1959. He started the Finals in fifth place and ended up second in the Calf Roping event riding his popular mount, Poker Chip. Both the team roping and steer roping events were held in Clayton, New Mexico. Smith ended up in ninth place in the steer roping, and with partner John Clem he finished the team roping in the fifteenth slot. He rode Shady in these two events. It wasn't until 1966 that another cowboy qualified in three events for the Finals in the same year—Larry Mahan qualified for all three rough stock events. Tom Ferguson qualified for calf roping, steer wrestling and steer roping in 1979. The third roper to make that distinction was Trevor Brazile in 2003. The only other two to have this distinction were Ty Murray and Bobby Berger.

At the first National Finals the calf roping was an exciting event. Olin Young, of Lovington, New Mexico, at the end of the ninth go-round was standing third in the average with a total time of 177.4 seconds. Two other ropers from New Mexico were ahead of him: Monroe Tumlinson of Carlsbad with a time of 176.3 seconds, and Sonny Davis of Kenna scoring 173.1. The last go-round would tell the tale. Tumlinson roped in 16.1 and Davis scored an 18.7. Young tied his calf in 13.9 and won the average with a total score of 191.3 on ten head. His total earnings for the year were $17,732, and he finished fourth in the world. He won the NFR average again in 1962 and 1963. In 1963 he won it by only seven-tenths of a second with a score of 112.6. Sonny Worrell was second with a 113.3 time.[A23]

AUSSIE COMPETITION

In Australia the bushmen's carnivals and agricultural shows had been going on for many years. The word "rodeo" was seldom used in that country, but similar competitions, as our rodeo events, had been happening there since Europeans came to the island country. Most of the competitions were called buckjumping (saddle bronc riding) and bullock riding (bull riding). Alvie Gordon and a team of American cowboys, plus a Canadian team, went to Australia in 1938 and 1939 to represent their countries in competition. But roping was not an event. The Australian cowboy was ready to compete by the late 1950s in professional rodeo throughout the world, mainly the United States. Most rodeos in Australia included buckjumping, bullock riding, then they added bareback buckjumping, and *"the two American competitions,"* which were roping and steer wrestling. By the 1960s the Australian Rough Riders Association (ARRA) required all committees to include roping as one of the five events when hosting national championships.[41]

The Rodeo Information Commission reported that rodeos approved by the Rodeo Cowboys Association in 1958 drew a total attendance of 14,113,200, an increase of 1.6 million fans over 1957. California was the biggest rodeo state in the United States, and second was Texas, which had been the biggest until California took over three years previously. California had 66 RCA approved rodeos, Texas had 64 and Colorado came in third with 36.[A11]

ROPERS OF THE FIFTIES

RAY WHARTON. Born in Kerr County, Texas, to Lee and Ruth Wharton. His dad ranched and Ray learned to rope by working on ranches when just a kid. At 6 years of age he saw his first rodeo at Mansfield Park in Bandera. That same year he bruised his arm badly and had to have several operations. The bone slivers in his arm would work their way toward his skin and the doctor would cut him *"with the dullest knife,"* Ray remembered, when the doctor needed to get the bone splinters out. He was told his arm would not grow because of the affliction, but he went on using it and it did continue to grow. This did not stop his roping.

He traveled with Bob Mansfield (Toots' older brother), Buddy Groff, Don McLaughlin and Jim Bob Altizer. When asked who his biggest competitors were he named the same guys, and added Toots Mansfield, Dean Oliver, Troy Fort and the Goodspeed boys. Ray had good horses and says, *"You can just look and see who's riding the best horses. To win steady you have to be on the best horse."* Some of his best horses were Bones, Rusty, Scrap Iron, and Cindy. He traded for Cindy when going to Madison Square Garden because they penalized a roper ten seconds if they jerked a calf down. Wharton became the World

Champion Calf Roper at the age of 36, in 1956. When reviewing that winning year Wharton said, *"I didn't win a lot of firsts but I did win a lot of seconds. I only missed one calf all year."* He was fourth for the year in calf roping in 1955 and again in 1957. Today he and wife, Ada, live near Bandera, Texas.

GARY GIST. Gist was born September 6, 1945, in San Diego, California. He became the youngest member of the RCA when he joined on May 8, 1958. He was twelve years old. He, heeling, and Chick Davis, heading, teamed roped at Lonepine, California. They won fourth in the first go-round and split $70 with an 11.1 seconds time. In the second go-round, a 10.3 made them winners, getting $140 each, and with the top average of 21.4 seconds, they got another $140 each.

Gary Gist roping at the Buddy Peak Roping in Tucson, 1965.
—Photograph by and courtesy of Louise Serpa

Gist began team roping with his dad, Byron Gist, who roped almost all year when he could leave his job as manager of an ornamental iron works firm. Byron was the header and Gary heeled. A proud moment was being the best and beating 200 other teams at the 1958 Oakdale, California, Roping, one of the largest jackpot roping events in the country for many years. They roped in 8.7 seconds to win the fifth go-round, and in the 8th go-round had a time of 7.3 seconds, best of all 1,888 steers roped.

"I crossfired the steer, which I don't think had been seen done by a kid up to that time. That is why we had such a fast time," said Gary. (Crossfire is when the heeler throws his loop before the completion of the initial switch in direction of the steer by the header). They won $1,253.28, plus clothes and tack. The 7.3 seconds record held for many years before it was broken, and then the scoreline had been shortened.

The success of this youngster in a man's world was unusual, but it also caused him to not be able to participate in junior rodeos like his young friends. Therefore Gary had to compete in the big league with the older men. Gary went to twelve National Finals Rodeos and finished second in the world team roping standings in 1964, the year he and his dad won the average. He and his dad were partners seven times, three times with Bucky Bradford, once with Bill Darnell, and once with Joe Murray.

Gist's career making outstanding trophy buckles is known far and wide in the rodeo world, however, he and his dad, in his mid-eighties, still team rope at USTRC events. Gary won a gold buckle, of which he is very proud, at a contest in Tulari, California, not long ago. Not bad when you can still win after six decades of roping.[A11]

HOWARD "SHOAT" CHOUTEAU WEBSTER. Born January 23, 1925, to Alan Clayton and Mary Francis Webster. He had aspirations of being a detective until his Aunt Kate Chouteau married Fred Lowry and he discovered roping. Shoat moved in and worked for him, every day milking the cows and separating the milk. Then they would rope ten to twelve calves. He was even known to rope his sisters and the chickens—everything was fair game to Shoat.

When he was thirteen or fourteen years old he went to a 4th of July gathering at Nowata, Oklahoma, and his Aunt Kate entered him in the calf roping. He weighed about 140 pounds and the calves weighed about 350 pounds, but he won. Shoat and Fred Inman, a fair roper who had a truck, went to rodeos and ropings at night after the work was done.

Lowry was truly Webster's mentor, *"I patterned myself after him. He'd always say 'Lay 'em down easy,' which I always tried to do,"* relayed the champion roper. His first real money in competition didn't come until he was in his twenties. He joined the Turtles in 1943, and went to Madison Square Garden in 1944. Webster considers his biggest win at Pendleton the Sam Jackson Trophy. It had been offered for twenty-one

Shoat Webster of Nowata, OK, won permanent possession of the Sam Jackson Trophy, now on display at the ProRodeo Hall of Fame, Colorado Springs, Colorado.
—Photograph by Lucille Stewart.
Courtesy of *Hoofs & Horns* Collection

years and to take it home you had to win the All-Around three times. Webster also won Cheyenne four times, and the Ben Johnson Memorial Roping 6 years.

When explaining how to win at steer roping, he said, *"To get your trip right you should have it above the hock and below the hip, when the steer falls on his right side, the horse will step to the right, which helps roll your steer over and down, then hurry and make a right hand tie."* When asked who he thought were his biggest competitors, he named Jim Snively, Don McLaughlin and Sonny Davis. He won the World Champion Steer Roping title in 1949, 1950, 1954, and 1955. He and wife Shirley live near Lenapah, Oklahoma.

BEN JOHNSON, JR. Born in Foraker, Oklahoma, in the Osage country, June 13, 1918, to Ben, Sr., and Ollie Johnson. Young Ben had not planned to do anything other than follow in his father's footsteps. He planned to work on a ranch and compete in rodeos. However when he was called upon to deliver sixteen horses to Flagstaff, Arizona, to a movie set for *"The Outlaw,"* and was given a check for $300 by Director Howard Hawks, his life changed. He was hired to be a stuntman and wrangler by Howard Hughes, who recognized his cowboy abilities and tall rugged looks. He became a stunt double for actors such as Joel McCrea, Gary Cooper, Henry Fonda, Gene Autry, Roy Rogers, and Wild Bill Elliott. But the turning point in Johnson's career was when he spotted a team of runaway horses heading the wrong way on the set of the John Ford movie, *"Fort Apache."* He rode his horse alongside the team, jumped on the lead horse and stopped the team, just before they ran into a rock wall. Ford was so impressed he sent him a seven year contract at $5,000 a week and his destiny was set.

Although his financial worries were behind him, Johnson took 1953 off from the glitz of Hollywood and competed as a team roper in professional rodeo, winning the RCA World Champion Team Roping title. He said he went home to a "mad" wife with just $3 in his pocket. His generosity had paid many of his friends' entry fees along the way. His world championship in rodeo was the highlight of his life, although he was also honored by winning an Academy Award for Best Supporting Actor in *The Last Picture Show*. He also received many other movie honors and was inducted into both the National Cowboy & Western Heritage Hall of Fame and the Pro Rodeo Hall of Fame. Johnson died in Mesa, Arizona, March 28, 1996, of a heart attack.

GOOD HORSES

SHORTY. *"A sorry looking little fellow"* that no one seemed to think would turn out to be anything special. He had been bred well by George Smith, a customs officer on the Mexican border. Smith, unimpressed, gave the colt and his mother away. The colt went to a friend of Smith, Cliff Whatley, who had come with his family to the Douglas-Benson area of Arizona from New Mexico. Whatley was recruited by the army shortly after receiving the colt. He named him

Shorty. It seemed Whatley's furloughs always coincided with Arizona rodeos.

When Whatley completed his tour of duty, he made Shorty a multi-purpose mount. He could compete in the calf roping, team roping (both as a header horse and heeler horse), and even steer wrestling. Shorty never got mixed up. He never wasted an inch or a fraction of a second. He could shortcut and get his rider in a good roping position and outguess the steer.

Whatley and Shorty won day money the first two days in all three events at the 1950 Prescott rodeo. Although Whatley is left handed, other right-handed ropers such as Buck Sorrels, Olan Sims, Roland Curry, and John Rhodes have won on him. On a trip to Tacoma, Washington, unknown to Whatley and travel partner, Lex Connelly, the steel divider in the trailer broke off where it was welded and ended up in Shorty's left rear leg, cutting the hoof half off and severely cutting the hock. Two veterinarians advised putting him down, but Whatley would have no part of that. He had heard of an 80-year-old retired vet in Klamath Falls, Oregon, and immediately took Shorty to him. The senior vet fixed the wound, and taught Whatley how to care for him. In five months Whatley and Shorty were competing in the Tucson area and Whatley had won the all-around with his calf roping and team tying scores. Shorty's foot had healed properly and he had no lameness or need for a special shoe.[A19]

CHAPTER SEVEN

THE RODEO REVOLUTION

Hippies, flower children and protests were not all that the sixties era held for Americans. In the world of rodeo, innovations and prosperity was full speed ahead. The *Rodeo Sports News*, the official RCA magazine, was chock full of rodeo results and improvements in the sport. Headlines on the front page of the August 15th issue touted, *McLaughlin Takes All Around Honors at Cheyenne,* and *Bill Harlan Steer Roping Leader.* That issue also announced that the Steer Roping Finals at Clayton, New Mexico, had been set for October 7 and 8, earlier by five weeks than last year's Finals, in order to assure better weather for the contest. The Team Roping Finals and the Girls Rodeo Association Barrel Racing Finals were held for 1960 on November 19-20 at Scottsdale, Arizona.

Harry Charters of Melba, Washington, won the Calf Roping and All-Around at Pendleton RoundUp in 1960. He tied his first calf in 16.9 to win fourth in the first go-round, scored the fastest time in the contest, a 13.5, to win the second go-round, won second on the final calf in 14 flat, and first in the average with a total time on three head of 44.4 seconds. By October 1 that issue reported there was only six dollars between first place steer roper Don McLaughlin and second place held by John Dalton. Fourth place was held by Bill Harlan at just $658 behind the leader going into the Finals. McLaughlin won riding a horse called Peter Hancock, owned and trained by John Pogue of Miami, Oklahoma. Jim Rodriguez, Jr., and Gene Rambo won the Team Roping Finals for 1960.

Two innovative calf ropers, Clifton Smith and Harry Charters, qualified for the National Finals calf roping, in 1960, by using the right side dismount. In fact, Charters roped a calf in 10.1 seconds, a National Finals record. Dean Oliver said, *"It's harder to keep a horse working when you get off on the right. A right-handed roper has the rope going down the right side of the horse. Horses are more apt to jump to the*

116

left if everything is happening on the right side."A11 After much experimentation and decisions as to which side made for a quicker tie and much practice—practice—practice by ropers, two decades later the right-side dismount was "the only game in town."

The Steer Roping Championship was held at Laramie, Wyoming, in 1961. The scores were so close the winner was not determined until the tenth round. Clark McEntire of Kiowa, Oklahoma, won by a mere $94 over Joe Snively of Pawhuska, Oklahoma. McEntire had a final dollar amount for the year of $3,877 to Snively's $3,783.[46]

SLEET AND SNOW WON'T STOP A ROPER!

A dedicated roper would "give away his first born" to get to a roping. There is nothing comparable to the determination and lengths a roper will go to be able to perform his skill. Unless, just maybe, it would be salmon spawning upstream, but I would guess the salmon would come in second.

A good case in point is when Jack Stricklin, who needed to get from Abilene, Texas, to Chickasha, Oklahoma, to a roping in mid-February. It was the dead of winter and a snow storm blew in. The Texas Highway Patrol issued warnings to stay off the highways unless it was an emergency. An old-timers roping club was having a competition in Chickasha and Jack was determined to go. He and wife, Cozette, loaded up Jack's two roping horses in the trailer and headed north.

By the time they made it to Weatherford, Texas, the snow was really coming down. Big flakes and lots of them. It was tenuous going, but turning back was not an option. By the time they reached Lawton, Oklahoma, the roads were solid ice. They passed cars and trucks in the ditch all along the way. Jack kept going, inching along.

About twenty miles from their destination they slid off the road and buried the car and trailer in deep snow. At first Jack was not too concerned, but it was soon apparent he could not get out of the drift without help. He suggested Cozette take both horses out of the trailer, and walk them toward Chickasha. It was snowing so much there was very little visibility, but according to Jack's calculations the town was "just up the road." Meanwhile he would stay with the car and trailer and try to dig out and hope help would come by.

—Illustration by Gail Gandolfi

It wasn't too long before an Oklahoma Highway patrolman came by and helped Jack. The officer couldn't resist saying, *"Just where in hell are all you Texans going with these horses in trailers in this weather?"*

Meanwhile Cozette was trudging through the deep snow, holding onto the horses' halters. Her arm began to ache, her fingers were frozen, but she kept walking along the road.

Jack got the vehicles out of the drift and started toward their destination. He was concentrating on the treacherous driving so hard he never noticed when he passed Cozette leading the horses. When a car came by her, a passenger rolled down the window and shouted, *"Why don't you get your fat fanny off the highway with those damn horses!"* She was tempted to pick up a rock and hurl it through the car window, but she was too cold to bend, and her fingers probably couldn't have picked up a rock.

Eventually Jack did find Cozette and the horses. Everyone thawed out and they made it to the roping. Mission accomplished![35]

SCHOOL AND MORE SCHOOL

Don McLaughlin's first roping school, in Fort Collins, Colorado, was announced in the *Rodeo Sports News* in 1962. It was limited to the first twenty who registered. They would rope from 8 A.M. until 3:30 P.M., five days a week. After the first year, the school was scheduled for June, sometimes April and December.[A11] By 1966 he had an indoor arena 205 feet by 56 feet, and an outdoor arena 450 feet by 120 feet, box stalls, tack rooms, plenty of fresh roping calves, and a western store. A morning session would include legging, flanking, and tying calves. The afternoon session would include saddling horses and roping. Don was judge, jury, and instructor all rolled into one for his students, who often repeated the schooling to improve their skills.[A13]

Don McLaughlin, roper and world champion at National Finals Steer Roping at Pawhuska, Oklahoma, 1964.

—Photo by Bern Gregory. Courtesy of National Cowboy & Western Heritage Museum

SPECIAL RECOGNITION

Everett Shaw was top man at the Steer Roping Finals held in Douglas, Wyoming, in 1962. That same year the Team Roping Finals became part of the National Finals Rodeo, which was held in Los Angeles. Dean Oliver, of Boise, Idaho, stayed in the lead almost all year for the All-Around, but Tom Nesmith came on strong toward the end of the year and beat him by a little over $2,000. Don Fedderson's sorrel rope horse carried various ropers and won big for most of them, including Oliver, Nesmith, Herb Doenz, and Jim Bob Altizer. Altizer won $8,400 riding him on the first eleven calves he roped.

Nesmith was honored by the Oklahoma State Legislature when they issued a State Resolution saying; *"A Resolution commending and congratulating Mr. Tom Nesmith of Bethel, Oklahoma, upon his winning the title of 'World Champion Cowboy,' and for possessing and displaying those admirable qualities which truly make him a champion in his own right."* The Senate also had a Resolution for Freckles Brown that year, who won the Bull Riding Championship, and it said: *"A Resolution commending and congratulating Mr. Freckles Brown of Lawton, Oklahoma, upon his winning the title of 'World Champion Bull Rider,' and his courageous efforts in carrying forth this western tradition."*[A11]

The top fifteen Team Ropers who went to the Finals competition during this era were generally from California and Arizona, with an occasional New Mexican. The year 1962 was no different, with Jim Rodriguez, Jr., of Castroville, California, winning it. Fifteen-year-old Ace Berry, Jr., of Escalon, California, qualified with partner Bud Corwin. The teenager finished 11th for the year, but it was no fluke. He qualified for the National Finals at least eight more times.[45]

NEWSPAPER COVERAGE

The Rodeo News Bureau was formed in 1955 for the sole purpose of getting rodeo recognized and reported on the sports pages of newspapers across the country. By 1963 they were working at breakneck speed to keep wire services and the press informed of rodeo happenings. Sent to the 539 approved rodeos in RCA were 735 Press Kits. The *Parade*, a popular Sunday newspaper supplement magazine, did a

This photograph was Louise Serpa's first Hoofs & Horns *magazine cover. Roper is Bill Benton, 1962 at High School Finals, Douglas, AZ.*

—Courtesy of Louise Serpa

photo coverage of Pendleton RoundUp. Red Smith, nationally syndicated sports writer, sent out five columns during the year on rodeo, which was more than any other sport other than football, baseball, and horse racing. *Life* magazine did an article on Wick Peth, the bullfighter. *Time* magazine did two articles on rodeo, one on Joe Kelsey's bull, "0," and the second article was on the matched roping between Dean Oliver and Jim Bob Altizer. Dale Smith was one of five professional athletes to be considered for the honor of Athlete of the Year in his home state of Arizona. This was the first time a rodeo competitor had been picked for this award. The other four were jockey Dean Hall, hunter and guide Bob Housholder, Phoenix golf pro Bill Johnson, and Los Angeles Angels pitcher Don Lee, who lived in Tucson. Lee won the award.[A11]

Dale Smith riding the well-known Poker Chip to win first place in the fourth go-round of the National Finals Rodeo, 1961.

—Photograph by and courtesy of Ferrell Butler

The eastern sector of the United States was becoming more active in the rodeo world and competitors from that section were able to compete closer to home at more rodeos than ever before. Howard Harris, III, began the Cowtown, New Jersey, rodeo at Woodstown every weekend during the summer season. Leesburg, Virginia, held a rodeo every Sunday in the summer, just six miles from Dulles airport at our nation's capitol.[A11]

During the sixties numerous rodeo committees wanted to expand their events and entice more competitors to attend. They also decided it would be appropriate to entertain visiting contenders. Golf games and tournaments began to be advertised in the *Rodeo Sports News*, in conjunction with various rodeos. This idea proved to be an excellent way for competitors to continue their aggression toward winning, and yet enjoy the camaraderie of their hosts and local people. The golf games are still being held at many rodeos and rodeo venues throughout the country.

When the top Team Ropers in the RCA were announced at the end of 1964, they then selected their team partners. Leading the competition that year was Billy Hamilton, who chose #4 in winnings, Ted

Ashworth, as his partner. Gary Gist, #2, partnered with #6 Byron Gist; Jack Gomez, #3, roped with Ron Bigon, who was #12, and so on.[A11]

ROPE SCARCITY OVER

Lariat rope was unavailable for many years and ropers guarded and protected their ropes with a vengeance. The Plymouth Cordage Company stopped making the precious rope and it took quite a few years to get them to put it back into their manufacturing program. By the mid-sixties advertisements in magazines such as the *Rodeo Sports News* touted, *"Attention Calf Ropers. Here's the rope you've been look-ing for. Plymouth Silk Manila Lariat, stretched, singed and hand rubbed, 27 feet long with straight Honda and handsewn leather burner, 33 or 36 thread for $7.50. Cut lengths sold for 20 cents per foot. Also Nylon Lariat, stretched and aged, for steer ropers and team ropers. Made up from ⁷/₁₆"*

Everett Shaw, roping at National Finals Steer Roping, 1964. Always known as the ropers' roper.

—Photo by Bern Gregory. Courtesy of National Cowboy
& Western Heritage Museum

weighted pay nylon that has been properly stretched and aged outdoors for six months. Length 30 feet before tying, for $12.50. The extra hard twist piggin' string is $1.75."[A11]

Mike Hudson went to college at Sam Houston State College in Huntsville, Texas, in 1965. He was a serious student but also rode bulls and saddle broncs. He came from the central part of Texas and had participated in youth rodeos through the American Junior Rodeo Association (AJRA). There were other youth groups in Texas other than the AJRA. For example in the southern part of Texas, the Texas Youth Rodeo Association (TYRA) was most active. Each association had their own competitions and seldom did the competitors of one group meet the competitors of the other organization.

When Hudson arrived at college he was assigned a room in the

Bill Harlan roping in the second go-round at San Angelo, Texas, 1962.
—Photograph by and courtesy of Ferrell Butler

freshman dorm. The first person he met was his roommate, Phil Lyne, from George West. Hudson had heard about Lyne's reputation with the TYRA but Hudson admitted, *"As kids we were glad we were competing in the AJRA youth rodeos, and hadn't had to compete against Lyne. He'd won practically everything there was to win by the time he got to college."*

Hudson said it was evident Lyne was a natural athlete; he was always on an even keel. He worked every event in college rodeo and either got first or second. *"We went to college to compete in rodeos,"* said Hudson, who is presently in veterinarian pharmaceutical sales and a former Coors rodeo representative. Lyne transferred to Southwest Texas State College and was part of their 1968 National Intercollegiate Rodeo Association (NIRA) team. He transferred back to Sam Houston State University and was part of the 1969 NIRA Championship team from that school. Sonny Sikes, college rodeo coach, said, *"If we could get Lyne to wear a wig and enter the barrel racing we could win every event!"*

Lyne won the Calf Roping Championship and the All-Around Championship his junior and senior year in the NIRA.

Two new steer ropings were added to the RCA in 1965. Wheatland, Wyoming, added the classic roping event to their schedule, as well as Team Roping. This was the only rodeo to hold both

Gary and Byron Gist in the fifth go-round at National Finals Rodeo. They won the average at the 1964 Finals.

—Photography by and courtesy of Ferrell Butler

events that year. Sidney, Nebraska, also added Steer Roping to their program.[A11]

RODEO BEWARE!

The State of Ohio passed a bill, #451, in 1965, outlawing rodeo in that state. There was a total lack of opposition to this bill. RCA was not contacted until after the bill passed and therefore no defense was made. It was pointed out that RCA had seventeen rules, on pages 61 and 62, of the official rule book, which guarantee humane treatment of livestock. The shock throughout the rodeo world when this bill passed caused the RCA to realize if this could happen in one state, it could happen in others, if representatives weren't there to defend rodeo.

Following the Ohio fiasco, during the next few years anti-rodeo bills were introduced in Wisconsin, Virginia, Illinois, Rhode Island, Michigan, Connecticut, New York, Pennsylvania, and California. Primary representative for RCA was Clem McSpadden, who made sure the rodeo side of the story was presented. Headlines in 1967 were *"the Ohio Bill was unconstitutional!"* Fortunately for rodeo, from then on not one anti-bill was passed, thanks to conscientious attention to the matter by cowboys who cared.[A11]

RCA announced that stock contractors, for the first time in the history of RCA, would be represented on the Board of Directors in 1966. Harry Knight of Fowler, Colorado, was chosen as their representative. At the American Veterinary Medical Association's convention in Portland, Oregon, president-elect Harry E. Furgeson of Anaconda, Montana, was asked if rodeo was cruel to animals. His answer, *"No, it's cruelty to cowboys!"*[A11]

The 13th Annual Steer Roping in San Angelo, Texas, in 1966 had Tim Prather of Post, Texas, holding onto the lead. Not at all superstitious, he was the 13th roper and drew steer number 13 on his first go. Toward the end of the contest Don McLaughlin was the only one who could take Prather out of first place. If McLaughlin caught his steer in 23.6 seconds, he would win. When Clem McSpadden announced that time for McLaughlin was 24.2, Prather let out a wild whoop. On four head Prather had 60.1 seconds, McLaughlin's score was 60.5, and third was Olin Young with 60.8.[38]

NEW HALL OF FAME OPENS DOORS

The first group of cowboys to be inducted at the newly opened (June 26, 1965) National Cowboy Hall of Fame & Western Heritage Center in Oklahoma City in 1966 included two ropers, Bob Crosby and Clyde Burk. The other three inducted by the Board of Trustees were Lee Caldwell, Doff Aber, and Kid Fletcher. Bill Linderman was also honored that year for his All-Around Championships.[A11] According to the Cowboy Hall of Fame, the very first person inducted was Jake McClure in 1955. The next inductee was Pete Knight in 1958, followed by Thad Sowder in 1960, Paul Carney and Ben Johnson, Sr., in 1961. Lewis Bowman was honored in 1962, Oral Zumwalt in 1963, Coke T. Robards in 1964, and Leonard Stroud in 1965.[3]

Ropers at Steer Roping Finals held at Pawhuska, Oklahoma, 1964. Left to right: Don McLaughlin, Jim Bob Altizer, Everett Shaw, Clark McEntire, Shoat Webster, unknown cowboy holding child.

—Photograph by Bern Gregory. Courtesy of
National Cowboy & Western Heritage Museum

BROKE A ROPE, OR TWO

Dean Oliver was headed toward his eighth World Championship in Calf Roping in 1966 when bad luck plagued him like you wouldn't believe. In the 7th round and again in the 8th round of the National Finals, ropes broke during his run. He missed being the champ by $96 when he was beat by Junior Garrison of Marlow, Oklahoma. Oliver didn't make his eighth world championship until 1969.

Cheyenne Frontier Days closed their books in 1969 with a record

Les Hirdes, the top Team Roper of 1963.

—Photograph by Allen.
Courtesy of *Hoofs & Horns* Collection

Sonny Davis on "Ol Yeller" roping at Ben Johnson Memorial Steer Roping, 1964.
—Photograph by Bern Gregory. Courtesy of
National Cowboy & Western Heritage Museum

Clark McEntire roping in the fourth go-round at the 1963 Steer Roping Finals,
Pawhuska, Oklahoma.

—Photograph by and courtesy of Ferrell Butler

706 entries in six events. The calf roping event had 251 entries to top the list. Winning the calf roping was Dean Oliver, taking home $4,445, with Sonny Worrell second, followed by Sherrell Overturff, Bob Ragsdale, Mark Schricker, and Gene Stamm. The single steer roping event was next with 165 entries. Walt Arnold won $2,610, followed by Bud Tillard, Shoat Webster, Jack Newton, Joe Snively, and Ken Patterson. That same year Calgary Stampede had $68,443 in prize money. Dean Oliver won the calf roping there and took home $4,464, with Bob Ragsdale second, Buttons Howard third, followed by Barry Burk, Mark Schricker, and Ervin Carlson in that order. Pendleton RoundUp had a purse of $44,788, with Olin Young winning the calf roping and Don McLaughlin winning the Steer Roping. RCA Rookie of the Year honors went to Phil Lyne, who entered all six events and earned $12,565 for the year.[A11]

MASTERS OF THE HEMP

DEAN OLIVER. Born in 1929 in Dodge City, Kansas, one of seven children. His father was killed in an airplane crash when Dean was only ten years old. Everyone had to help to keep the family going. He dropped out of school when only a sophomore. The family was on "relief" and any monies that were earned were used strictly for necessities.

Although they lived in Idaho, where rodeos abound, Dean was nineteen before he saw a rodeo. As he watched cowboys rope for a few seconds and win as much as $250, it looked like the solution to Dean's family financial problems, he thought. All he had to do was learn to rope. While working on a dairy farm, he found a piece of rope he could use as a piggin' string, and he began tying calves and practicing steer wrestling on the milk cows. Of course all this practice had to be done while the owner wasn't watching, and often it was after dark.

Oliver was a self-taught roper. He knew good horses and was always well mounted. Only a short seven years after seeing that first rodeo, he won his first calf roping title in 1955. He won seven more in 1958, 1960 through 1964, and again in 1969. He also learned to steer wrestle and won enough to become the All-Around Cowboy of the World in 1963, 1964, and 1965. He said about ropers, *"Ropers are always accused of being about as single tracked, when it comes to their*

Dean Oliver, losing his eighth World Championship in 1966, when his rope broke in the eighth go-round.

—Photograph by Bern Gregory. Courtesy of
National Cowboy & Western Heritage Museum

Ferrell Butler's photo of the same incident, when Dean Oliver lost the World Title in 1966.

—Courtesy of Ferrell Butler

Dean Oliver, calf roping and All-Around Champion, was also top-notch in the administrative end of rodeo.

—Photographer unknown.
Courtesy of *Hoofs & Horns* Collection

thinking and talking, as any bunch of guys anywhere. And it's true. I know I spend most of my time thinking and talking about roping. But it's a much better event to watch if you know what both the roper and the horse are trying to do when they make each move."[A32]

Oliver married Martha when he was 20 years old. They had five daughters. Today they live and ranch in Greenleaf, Idaho.

JIM RODRIGUEZ, JR. Born September 9, 1941, in Watsonville, California. His dad, Jim, Sr., was a calf roper and a team roper. Jim, Jr., won the All-Around at a Salinas Junior rodeo when only seven years old, with competitors up to age eighteen.

In 1958 he and Gene Rambo competed in the Oakdale, California, roping against 132 other teams and won. This town made tandem dally roping famous in rodeo. On ten head they dallied in 132.8 seconds to beat out Al Hooper and Everett Shaw who were second with 135.8 seconds.[38] Rodriguez joined RCA in 1959 at age eighteen and won the Team Roping Championship that year with Gene Rambo. He was the youngest cowboy to win a World Title. He followed that win with World Championships in 1960, 1962, in spite of being shut out at the Finals, and in 1965. Rambo was his partner in the first three wins, then Ken Luman partnered with him for the last win. He also won the National Finals average in three decades, 1959–1966 and 1973. He qualified for the National Finals Team Roping for twenty years in a row (1959-1978).[46, 45]

WANDA HARPER BUSH. Born in 1931, she was raised on the family ranch near Mason, Texas, where she still resides. Growing up roping and helping her dad gave her plenty of practice. When she joined the Girl's Rodeo Association, later to be called Professional Woman's Rodeo Association, she won 29 World Championships from 1951 through 1969, including nine All-Around titles, eleven Calf Roping championships, seven Ribbon Roping titles, two Cutting Horse wins, two Barrel Racing titles, and one Flag Race win, according to the WPRA 2005 Media Book. After retiring, she trains and sells horses. She was inducted into the National Cowgirl Hall of Fame in 1978, and the Rodeo Historical Society Hall of Fame in 2001.[A25]

FINE ROPING HORSES

POKER CHIP. Foaled May 16, 1950, on the Peake Ranch near Lompoc, California, an offspring of Driftwood by Katy Peake, and Sage Hen by Waggoner.

During a career of ten years, Poker Chip carried Dale Smith to win over $125,000, not counting the jackpot and matched ropings they won. Smith said about the 1,200 pound, 15 hands high, big, stout horse, *"He was loaded with ability and coordination. And he had balance and timing. He could do everything. The reason I think he enjoyed roping so much is because even after he got crippled he'd kind of prance a little bit and he never hesitated about going into the barrier. He always acted like he was eager to get in there. I always let him gallop into the box or trot in. He wanted to get in there in a hurry. And I just ran him, turned him around and backed him up. He didn't like to stay in there too long and I didn't like to hold him there too long. If a calf was pretty decent I'd call for him right now."*

Willard Porter said he wouldn't cheat his owner or any other rider. He went to a calf the same every time—as hard as he could go—and he would not quit running until the calf had been caught and the slack rope pitched out of the way. Then he would stop on cue as his rider dismounted. He worked the rope well. When a calf was down or bounding around on the end of a rope, Poker Chip seemed to be aware of the exact amount of pressure to put on the rope to help the roper throw or tie the calf. He rarely choked a calf. He never let one get up or slam his head around on the ground.

Someone once said Poker Chip was more famous than his owner, Dale Smith. Smith laughed and remarked, *"That's OK, he gets all the glory and I get the money."* Willard Combs offered Smith $10,000 for him, but he wasn't for sale. In January 1963, near Vega, Texas, the trailer in which Poker Chip was riding jack-knifed and overturned.

His spine was broken in three places, his withers broken, both knees busted open, foretop knocked off, both back ankles badly lacerated and a muscle in his right hip smashed completely in two. After two weeks in Amarillo, the horse was taken to Dale's brother, Max Smith, a veterinarian in Safford, Arizona. In three months he had recovered from all injuries except the muscle in his hip. By mid-summer Smith won the Prescott and Payson, Arizona, ropings with 10 second runs on the recovered horse. The following winter a calcium deposit had formed around the hip injury. Surgery was performed and the calcium removed but Smith never competed on him again. Poker Chip was retired in 1964 and had certainly earned it. The horse died of an apparent heart attack on the Smith ranch December 20, 1977.[A11]

Sonny Worrell ropes a steer at McSpadden's Bushyhead, Oklahoma, Roping, 1976.
—Photograph by Bern Gregory. Courtesy of
National Cowboy & Western Heritage Museum

Tom Prather laying a trip.
—Photograph by and courtesy of Ferrell Butler

CHAPTER EIGHT

INNOVATION & GROWTH

The timed events were so popular by the 1970s, there were so many entries at most rodeos it caused committees to become very flustered, especially at the larger rodeos such as Houston, Fort Worth, El Paso, Phoenix, and Albuquerque. The large number of entries required stock contractors to provide more and more roping stock, as well as steer wrestling steers. The dilemma was how to handle the overflow of entries so the roping events within a performance wouldn't get tedious to the spectator. The RCA officials discussed it, "cussed" it, and worked with it for some time. Early on it was determined that limiting entries was contrary to the Association's long-time rule on this matter. It was also decided it would hurt the rodeo business overall. In other words, the Cowboy's Turtle Association, and then the Rodeo Cowboy Association, both ruled that if you were a member you were entitled to enter any Association rodeo and compete.

The following account was reported in the book, *Bridlewise & Otherwise*, by Rusty Bradley, and with permission I relay it here.

"There was a team roping in Post, Texas, summer, 1970. Martin Fryar is a roping son-of-a-gun. The match was a close one. Martin drove this old calf to the back end of the arena, and when the calf made just a little bend to the right, Martin put his string on him. He roped him like a cowboy, dismounted and started down his rope to the calf, and then we had an accident in the making. Martin got tangled up in his rope, and his horse became frightened and sold out! I mean he left there in a hurry. Out of a cloud of dust following this horse one could see the calf momentarily, then Martin would become visible. He would hit on his head and bounce high into the air, come down and slide along the ground—plowing up the arena with his head. A runaway horse dragging an object or two is not the easiest thing to stop. Finally a miracle happened, Martin became untangled and the horse and the calf went on, until the cowboys got him stopped.

Now the dilemma was, could Martin continue in the competitive roping for his team or would it be necessary to find someone to take his place. One of Martin's spurs was missing, one knee was out of his Levis and a small stream of blood was making its way into his boot; his belt buckle was as shiny as it could get after being polished vigorously in the sand of that arena. His shirt was completely gone except his collar and the part where the buttonholes were. One sleeve was still attached to the collar by a few threads. There were raw red spots all over his body. No one could see how he could continue to rope.

But those who are acquainted with ropers well know that they are a very unusual group of folks.

A group of three ropers were appointed to determine if Martin's team should get a replacement for him. The team, of course, would want someone of Martin's ability or better. The opposing team, naturally, would like his replacement to be of lesser roping skills than Martin. The match was very close. After thoroughly examining Fryar it was determined that he had sustained 'no permanent damage, except his chew of tobacco was very gritty,' but that's no cause to hold up the proceedings. Let's rope! And they did."[35]

—Illustration by Gail Gandolfi

DUES GO UP, STEER ROPINGS GO DOWN

The dues for RCA went up to $50 a year in 1971, from the previous amount of $35. Permit holders were to pay $35, instead of the $20 a year formerly charged. Only nine sanctioned steer ropings were held through RCA that year. The only states to hold steer ropings were

Ronnye Sewalt, top calf roper in the 1960s and 1970s.
—Photograph by and courtesy of Ferrell Butler

Troy Fort wins first in second go-round of the 1970 National Finals Steer roping in Pecos, Texas.
—Photo by and courtesy of Ferrell Butler

Wyoming, Nebraska, Oklahoma, Washington, and Oregon. By August 15, 266 RCA rodeos had been held and $2,075,351 in prize money had been paid.[A11]

How often do you see a five-way split for first place? It happened at the Sandhills Rodeo in Odessa, Texas, when five ropers had a time of 10.2 in the calf roping. Those ropers were Barry Burk, Jeff Copenhaver, Kenny McMullan, Paul Petska, and Tim Prather, who each went home with a fifth of first place—$389. In 1972 The Winston Rodeo Awards program, sponsored by the R. J. Reynolds Tobacco Company of Winston-Salem, North Carolina, gave $105,000 total to rodeos sanctioned by RCA, to be paid in each of six events. It was divided in two parts for the year, plus an overall yearly amount. Winner for the first half of the season in calf roping was Dean Oliver and in team roping was Gary Gist. The second half of the year the calf roping winner was Phil Lyne, and Leo Camarillo won the team roping. Phil Lyne won the year's final payoff with $10,000 for the All-Around title and $5,000 for the Calf Roping Championship. Winston also paid $5,000 to the top five money winners in steer roping. Top steer scorer was Allen Keller.

The Canadian Rodeo Cowboy Association for 1972 found Kenny McLean of Vernon, B.C., the All-Around Cowboy, as well as winning the steer wrestling and calf roping crowns. The versatile cowboy also competed in the saddle bronc event.

Each decade it seemed the calf roping time improved a few seconds. For example, at Burwell, Nebraska, in 1930, the fastest calf roper was Jake McClure in 17.8 seconds. In 1941 Toots Mansfield roped the fastest calf in 13.8; Red Nixon was the fastest in 1950 with 12.9; and in 1964 Barry Burk had the fastest time at 12 flat. By 1970 Ronnye Sewalt roped the fastest in 11.1 seconds.[33]

Barry Burk and son, Blair, at 1973 National Finals Rodeo.

—Photograph by and courtesy of Ferrell Butler

Walt Arnold, 1969 World Champion, steer roping in fourth go-round at Pecos National Steer Roping Finals, 1970.

—Photograph by and courtesy of Ferrell Butler

YOUTH RULES

J. D. Yates made the 1975 National Finals team roping, at the age of fifteen. He also has the distinction of another National Finals record. Yates, along with his dad, Dick, and sister, Kelly, are the only father-son-daughter combination to compete at the National Finals in the same year. J. D. also roped calves and steers and eventually competed in 18 NFRs and three National Finals Steer Ropings.

Ace Berry, another team roper, who qualified when only fifteen, also had an additional NFR record of being one of only two men to win two NFR averages the same year. In 1972 he won both the bareback riding and the team roping averages. It certainly pays to start young!

College rodeo competition of the 1970s boasted the likes of Phil Lyne, Tom Ferguson, and Roy Cooper, all of whom later made big marks in professional roping history. Team Roping became a college rodeo competition in 1975 and the name Mike Beers began appearing on rodeo programs.[34]

Phil Lyne won the RCA All-Around and Calf Roping titles in 1971 and 1972. At what everyone thought was the top of his rodeo game, Lyne announced in 1973 that he was retiring from full-time rodeoing. He bought cattle with his winnings and decided to ranch and just make a few near-by rodeos. *"When I found I wasn't concentrating on my rodeo events any more, I knew it was time to quit,"* said Lyne at an interview in 2006.

Bob Ragsdale, current RCA President, announced in 1973 that the "no jerk-down rule" was not working out. At recent rodeos when a judge determined a calf roper had jerked down a calf and was penalized, the fans' response was to boo fiercely. It was determined the judge did not have to have that responsibility. If the stock contractors were concerned with injury to their roping stock, the problem might be the condition of the arena or the condition of the calves. A test of the rule was put into effect. How else does a rule change or suggestion of merit get consideration if it is not tested under regular circumstances?[A11]

The Australian Rough Riders Association, equivalent in their

Phil Lyne, World Champion Calf Roper and All Around, also rode bulls. Taken at the National Finals in 1971 as he rode Beutler & Sons' bull, T3.
—Photograph by Bern Gregory. Courtesy of the National Cowboy & Western Heritage Museum

country to the U.S.A.'s RCA, crowned their All-Around Champion, Gary McPhee, for the fourth time in 1974. He took the honors in three events: bull riding, calf roping, and steer wrestling. He also competed in the bareback riding event. At the Australian National Finals Rodeo he won the roping, the doggin, and two go-rounds on the bulls. McPhee's abilities earned him eight event titles in a four year period.[A11]

Flaxie Fletcher, long-time secretary of the Rodeo Historical Society (RHS) wrote in her newsletter, EXTRA!, *"The National Rodeo Hall of Fame has come around full circle. This year it is enshrining a cowboy in his own time. Heretofore the Honorees of the Rodeo Hall of Fame have taken the long trail home. As its 1975 Honoree, The Cowboy Hall of Fame has elected a mighty atom of the Steer Roping world to its halls."* Ike and Cleo Rude and family were honored at the Rodeo

Eddie and Alvin Brownings of Willcox, Arizona, team roping at Sonoita, Arizona, 1973.

—Photograph by and courtesy of Louise Serpa

Historical Society's Luncheon of Champions, on December 12, 1974. Ike was inducted into the Hall of Fame at the National Finals Rodeo that evening. The ceremony was done on horseback with RHS president Andy Curtis presenting the award and western singer Rex Allen, Cowboy Hall of Fame Trustee, reading the citation. Ike rode around the arena to a standing ovation.[A28]

NAME CHANGE TO PROFESSIONAL

No fanfare was made when it was decided to add "Professional" to the title of the RCA in 1975. The April 1 *Rodeo Sports News* presented the Professional Rodeo Cowboys Association (PRCA) objectives. In summation it reported, *"The final objective, the most important, and a cumulative end result of our other goals and objectives, is the elevation of rodeo athletes to a monetary plane equal to professional athletes in other sports."*

In the very next issue the following statement was made under the heading, *"PRCA Board of Directors Confront Difficult Tasks."* It said, in part: *"The board finds itself in a position where it has to constantly make decisions affecting all segments of the sport. Considering some 3,500 cowboys and contract members, about 40 stock contractors and hundreds of committeemen, that's a lot of people to please, or madden, depending on which side of the fence you're on and who you're talking to."*[A11] A group not mentioned in this article was the rodeo fans. Although they are not directly involved with the organization, as those listed above, they are probably the most important group to consider because without spectators and fans there would be no rodeos.[A11]

CIRCUITS ESTABLISHED FOR "STAY AT HOME" COWBOYS

During this same time period the Circuit System was put into effect. Professional rodeo recognized that there were cowboys who were unable to travel long distances to compete, due to their employment or family obligations; however, they were just as serious about the sport as cowboys who were able to travel. Twelve cir-

Tom Ferguson at National Finals 1973 in eighth go-round. Soon to become a six-time All Around World Champion.

—Photograph by and courtesy of Ferrell Butler

cuits across the United States were formed and an award system within each circuit was encouraged for those competitors who had to limit rodeo efforts primarily to weekends. Each cowboy chose a circuit at the beginning of the year, or was assigned one, according to his home address. They earned points throughout the year and those points earned in the cowboy's home circuit applied toward his standing in the circuit. At the end of the year each circuit would hold a final competition with the eligible cowboys who had earned the most points.[A11]

A TIE

The World Champion All-Around Cowboy contest in 1975 was between Tom Ferguson of Miami, Oklahoma, who competed in Calf Roping and Steer Wrestling at the National Finals, and Leo Camarillo of Oakdale, California, who competed and won the Team Roping at the Finals. They each ended the year with $50,300 and split the honors that year. Ironically, the following year, 1976, a tie happened for the World Champion Saddle Bronc title between Mel Hyland and

Monty Henson, when both finalized their year earnings of $4,473. The very next year, 1977, Donnie Gay and Randy Magers tied for the Bull Riding Championship with totals of $6,521. With so many ties occurring during such a short period of time, PRCA decided to have a "ride-off." Gay won.[A4, 46]

Roy Cooper entered professional rodeo in 1976 and won his first world championship title in calf roping. People began to notice this young man because of the way he held his slack. Rather than waiting for the calf to hit the end of the line, like other ropers were doing, he put his foot on the ground nearly the instant the rope settled around the calf's neck. He gave credit to Butch Bode for doing this first, but Cooper took it a step beyond by holding the rope's slack as he dismounted. He didn't let go of the slack until the calf was nearly at the end of the rope. The new technique helped speed up a run by keeping the calf on his feet. As he gained more titles, other ropers began copying his style and shaving milliseconds off their times.[A11]

Gerald Russell calf roping at Pocatello, Idaho, 1971.
—Photograph by and courtesy of James Fain

PRCA made it mandatory in 1976 for a number of rodeos in the west to have Team Roping as a standard event in order to be sanctioned. Team Roping had been a very popular event in certain areas, especially California. The Saint Paul, Oregon, rodeo committee was hesitant, and did not want to include team roping. After much deliberation, it was added. They did not, however, give a belt buckle to the winners of the team roping event, as they did in the other events. It wasn't until 1985 they finally honored the team roping winners with a buckle.[39]

PRCA ADDS PROCOM

PROCOM, a central entry office for all rodeos sanctioned by PRCA, went into effect in 1976. Prior to this time cowboys were required to spend a significant amount of time on the telephone talking with the secretary of each rodeo they wanted to enter. The phone lines were jammed with calls. T. J. Walter told of taking seventeen hours to enter the rodeo at Prescott, Arizona, and when he called back he learned, *"It was midnight when I found out we were up the next afternoon and we were in Calgary, Alberta, at the time."*

The new PROCOM program allowed competing cowboys to reach one of forty operators who sat at terminals. The entire system was computerized—a giant step toward improving rodeo for the competing cowboy.[A11]

Statistics on professional rodeo grew during this time. In 1977 there were 579 PRCA rodeos in 37 states and four provinces in Canada. Fourteen million spectators paid to see rodeo. Prize money rose to seven million dollars. Membership in PRCA totaled 4,322 and 3,026 permit holders.

During Cheyenne Frontier Days, the PRCA Board of Directors signed an agreement to issue municipal bonds for construction of the ProRodeo Hall of Champions and PRCA National Headquarters in Colorado Springs, under the direction of president Dale Smith. That same year timed-event contestant, Jack Hannum of Ogden, Utah, became the first PRCA competitor to win more than $10,000 at a regular season rodeo. At Cheyenne Frontier Days he pocketed $10, 843 by winning the calf roping and the All-Around honors.[A11, 26]

CHANGES GALORE

Overall Rookie of the Year, in professional rodeo, had been recognized since 1956. The first year RCA member to win the most monies was awarded this honor. The Rookie of the Year, in each event, was recognized for the first time in 1977. In the roping events, Jimmy D. Brazile won $889 for the steer roping rookie seat, and team roper Brian Murphy was the best rookie, as was Steve Bland, who was the top newcomer in calf roping and steer wrestling. Jerry Jetton of Stephenville, Texas, a PRCA rookie, tied the fastest calf in PRCA history at Watonga, Oklahoma, on the weekend of May 19 and 20, 1979. His time, 7.3 seconds, was one-tenth of a second faster than a record set in 1977, at Ponca, Nebraska, by North Dakota roper Tom Needham.[A11]

Significant changes were being made in various ways throughout professional rodeo. The Pro Judging System was introduced by the association in 1978. Administered by a judge commissioner, the program called for twenty full-time, salaried judges and an equal number of part-time associate judges, all experienced in competition, to judge most PRCA approved rodeos for the year. The funding came from various sources, producers, committees, contestants, and a percentage of the purse. Cowboys to be considered as judges had to attend Pro Judging seminars, held periodically throughout the country. The concept expanded in 1982 and was renamed the ProOfficial System and was underwritten by Wrangler.[10, A11]

AUSSIE FACTS

The Australian professional cowboys, called rough riders, were not too far behind the United States in forming rodeos, called buck-jumping events. They did not hit their stride in the calf, steer, and team roping events until the 1970s and 1980s, in part because most Australian cowboys carried just one horse and expected him to be versatile enough to be a steer wrestling horse and a good roping horse, too. Eventually they learned it took an exceptional and specialized mount to do their very best at roping.[41]

In the spring of 1979, eleven PRCA cowboys from the United

States traveled to Australia for a two-week rodeo experience, hosted by Kooralbyrn, Queensland, with a purse of $50,000. This was the second trip in a year for PRCA cowboys The first was a rodeo in Adelaide, South Australia, and the three-day rodeo had a purse of $35,000. Dave Brock, world champion calf roper for 1978, who won $10,000 "down under," said, *"We paid entry fees, just like we do in America. The competition was tough in the bulldogging, but I think the Australian cowboys are just a little behind us in calf roping. For instance, I won the roping rounds with 10.3 and 11.0 seconds, and the closest roper to me had a 13 seconds run."*

The PRCA timed event cowboys used a roping and steer wrestling horse belonging to Australian Gary McPhee. *"They won about $10,000 on the horse in Adelaide, and about $6,000 in Kooralbyrn,"* said Harley May. The stock was very good and Bob Tallman did the announcing. It was reported that the Australian audience was not as accustomed to being informed about rodeo and Tallman did a bang up job of educating the fans.[A11]

COWBOYS OF THE TIMES

TUFFY COOPER. Tuffy Cooper was born on the 1905 family homestead in Lee County, New Mexico, near the town of Monument, where he still resides. He was born in 1925 and had one brother, Jimmy, fifteen months younger.

When the boys were fourteen and fifteen, they were hired by a large ranch to help with the screw worm epidemic. The rancher knew Tuffy and Jimmy could rope and he taught them the rest they needed to know to help out. Tuffy attributes his success in rodeo to this first job. *"It was a wonderful life,"* said the lean roper, *"$45 a month, plus room and board, furnished ropes and horses, good food, good place to spend the night. Mother didn't like her kids working at that age, but we had to, too many men in the service and no other help available in 1941."*

Tuffy entered his first rodeo at age ten, with the help of his aunt. He borrowed a horse, spurs, and a rope, and won it. Sixty-eight years later Tuffy was still winning, *"In 2003 I won the best saddle I'd ever won. Booger Barger put on a roping at Albuquerque, New Mexico, and I won as top senior roper."*

Tuffy married Betty Rose Hadley, whom he met while competing

Tuffy Cooper of the "Cooper Roping Clan" and grandson Collin Cooper, age 13, on the Horned Five Ranch, Monument, New Mexico.
—Photograph by and courtesy of Gene Peach

at college rodeos. He won the calf roping National Intercollegiate Rodeo Association (NIRA) title in 1950. They had three children: Betty Gayle, Roy, and Clay Tom. *"Betty Rose is a great rodeo wife. She can drive that car, have the horses ready, know which ropes I need. She also hauled those kids to rodeos for years. Good advice for any cowboy is to get a partner (wife) that understands cowboy life. It's awful hard to explain to a 'town girl' what rodeo is like."*

Tuffy taught his children everything he could about roping. *"I studied roping and ropers all the time. I'd pick out the best things from everybody and try and instill them in my kids."* Oldest child, Betty Gayle, captured the NIRA 1972 breakaway roping championship. Son Roy's accomplishments were PRCA Rookie of the Year in 1976, World Champion Calf Roper in 1976 through 1978, and 1980 through 1983. He was Steer Roping World Champion and All-Around Cowboy of the World in 1983. Youngest son, Clay, competed in both college and professional rodeo finals, as well.

Tuffy hails from Lea County, in southeastern New Mexico, that has claim to many rodeo greats, such as George Weir, Richard Merchant, Jake McClure, Troy Fort, and then there are the Coopers, plus Bob Crosby, who was born just over the county line, *"But we sure like to claim him,"* said Cooper. When asked why so many good cowboys come from one area, he said, *"Survival. You either have to rope or work."*[A6]

PHIL LYNE. Born in San Antonio, Texas, on January 18, 1947, to Joe and Mary Jo Lyne. The Lyne family ranched at George West, Texas, just north of the Rio Grande Valley.

Phil, his brother, Poochie, and his dad had lots of opportunity to rope, raising their cross-bred cattle. He entered his first youth rodeo at Alice, Texas, when he was four years old, and competed in breakaway calf roping and ribbon roping.

His first championship came in the Texas Youth Rodeo Association (TYRA) in calf roping for 1962, which he continued through 1965. He also became TYRA All-Around in 1964 and 1965,

Phil Lyne calf roping in the eighth go-round of the 1973 National Finals Rodeo.

—Photograph by and courtesy of Ferrell Butler

adding bareback riding, steer wrestling, and bull riding championships in 1965. That year he also won the National High School Calf Roping Championship. In college Phil was part of the 1968 National Intercollegiate Rodeo Association championship team from Southwest Texas State College, located in San Marcos, Texas. The following year he transferred to Sam Houston State University and was part of their championship team for NIRA. In both his junior and senior year he won the All-Around Championship and the Calf Roping Championship for NIRA, the junior year for Southwest Texas State University and the senior year for Sam Houston State.

By the time he entered the Rodeo Cowboy Association he was a seasoned competitor with an array of wins under his belt. He finished 1969 as RCA Rookie of the Year and became the World Champion Calf Roper and All-Around Champion in 1971 and 1972.

Lyne's versatility in the arena is well known. He is often compared to Gene Rambo in his ability to compete in any event. On occasion he was entered in as many as seven events. He was known as being a member of the "new breed of cowboy," and proved it by buying a 201 Cessna plane with T. J. Walter, getting his pilot's license, and traveling by plane to many rodeos throughout the country. This meant using horses belonging to others. In 1971, the first year he won the RCA calf roping title, he competed on 47 different horses.

Although RCA announced that Lyne had retired from rodeoing full time in early 1973, he still competed in nearby rodeos. In 1974 he was invited by James Allen to come to his ranch and practice steer roping under Allen's tutelage. Lyne qualified for the National Finals Steer Roping ten years and won the Championship in 1990. He also won first in the National Finals average in 1983 and 1986.[46] Lyne is the only cowboy who has won the National Finals average in three different events: Bull Riding average in 1972, Calf Roping average in 1972, and Steer Roping average in 1983 and 1986. He also won the Linderman Award four times, in 1970, 1971, 1972, and 1976. The Linderman Award is given to a member who has won the most money, and at least $1,000 in three different events during the year.

When interviewing Lyne he said, *"Ronnye Sewalt used to tell me I was born under a lucky star."* I disagree with Sewalt in that I believe Lyne has proved again and again that he has the natural ability to be a world champion and that luck played a very small part in his accomplishments. Many cowboys of his era and before have said Lyne is the best All-Around Cowboy of any time.

Leo Camarillo in 1969, soon to become an All Around and Team Roping Champ.
—Photograph by and courtesy of Ferrell Butler

LEO CAMARILLO. Born January 25, 1946, in Santa Ana, California. His dad, Ralph, also a rodeo competitor, ran ranches and kept his children involved in competitive roping events. Leo, the oldest boy, was a team roping header for the younger Camarillos. During this time he admits he saw opportunities to heel that others didn't see.

It wasn't until he was sixteen that he began heeling. He competed in team roping, steer roping, and calf roping. He joined the RCA in 1968, qualified for the National Finals that year, and won the first of six National Finals Team Roping Averages. He also won the National Finals average in 1969, 1970, and 1971, then again in 1980 and 1982. He won five world titles, four as World Champion Team Roper in 1972, 1973, 1975, and 1983, and was co-champ with Tom Ferguson for the All-Around World Championship in 1975. He also won the PRCA Team Roping Championship in 1976 (one of those years they determined the World Champion by who won the National Finals).

"My dad kept us in a confident mood by entering us in major ropings in our area of California. They had Calcuttas, and I was always the highest one sold," recalled Camarillo. A Calcutta is bidding on the contestants prior to the event, and the highest bidder pays that amount for his roper. If the bidder's roper wins, he gets a much greater amount of money, accumulated from all the other bids on other contestants.

Camarillo remembered "going down the road." *"We're blood, we're family and real close. It was fun going up and down the road with my* brothers. *We didn't have to worry, we trusted each other, and we each had our job to do—feeding the horses, getting the entries."*

Walt Woodard, a team roper from California said that Leo Camarillo was an "intimidator." He and Camarillo were competing in a jackpot roping near home and everyone put up money or a check as their "entry fee." When the roping was over, Camarillo won Woodard's check. When he endorsed it, he wrote on the back of the check, *"Thank you very much for coming. I'm going to spend the money on myself, or I might buy something nice for my wife. Thanks again. Leo."*[31]

At age 59, Camarillo, admits 2006 was one of his best years. He won four events in Senior Rodeos. *"I still feel like I'm at the top of my game,"* he said with a chuckle.

TOM FERGUSON. Born December 20, 1950, at Tahlequah, Oklahoma. His father, Ira, and brother were also competitive cowboys. Tom was a versatile cowboy who won world titles in steer wrestling twice, calf roping once, and six All-Around honors in a row.

From Miami, Oklahoma, he worked calf roping and steer wrestling for fifteen years. He earned twenty-three qualifications to the National Finals, and also qualified for the Steer Roping Finals in 1979.

Tom Ferguson steer roping at Pendleton RoundUp, 1978.
—Photograph by and courtesy of James Fain

This record-setter was the first cowboy to earn more than $100,000 in a single season with $103,734 in 1978. In 1982 he set the PRCA record with the most money won at a single rodeo when he won $17,225 at the Houston rodeo. In March 1986 he was the first professional cowboy to cross the million dollar mark.

CLEM McSPADDEN. There was never a rodeo announcer who knew more about roping cowboys and roping horses than this man. He was always interested in roping, even as a little tyke.

Clem was born near Bushyhead, Oklahoma, on November 9, 1925. When he was two years old, his dad, a nephew of Will Rogers, moved them to the Rogers Ranch at Oolagah. His dad was not a professional roper but did rope with some of the best of his day at Dewey and Vinita.

As a small boy, a game Clem played with his mother involved his mother announcing all the good ropers of the day, and their imaginary times at roping. Then Clem would rope, and of course, mother saw to it he always beat them all. His rope target in those days was a bucket. Clem did some competitive roping growing up, even did a little steer wrestling, but he found his forte in another field.

Monroe Veach was putting on a rodeo at Story City, Iowa. When

—Illustration by Gail Gandolfi

the Saturday evening performance got rained out, it was necessary to hold both performances on Sunday. Veach's son-in-law, George McAlister, the regular announcer, was sent back to Trenton, Missouri, to open the Veach Saddlery on Monday morning. McAlister recommended Clem to Veach, and that was his first job as rodeo announcer.

The rest is history—Claremore, Vinita, Kissimmee, Florida, Salt Lake City, Utah, and so many other rodeos throughout his career. He was the first American announcer to be invited to Calgary Stampede. He also worked Hawaii and Mexico and the first National Finals Rodeo.

In 1975 Clem began holding the "World's Richest Roping" at his Bushyhead Ranch. They had an arena where events were held, but they also held a pasture roping, with a 101 foot scoreline. The reason the scoreline was 101 feet was because Texas had originated the pasture roping with the 100 foot scoreline, and Oklahoma had to outdo them! Clem remembers all the great ropers, and horses, too. Clem also represented his home state of Oklahoma as a senator for eighteen years, and was then elected to the U.S. Congress. Today, he and son Bert have a lobbying firm, McSpadden & Associates.

TOP RATE ROPING HORSE

STICK. Leo Camarillo saw Stick for the first time in 1969. Stick was once owned by a school teacher who was at a team roping school Camarillo was putting on in South Dakota. The Oakdale, California, team roper was very impressed with the horse and his owner let the instructor use him for demonstration purposes. He also rode him in a local jackpot roping and won. The owner refused to consider selling him. That was 1969, but by late 1971, Camarillo had persisted with his offer to buy the six-year old Stick. The owner finally sold him for $2,500, and delivered him in the middle of the National Finals that year in Oklahoma City. For the next fifteen years Stick was one of the most celebrated heeling horses in rodeo and teamed with Camarillo to win numerous world championships. When Stick was 21 years old Camarillo gave him to a kid just learning to team rope and he continued to rope off him during his high school years. Talk about longevity in horses, Stick must have loved being part of a roping team.[A9, A11]

EASY COME, EASY GO

The world was on a roll. Money was flowing and it was a time normal people began to get a little crazy. New trailers, new trucks, high priced horses, the best tack were all available. Loans were easy to get and many took advantage of the situation. Halfway through the era, however, when the FDIC requested the banks to pull in their loans, the spending slowed down. In fact, in places it came to a screeching halt!

The National Finals All-Around title was won by ropers the first half of the 1980s—with Paul Tierney, Jimmie Cooper, Chris Lybbert, Roy Cooper, and Dee Pickett wearing the crown. At the 1980 National Finals Tee Woolman of Llano, Texas, partnered with Leo Camarillo, former world champion, in the team roping. They won five go-rounds and the National Finals average. Woolman's $49,983 for the year also broke the season record. In 1981 Walt Woodard and Doyle Gellerman won the Team Roping world title. It was the first time there was a tie and the header and the heeler shared the World Champion title. (In 1978 they had won the PRCA title, which meant they had won the most money during that year, but that was one of the three years the PRCA declared the World Champion based on monies won at the National Finals only. This was done from 1976 through 1978. In 1979 it went back to the former way of honoring the World Champion, monies won throughout the year, including the National Finals.)

The 1981 All-Around title was neck and neck between Jimmie Cooper of Monument, New Mexico, and cousin Roy Cooper of Durant, Oklahoma. When the last rope was thrown and the last calf tied in the tenth round of the National Finals, Jimmie beat Roy by two-tenths of a second, and by $47. His year's take was $105,861. Talk about a nail-biter! When Jimmie Cooper was given the gold buckle for becoming the All-Around Champion of the World at the awards ban-

Jimmie Cooper, 1981 All Around World Champion, calf roping at Buckeye, Arizona, in 1983.

—Photograph by and courtesy of Louise Serpa

quet, he stopped, took off the buckle he was wearing, put the gold buckle on before he spoke. He then said, *"From the time I was a little boy, I dreamed of winning this buckle. Ever since I was a boy I've worked to some extent for it. I guess early in my life I didn't work hard enough, because I didn't win very much."* He got his degree in agriculture economics in 1978 from New Mexico State University, then stormed through his rookie year in professional rodeo in 1980. He broke all-time winnings for a first year member of PRCA. He won both the calf roping and steer wrestling rookie titles, which cinched winning Rookie of the Year. He won $65,000 in arena earnings, and then picked up another $9,500 at the National Finals. He gave much credit to Tom and Larry Ferguson for teaching him about rodeo. *"Tom has forgotten more about the rodeo business than most champions know,"* said the appreciative titlist.[A11]

STEERS, AND MORE STEERS

Guy Allen, steer roper, won his first World Champion Steer Roping title in 1977, just a year after he began his PRCA career. His second world title was in 1980, again in 1982 and 1984, and so on. In a 1982 *ProRodeo Sports News* issue Allen was asked how his event could experience additional growth, and his answer was, *"I'd like to see equal national sponsorship for single steer roping. This could be done in a way to better educate the public about this event, which dates from the beginning of rodeo. To enhance this event for the fan and make it safer for the stock, the score has been shortened and the steers are now lighter in weight. This has kept injuries to a minimum. It has also made for some very surprising fast times. My 10.2 seconds at the last National Finals Steer Roping was a real surprise to me. I know when I am having a fast tie but never quite how fast."* Allen who was raised on the family ranch in Santa Anna, Texas, tied his first steer when he was twelve. His practice included tying 50 head a day with his dad and brother.[A11]

Pendleton RoundUp always had good steer roping. In 1982 the roping steers arrived in June for the September event. Livestock director Holmes expected them to weigh around 650 pounds by RoundUp time. Paul Hughes roped a steer in 11 flat, with Roy Cooper and Paul Tierney both in contention for the all-around title. Cooper won the All-Around, but Guy Allen won the steer roping that year with an average time of 13.8$^1/_3$ seconds. Pax Irvine won the calf roping.[13]

Craig Hamilton and Cody Woodson get a 7.1 seconds time at Prescott, Arizona, 1982.

—Photograph by and courtesy of Louise Serpa

George Aros and Jerold Camarillo team roping at Prescott, Arizona, 1982.
Photograph by and courtesy of Louise Serpa

Always willing to find new ways to improve the sport of rodeo and expose it to the most people, the PRCA held a Rodeo ProTour USA with a five month television series in 1982. Five preliminary qualifying rodeos were included and the Finals were held in October in Casper, Wyoming, with the top four winners in each preliminary rodeo competing in each event of two rounds, with the top eight contestants in a semi-final round. Then the top four competed in a final round. More than $100,000 in prizes were in contention, including bonuses offered by sponsors Coors and Nestea. In the roping events Walt Parke of Gooding, Idaho, won the calf roping with a 9.2 second run, with Scott Clements second, Larry Snyder third, and Roy Cooper in fourth place. The team roping was won by Charley Price of Hobbs, New Mexico, and Sterling Price of Tatum, New Mexico, with an 8.7 time. J. D. Yates and Dick Yates won second, and Jerold Camarillo and George Aros won third. In fourth place were Jim Rodriguez and John Paboojan.[A11]

Chris Lybbert won the PRCA All-Around title in 1982 by competing in calf roping and steer wrestling and going to the National Finals in both events. He was the first professional cowboy to break the $100,000 mark during the year before National Finals. His total for the year was $123,709.[45]

THE YEAR OF THE COOPER

The year 1983 belonged to Roy Cooper. He ended the year with the All-Around Champion Cowboy title, the Calf Roping World Championship and the National Finals average, plus the Steer Roping Championship. You can't get much better than that![45]

In 1984 PRCA put into effect the new "100 rodeos a year" rule. Previously a PRCA cowboy could go to as many rodeos as he wanted, but the organization decided to limit a cowboy to 100 qualifying rodeos a year. The scores the cowboy made for the 100 rodeos he picked to compete in, were the only ones counted in tallying his final score (based on dollars won) for the year. Dee Pickett won the All-Around title, plus the Team Roping Championship, with partner Mike Beers, and the Calf Roping average of the National Finals with a time of 114.0 on ten head.[45]

Paul Tierney calf roping at Tucson in 1984.
—Photograph by and courtesy of James Fain

Dee Pickett, calf roping winner, at Cheyenne Frontier Days, 1984.
—Photograph by and courtesy of Randall Wagner

NEW HOME

The National Finals rodeo found a home in Dallas, Texas, in Los Angeles, California, and in Oklahoma City, Oklahoma, but in 1985 they moved to Las Vegas, Nevada. The move was controversial, to say the least. Thomas & Mack Stadium at the University of Las Vegas (LVN) became the new home for this "Super Bowl of Rodeo." Benny Binion, of Binion's Horseshoe Hotel & Casino was instrumental in recommending the move to Nevada. He began paying entry fees for every contestant who qualified for the National Finals. After his death and when the family sold the casino (2002-2003), the Boyd Gaming Group took over paying the contestants' entry fees.[A11]

Malcolm Baldridge, Secretary of Commerce, heeling with Stan Harter at Tucson, 1983. He used this photo to describe to his Washington, D.C., political friends what a heeler did in rodeo.
—Photograph by and courtesy of Louise Serpa

The ProJudging System, put in place in 1978, continued to be finely tuned. By 1982 the concept was expanded and renamed the ProOfficials System. It was underwritten by Wrangler. Eight judges were hired by PRCA at $18,000 a year to judge twenty to twenty-eight rodeos a year. It continued to improve, but the bottom line was *"the decision of the judges will be final and may not subsequently be overturned by action of the PRCA, its officers or directors, or any other party. Any judge, however, who does not perform his duties in compliance with these rules, or who otherwise abuses his position, will be subject to disciplinary action by the PRCA board."*[10]

THE DODGE NATIONAL CIRCUIT FINALS

Reg Kesler, stock contractor from Missoula, Montana, and Rosemary Alberta, Jack Hannum of Ogden, Utah, Lonna Jean

Conroy and Lester Selders, both of Pocatello, Idaho, had a dream. It was an end-of-the-year event for the cowboys who stayed close to home and competed primarily in their circuit area. The dream evolved into the Dodge National Circuit Finals, which was started in 1987 in Pocatello, Idaho. After each of the 12 PRCA circuits across the United States held their respective finals, the top cowboys in each circuit, for each event, were eligible to compete in the Dodge National Circuit Finals Rodeo. The top two cowboys were: (1) the winner of the circuit finals in each event, and (2) the cowboy with the highest score for the circuit once the final was held, in each event. It operates under a tournament-style system. Those who are eligible compete in two preliminary rounds, then the top eight contestants in each event advance to the semifinals. The top four in each event move on to the final round, where national titles are decided. The titles are called Dodge National Circuit Finals Rodeo Champions.

Three outstanding ropers were polled by Kendra Santos, a reporter well versed in rodeo, for an article in the February 1988 issue of *ProRodeo Sports News.* Her question to them was to review the improved calf roping times through the evolution of the event. She chose as her subjects for this analysis, Dean Oliver, a World Champion with almost thirty years of success behind him; Roy Cooper, whose run of championships began with the World twelve years earlier; and Joe Beaver, who at this time had two World titles under his belt.

J. D. Tadlock flanking the calf at Tucson, Arizona, 1984.
—Photograph by and courtesy of Louise Serpa

"*The young kids have learned all the short cuts,*" said Oliver. Cooper added, "*I think all the roping schools have really helped improve the overall quality of ropers. In my roping school I tell the students everything and hold nothing back.*" Beaver also said, "*The days of running a ranch or other business during the week and hitching up the trailer and scoring big on the weekend is over. Today roping is the contestant's sole livelihood.*" Beaver continued with the fact that "*at any given rodeo 50 out of 70 ropers could win the top monies. You might tie a calf in 8.5 seconds and the next roper might tie in 8.4, and you don't even know who he is.*" Oliver agreed with him—to an extent, by saying, "*Anyone might win a day money, but to consistently win rodeos all year it is still the same tough few who win the championships.*"

Beaver continued by saying, "*Everyone takes a chance now because you can't afford not to. Ropers reach farther for their calf today, as the calves aren't as big, wild and fresh as they used to be. If we get our rope on the calf quickest we have more time on the ground.*" Santos stated Cooper single-handedly revolutionized roping so much he was definitely a target for criticism. The old-timers would say, "You should

Jerry Jetton tying the calf, Tucson, Arizona, 1984.
—Photograph by and courtesy of Louise Serpa

Left: *Mike Ray completing the tie, Globe, Arizona, 1984.*
—Photograph by and courtesy of Louise Serpa

Below: *John W. Jones, World Champ in Steer Wrestling, competes in the calf roping event, Tucson, Arizona, 1984.*
—Photograph by and courtesy of Louise Serpa

have roped the bigger calves we roped." Cooper thinks the size of the calf isn't the biggest difference. It is the way they are roped and tied.

Beaver followed Cooper's lead and took it further. *"The main thing a guy needs to do today is handle his slack so it doesn't handle him."* Oliver recalled that Toots Mansfield started ducking under the rope after stepping off his horse, and "flanking" the calf (picking him up with the rope at the neck of the calf and the other hand on the calf's flank). Flanking calves eliminated the extra step of having to step across the animal's body for the tie. It didn't take ropers long to figure out that getting off on the right side of the horse would save considerable time.

Cooper's biggest contribution to the advancement of calf roping was his "shortwrap" method of tying. His dad, Tuffy, watched Don McLaughlin trying it on his first wrap. The Coopers refined the concept and Roy was the first to master it.

The three experts agreed that the rope has changed considerably. The earlier grass ropes made of Manila hemp felt good but were apt to break when the calf hit the end. *"I broke two ropes at the 1966 NFR,"* Oliver said, *"and it cost me the world championship."* Hemp rope is still used but the addition of poly rope makes them much stronger. The second change these experts all agreed on is that horse training and rodeo roping don't mix. Oliver said it best, *"Today you keep yourself tuned and let somebody else tune the horses."* The article ended with Oliver saying, *"Ropers keep learning new tricks to be better. But I don't see how they can make it much faster."* Cooper agreed by saying, *"I think roping has come to the point where calves are being tied as fast as they can be tied. Though Joe Beaver is capable of anything."*[A11]

OOOOOOPS!

Accidents and injury are a given in the rodeo world. Roping competitors, however, have a special kind of injury that is specific to their event, and that is injuries to the hand, especially the fingers. Peggy Veach Robinson is a second generation roper and runs the family saddle shop, Veach Saddlery, in Trenton, Missouri, with her husband Robert and son Craig. On Sundays, when the store was closed, they enjoy attending and participating in jackpot ropings in their area.

The Robinsons were holding a roping at their place in October 1988, and ten or so people had arrived and were practicing. A young roper was learning to team rope, and Peggy was heeling for him. Craig was giving him instructions. They had been roping for some time when Peggy threw her loop, caught the calf's hind feet, and dallied. *"I just didn't dally deep enough around the horn, and my rope just popped off, wrapping my right thumb in the process,"* explained Peggy.

In a matter of seconds her right arm went numb. When she looked down and saw her bloody gloved hand, she knew immediately what had happened. Her right thumb had been cut off! Without removing her glove she called for Robert or Craig to come help her down from the horse. Immediately Robert called for one of the ropers to bring his ice chest to them and Peggy immersed her gloved hand, up to the wrist, in the ice.

They rushed her to nearby Trenton hospital where the doctor on call removed the glove. He determined that she needed to be taken at once to a Kansas City hospital where experts could try to re-attach the thumb. This procedure was not done in the small hospital in Trenton.

The thumb was placed on ice, and Peggy—and her thumb—were transported by ambulance to Kansas City, some hour and a half distant.

Quickly surgery was performed and the thumb was re-attached. When Peggy came to after surgery, she realized the room was extremely warm. The temperature remained at 85 degrees, which is necessary when re-attaching a limb. The first 24 hours were touch and go, no one knew if her body would accept or reject the thumb. Probes were attached to the thumb and fingers to monitor what was happening to the hand. The doctor even discussed the possibility of using one of Peggy's big toes and doing a transplant, if the thumb was rejected.

Fortunately, the surgery was a success. Peggy admits today that the first three years were tough. The thumb was black, there was no feeling, and the joint would not bend. Since she was right handed, she had to learn to use her left hand for many chores. *"I like to tore up my mouth, learning to brush my teeth with my left hand. But I got to go to the beauty shop a lot!"* reported Peggy, who admits she still has a weak grip with her right hand. She and her family still rope on Sundays.

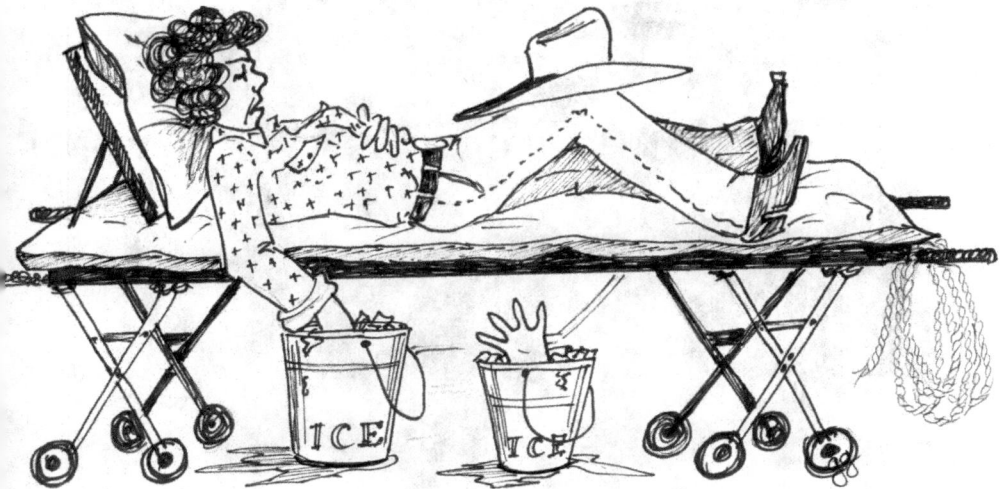

—Illustration by Gail Gandolfi

OLYMPIC GOLD

The February 1988 XV Winter Olympics were held in Alberta, Canada. To entertain the fans, an exhibition rodeo was held between the best cowboys and cowgirls of Canada and the United States. It was called the Calgary Exhibition and Stampede Rodeo '88 Challenge Cup.

Five events were held: saddle bronc riding, bareback riding, calf roping, steer wrestling, and women's barrel racing. Three competitors from each country were featured in each event. For the United States, the calf roping team consisted of Joe Beaver of Victoria, Texas, D. R. Daniel of Okeechobee, Florida, and Darrell Lambert of Abilene, Texas. The three Canadian ropers were Mark Nugent of Water Valley, Cliff Williamson of Madden, and Greg Cassidy of Donalds, all in Alberta. The outcome found the United States bringing home the gold team medal, and five of the six individual gold medals. Joe Beaver won the calf roping gold medal over Canadian Greg Cassidy.[A11]

Roping schools were being held across the country. Teachers were

Roy Cooper at Las Vegas slack, 1984.
—Photo by and courtesy of James Fain

former roping champions and multiple-times NFR contestants. Some concentrated on calf roping, but team roping was becoming a major event.

Tee Woolman and Bobby Harris held a team roping school in Colorado Springs, Colorado, during the summer of 1988. Those who attended were headers and heelers. The headers roped the dummy steer, while the heelers roped the legs of the sawhorse, but this was a quick exercise. The bulk of their day was spent in the saddle. *"You can only show someone so much on the ground,"* said Woolman. The instructors kept it simple. Woolman taught the headers to rope the right horn first, then push your loop across and rope the left horn. Harris had a four-step method for the heelers; *"Position, target, swing, and delivery—they all work together,"* he taught. Position refers to where the roper rides his horse in relation to the steer. A header should ride up close to a steer's left hip before making the throw. This also affords the heeler his best shot. Left-handed heelers ride the right hip. The former champ's parting words were, *"Practice consistency—that's where it is at."*[A11]

One of the most versatile cowboys of the 20th century was Chuck Sheppard, of Globe, Arizona. He was a four event man, competing in bronc riding, calf roping, steer wrestling, and team roping. He began his rodeo career in 1932, when only sixteen, and turned professional in 1937. He won the World Championship Team Roping in 1946. He also designed and produced the first RCA trophy saddles. He spent more than sixty years competing and in 1988, at the age of 82, took home $6,000 and a saddle from a Prescott roping event. He died at home with his family at the age of 89 on June 14, 2005.[A11, A27]

The PRCA introduced a new rule for heelers in 1988. All headers were started behind a barrier and in the event they broke the barrier, a 10 second penalty was added. The addition was that a Rodeo Committee or a stock contractor could request that a heeler start behind a barrier as well. If the heeler breaks the barrier, a ten second penalty is added, however, no more than one ten second penalty is added, even if the header and the heeler both break the barrier.[A11]

TEAM ROPINGS ABOUND

The Dodge City, Kansas, rodeo added a team roping matched competition in the mid-1980s. They pitted the reigning world champions against the team that won the National Finals average at the last Finals. In 1988 there were three teams as the National Finals average had been shared by the Walt Woodard/Jake Milton team and the Tee Woolman/Bobby Harris team. World Champions Jake Barnes and Clay O'Brien Cooper were the third team. When all the competition was over, Woolman and Harris won with a 57.4 seconds total on six steers.

Team Roping competition was added to the San Antonio Livestock Show and Rodeo roster in 1989. *"It is my hope that all the big winter rodeos, like Houston and Fort Worth, will add team roping, too,"* said Dee Pickett, All-Around and Team Roping Champion with Mike Beers for 1984. *"It would give the cowboys that are team ropers more of a chance at winning the All-Around and not just the event. They pay their entry fees just like everyone else."* Pickett was also second for the 1984 year in calf roping, behind Roy Cooper.[A11]

Oakdale Saddle Club Rodeo in Oakdale, California, began including a PRCA Gold Card Team Roping contest in 1989. The Gold Card is eligible to any PRCA member who is fifty years of age or older. Oakdale has a large number of competitive cowboys, primarily ropers and is called Cowboy Capital of the World. Cecil Nichol, age 54, and

Charles Pogue and Rickey Green team roping, Tucson, Arizona, 1989.
—Photo by and courtesy of Louise Serpa

Frank Ferreira, Sr., age 70, won the event by roping two steers in 21.9 seconds that year.[A11]

It is no secret that going-down-the-road cowboys are inclined to be in a few automobile accidents. A common reason for this is because their travel time is not when they are at their keenest. They want to be their best when they are competing. Often they travel during the night when long, straight roads get very boring and a cowboy's attention tends to stray. In May 1989 Shaun Burchett, the 1988 World Champion steer roper, and PRCA Steer Roping Rookie Ben Ingham were near Amarillo, Texas, after leaving a Kansas rodeo and were hit broadside by a train. Burchett incurred a ruptured spleen, torn kidney, broken nose, and multiple cuts and bruises. Burchett's World Champion gold buckle was mangled in the impact but apparently protected his stomach from a more severe injury. Ingham sustained a punctured lung and cuts. The impact threw the truck into the air and sheered off the trailer hitch. The horses in the trailer were unharmed.[A11]

BAN RODEO?? NO WAY!!

The State of Rhode Island banned traditional calf roping in 1989. The law, in an attempt to limit rodeo in the state, allows only breakaway roping, and requires that a veterinarian with at least two years of experience in large animal treatment be present at every performance. Violation carried a fine of $50 to $500. Doc Etienne of Salinas, California, attorney and chairman of the PRCA Rodeo Advisory Committee said, *"We weren't told about it until it was on the governor's desk and it was too late. We were unable to present the true facts and understanding of the event."* A 1988 injury survey conducted by on-site vets at several PRCA rodeos indicated that less than 8/10ths of one percent of the calves used in roping sustained any injuries. Nearly all of those that were hurt had leg injuries.[A11]

A special rodeo called Wrangler Jeans Rodeo Showdown pitted the United States team against the Canadian team. It was held in Scottsdale, Arizona, in October 1989. Five top competitors for each event from each country were selected to challenge one another for a total of $222,000, with $20,000 going to each of the seven events held, plus the Wrangler bullfights.

The Team U.S.A. calf roping representatives were Herbert Theriot of Wiggins, Mississippi, Troy Pruitt of Lennox, South Dakota, Mike Johnson of Henryetta, Oklahoma, Chris Lybbert of Argyle, Texas, and Jerry Jetton of Stephenville, Texas. The Team Canada calf ropers were Joe Lucas of Sundre, Alberta, Cliff Williamson of Madden, Alberta, Larry Robinson of Innisfal, Alberta, Mark Nugent of Water Valley, Alberta, and Garnet Smith of Wimborne, Alberta. The U.S.A. Team Roping members were Jake Barnes and Clay O'Brien Cooper, Bobby Hurley and Dennis Gatz, Matt Tyler and J. D. Yates, Jake Milton and Walt Woodard, and David Motes and Dennis Watkins. The Team Canada team ropers were Joe Lucas and Guy Chomistek, Dave and Bob Fraser, Doug Wilkinson and Todd Bogust, Don Depaoli and Jim Randle, and Rocky Callyn and Murray Linthicum. After five go-rounds the final Calf Roping winner was Mike Johnson (U.S.A.) with a score of 48.1 seconds on five calves. He won $4,875. Second was Garnet Smith of Canada, and third went to Larry Robinson of Canada, and fourth to Chris Lybbert (U.S.A.). The team roping winners were a sweep from the United States, with first being Bobby Hurley and Dennis Gatz with 41.2 seconds on five head, winning $2,875. Second was Jake Milton and Walt Woodard, third place went to Clay OBrien Cooper and Jake Barnes, and fourth was Dennis Watkins and David Motes.[A11]

ROPERS OF THE DAY

JOE BEAVER. Born October 13, 1965, in Victoria, Texas, to Walter and Bonnie Beaver. His mother can attest to the fact he cut his teeth on a piggin' string. She has a photograph of him in diapers roping the dog. They had a fenced-in area by the house that had been a garden and Joe spent hours each day, when four and five, roping the goats in the pen.

Bonnie started hauling Joe to youth rodeos when he was eight. He won his first saddle when he was nine. He started going to "open" rodeos when he was fifteen, and as they say, the rest is history. Bonnie Beaver said, *"Joe attended Saint Joseph Catholic High School in Victoria, and they worked with him real well, letting him off on Fridays to go to a rodeo. I had told them we probably had a drop-out, if they didn't as he loved roping so much. I knew how good he was and what talent he had."*

He joined PRCA in 1985 and was Overall Rookie and Calf Roping

Joe Beaver during second go-round at National Finals, Las Vegas, 1986.
—Photo by and courtesy of James Fain

Rookie that year, plus he won his first World Championship in Calf Roping. Mrs. Beaver calls 1985 "her year."

Joe has eight world championships, including three All-Arounds in 1995, 1996, and 2000, and five Calf Roping World Championships in 1985, 1987, 1988, 1992, and 1993. Injury has sidelined the Huntsville hero from time to time, but he plays catch-up real well, as his competitors will admit. Beaver presently competes in calf roping and team roping.

When asked of all his accomplishments which was the most thrilling, Beaver replied, *"Winning the $50,000 bonus at Calgary Stampede in 1994 because it was the result of a single tie. Every other win was a result of a build up, a win here, a second there. I'm looking forward to winning the $100,000 bonus they are offering this year!"* Beaver and wife Jenna and son Brody reside in Huntsville, Texas.

JAKE BARNES and CLAY O'BRIEN COOPER. Jake Barnes was born April 4, 1959, in Huntsville, Texas, and joined PRCA in 1980. He was named after the great roper Jake McClure. Clay O'Brien Cooper was born May 6, 1961, at Ray, Arizona, and joined PRCA in 1978.

Clay O'Brien Cooper with Tee Woolman at National Finals Rodeo, Oklahoma City, Oklahoma, 1984.

—Photo by and courtesy of James Fain

They both started roping as children. Before the two started team roping together, Barnes roped with Leo Camarillo and Cooper had Tee Woolman as his partner. When Barnes and Cooper got together, they became unstoppable. They won Team Roping World Championships in 1985, 1986, 1987, 1988, 1989, 1992, and 1994. They attribute their success to their game plan—to be a team, regardless. They also have said on numerous occasions they had a strong work ethic and rope continually. In 1994 they set a new NFR record of 59.1 seconds on 10 steers, beating the old record set in 1987 of 77.2 seconds by Tee Woolman/Bobby Harris and Jake Milton/Walt Woodard. Both team ropers qualified for twenty National Finals, although they weren't necessarily partners for all Finals, but when they were, they were hard to beat.

ROY COOPER. Born November 13, 1955, to Tuffy and Betty Cooper in Hobbs, New Mexico. He began his roping training when he was nine years old. When he was twelve he had competed in sixty rodeos and has only missed four calves. Roy came up through the rodeo ranks of American Junior Rodeo Association (AJRA) and the New

Mexico Junior Rodeo Association, then proceeded on to high school and college rodeos. He gives his dad, Tuffy Cooper, credit for his training. Tuffy taught Roy how Olin Young would always string a calf on the first wrap; how Don McLaughlin had a great second wrap; and Ronnye Sewalt's finished tie was the best. He encouraged Roy to practice and learn each of the procedures, until it felt natural to Roy, so he wouldn't have to think about it.

Roy Cooper at Las Vegas slack, 1984.
—Photo by and courtesy of Bern Gregory

Roy was Rookie of the Year in 1976, the same year he won his first calf roping world championship. He followed that win with more wins in 1977, 1978, 1980 through 1983. He also copped the All-Around title in 1983. It is a common opinion in rodeo that Roy Cooper revolutionized the sport of calf roping.

Roy suffered a broken wrist while practicing in June 1979. The pain was excruciating and surgery was required. The pain killers that were prescribed ruined his attitude. It was a bad time for Roy. When he began to heal and improve, he got on a serious training program, which included boxing, jumping rope, and finally he went back to roping, and eventually tying. It was necessary that he learn all over again. In addition to the last four calf roping titles, he won the steer roping World Championship in 1987.

Herbert Theriot, calf roper, from Poplarville, Mississippi, said of Cooper, "*I got with Roy last year (1983) and started learning everything I could. Mostly he taught me attitude. Confidence in myself. Roy never beats himself, he's a winner.*" Theriot was the 1994 World Champion Calf Roper. Dean Oliver said about Cooper, "*Every once in a while a guy will come along and change things. Roy changed things. He revolutionized the event. The way he got off the right side of a horse holding his slack and kept calves standing—no one had done the things he was doing.*" [48, 28]

CHAPTER TEN

THE LAST DECADE OF RODEO'S FIRST FULL CENTURY

From infancy, with little direction and no continuity, rodeo rose to a finely tuned, well established professional sport by the last ten years of the Twentieth Century. There will continue to be changes—nothing remains the same. But from a sport that developed from a cow pasture, and a cowboy's livelihood, it had become a professional well-run program with over 741 rodeos held with 2,128 performances in 1989 and more than $16,000,000 in prize money won by 5,560 members.

The American Quarter Horse Association gives Horse of the Year Awards each year to various horses in the rodeo world. In 1990 the AQHA calf roping horse of the year was Doc's Desperado, owned by Paul Zanardi and Joe Parsons. The Team Roping header horse was Mr. Roby Clerk owned by Matt Tyler. The Team Roping heeler horse award went to J. D. Yates and his dad, Dick Yates, for Flint's Friend. Tee Woolman and Mack Yates owned the steer roping horse named Cody Bar Skip.[A11]

Phil Lyne ended the 1990 year with $39,854 in steer roping and became the World Champion. He eased out Guy Allen of Lovington, New Mexico, who had won four earlier world titles in steer roping, by a mere $85. Ironically, Guy's dad, James, tutored Lyne in steer roping.

A SAD DAY FOR THE ROPING WORLD

In 1990 four calf ropers chartered a Cessna 210 airplane from Bob Card of Pendleton, Oregon, to get from St. Paul, Oregon, to Ponoka Stampede in Alberta, Canada. The plane crashed on Mount Ranier, about sixty miles southeast of Seattle. All four cowboys and the pilot were found still strapped in their seats when rescuers found the plane, intact on a glacier on the southwest side of the mountain. The Aeronautics Board representative confirmed it was weather related, no doubt a whiteout, which prevented them from seeing the mountain in their path. Those killed in the accident were Dave P. Smith, 1988 National Finals calf roper, who won the $50,000 showdown at Calgary that year; Mike Currin, who had won the 1988 Columbia River Circuit steer wrestling title and the All-Around at Pendleton RoundUp that year; David Bowen, a qualifier for the National Finals Rodeo in 1989 by a whopping $1.91, but ended up winning the Finals average and $36,830. He was the 1986 PRCA Resistol calf roping rookie of the year. The fourth was Randy Dierlam who went to the 1989 National Finals and finished tenth in the world in calf roping. All four young men had made the short round in calf roping at Ponoka and it was important for them to get there the quickest way and ready to compete.[A11]

Kelly Casebolt steer roping at Cheyenne Frontier Days, 1991.
—Photo by and courtesy of Randall Wagner

Tom Ferguson dismounting at 1994 Cheyenne Frontier Days.
—Photo by and courtesy of Randall Wagner

COWBOY MILLIONAIRES

Gas prices by the end of 1990 were affecting the roping world in a major way. $1.60 for a gallon of gasoline was hard on cowboys when it was not unusual to put at least 100,000 miles a year on a vehicle. Despite the gas crunch, four cowboys on the rodeo circuit managed to top the million dollar mark. Tom Ferguson did it in 1986, followed by Roy Cooper the next year. Lewis Feild and Dee Pickett went over a million in earnings by the end of 1990. All but Feild earned most of those dollars as prize money in roping competitions. No one admitted to having that kind of money in the bank, however. Everyone knows how much money it takes for a cowboy to get down the road, not to mention the cost of entry fees. By the end of the 1990 National Finals rodeo, two more cowboys went over the million dollar mark—Chris Lybbert, calf roper and steer wrestler, and Bruce Ford, bareback champion.[A11]

In an article by Kendra Santos about team roping, she wrote, *"Success in team roping is pursued by many and grasped by few. It is the right combination of men, horses and steers. It is as delicate as a young love, as lasting as a corner post. And it is truly rare."* She interviewed Rich Skelton, Clay O'Brien Cooper, and Jake Barnes, who were at the top of the game at this time. She listed the many reasons team ropers change partners, which included inability to win as a team due to being incompatible in roping styles, incompatible personalities, living too far away from one another to practice together enough, one member not having a horse that was good enough or not having enough horses to keep the hectic pace necessary. A good team has got to have a tremendous number of variables working in their favor to rise to the top of their sport.[A11]

In 1991 team roping was added to Pendleton RoundUp for the first time in the history of that rodeo. Steer roping had always been one of the favored competitions and the rodeo committee had always said "no" until now. It was hoped that many of the team roping competitors would also enter other events at RoundUp as well.

Although the original Madison Square Garden Rodeo ceased in 1959, a rodeo did return to the famous location from time to time. After a ten year absence, rodeo returned in 1969. Then in 1991, a two-day rodeo was held in November with Don Gay as chute boss, stock furnished by Three Hills Rodeo Inc., Burns Rodeo Company, and Cowtown

Jake Barnes and Allen Bach at an Open Roping, USTRC, Las Vegas, 1993.
—Photo by and courtesy of James Fain

Rodeo Company. Paul York of Mt. Morris, New York, won the calf roping with 9.2 seconds and picked up $1,617.[A11]

COMPUTERIZED RODEO

The PROCOM, a central entry system, used by the PRCA for
cowboys to enter all sanctioned rodeos originated in 1976. At that
time they had as many as sixty operators who took information by
telephone and hand wrote cards, which were later input into the system. In 1992 the PROCOM system became completely computerized
and operators could give cowboys information regarding the various
rodeos they entered, which was not available earlier. It was truly a
boon to the sport.

Bobby Motes and Mike Beers team roping at Tucson, 1995.
—Photo by and courtesy of Louise Serpa

OUR FAIR SHARE—DENIED

A temporary restraining order was requested and put on the National Finals purse with the top thirty team ropers who qualified for the 1992 National Finals as plaintiffs in a legal suit.

The request was denied on November 25, 1992, in the United States District Court for the District of New Mexico in Albuquerque, New Mexico. Their complaint was that the PRCA rules and regulations concerning the allocation of the contestant prize money among the NFR event purses violated sections I (restraint of trade) and 2 (monopolization) of the Sherman Antitrust Act. In simpler terms, contestant prize money should double the purse in team roping since it involved two men. The team roping purse at the 1992 NFR was

$462,150, which was split equally between the partners. The other five events had purses of $369,720.

The hearing was attended by PRCA Commissioner Lewis Cryer, PRCA Director of Rodeo Administration T. J. Walter, and PRCA legal counsel. Representing the team ropers were Clay O'Brien Cooper and J. D. Yates. The judge denied the plaintiffs' request for a temporary restraining order because (1) the plaintiffs had not shown a likelihood of the lawsuit's success on the merits of their antitrust claims, (2) the plaintiffs failed to demonstrate that they would suffer irreparable damage absent the requested injunction and they failed to show that they did not have an adequate remedy at law for money damages to compensate them for any hardship that may be suffered, (3) the plaintiffs had not shown that the hardship they might suffer would outweigh the hardship to the PRCA and other affected parties that would be caused by the injunction, (4) the plaintiffs had not shown that the requested injunction would serve the public interest, and (5) there was a question as to whether the New Mexico court had jurisdiction over the PRCA.[A11]

Dave Edwards roping calf at Cheyenne, 1992
—Photo by and courtesy of Randall Wagner

MORE BANS ON ROPING—C'MON NOW!

Animal activists were seeking for the fourth time to ban calf roping in Brown County, where Green Bay, Wisconsin, is located. The activists presented a petition with 802 signatures to ban calf roping, plus undocumented descriptions of calf abuse. Dr. Doug Corey, a veterinarian from Walla Walla, Washington, presented the PRCA point of view, plus a video on humane facts entitled, *Animals in Rodeo, a Closer Look.* The committee voted unanimously to deny the ban and felt this time the issue will be "put to bed," in Brown County.

The *ProRodeo Sports News* presented an article about injuries in the rodeo arena, by event. The most were sustained by bullriders at 37.1%, and bullfighters/clowns with 11.3%, followed by saddle bronc riders with 15.6%. Calf ropers only had 3.5% of the injuries, and team ropers ranked last with 0.8% of the injuries.[A11]

TRIBUTE TO TROY FORT

Roy Cooper broke ground in 1993 on his Museum of Champion Ropers, in Childress, Texas. On June 6 he held a reunion for all living world champion calf ropers. He called the day a tribute to the late Troy Fort, the 1947 and 1949 World Champion Calf Roper. Those in attendance were Don McLaughlin, Ray Wharton, Jim Bob Altizer, Glen Franklin, Chris Lybbert, Troy Pruitt, Fred Whitfield, Dean Oliver, Toots Mansfield, Jeff Copenhaver, Dave Brock, Ernie Taylor, Rabe Rabon, Phil Lyne, Tom Ferguson, and Cooper. Those unable to attend were Joe Beaver, Paul Tierney, and Jim Gladstone.

The longest scoreline for team roping and calf roping in the 1990s was at the California Rodeo at Salinas, with a forty-foot scoreline. Next was Cheyenne Frontier Days which had a thirty-foot scoreline for all three roping events. The next longest was at Guymon, Oklahoma, with a twenty-five-foot distance, followed by Pecos, Texas, with twenty feet. Cheyenne has the biggest arena at 665 feet long, followed by Salinas at 628 feet. Joe Beaver said that when roping on a long scoreline, the most important factors are (1) the draw, (2) how well your horse works, and (3) how good you rope. It's been said the long scoreline separates the men from the boys.[A11]

Roy Cooper steer roping at Frontier Days, 1993.
—Photo by and courtesy of Randall Wagner

Don McLaughlin at the 1993 Cheyenne Steer Roping.
—Photo by and courtesy of Randall Wagner

By 1994 the National Finals Rodeo had a payoff of $411,775. Calf roping paid each go-round $31,675, with $12,760 to first place. Second place received $9,502, third place $6,335, and fourth won $3,167. The calf roping average total was $95,025, with six places being paid. First place won $27,557, second place $22,806, third place $18,054, and on down to sixth place, which received $4,751. The Team Roping payoff was $39,600 for each go-round. Broken down, first place received $7,920 per header and the same amount to the heeler, second place $5,940 per man, third place $3,960 per man, and fourth place received $1,980 each. The average total was $118,800, paying six places with $17,226 per man for first place, second place $14,256 per man, third place $11,286 per man, and so on until sixth place paid $2,970 per man.[A11]

Herbert Theriot won the Calf Roping World Championship that year over Joe Beaver, five-time world champ, by a scant $14.81. Beaver broke the barrier in the ninth round. It was only the second barrier he had ever broken at the National Finals. Beaver said, *"I kind of backed off and I got beat for it."* Sometimes things like this have to happen to make a person get back to basics. When interviewed in March 1995 Beaver said, *"I've practiced more this season than since I was a kid of 18 or 19. I've been roping 50 calves a day and working on my team roping, too. It's paid off. I've had a good year so far."*

Ty Murray, who had won the All-Around title for the past six years, had knee surgery in June 1995 that put him out of commission for the rest of the year. Joe Beaver, who had been second to Murray's All-Around win three out of the last four years, tightened the reins and accelerated his program and literally entered more rodeos than he had been to in the last four years. He realized this opportunity for him to be the All-around Champ was the first time since 1984 (when Dee Pickett won it) that a timed event contestant could win this top spot. Not only did Beaver win the All-Around in 1995, but he won it again in 1996.[A11]

An announcement in the *ProRodeo Sports News* stated that after April 1, 1995, the "no jerk down" ground rule would affect all California PRCA approved rodeos. "Jerk down" was defined as "over backwards, with the calf landing on his back or head with all four feet in the air."

Marty Jones of Hobbs, New Mexico, tied a steer in 8.4 seconds at Coleman, Texas. Guy Allen had tied a steer in that time in 1991 at the Garden City, Kansas, rodeo. Twice before Jones tied record times made by Allen.[A11] Records are always made to be broken.

Gip Allen steer roping at Cheyenne, 1992.
—Photo by and courtesy of Randall Wagner

Jack Purchase makes a tie at 1994 Cheyenne Frontier Days.
—Photo by and courtesy of Randall Wagner

Kelly Banks throws his loop at Cheyenne Frontier Days, 1994.
—Photo by and courtesy of Randall Wagner

GONE, BUT NEVER FORGOTTEN

It happens, time and time again, but we are always shocked when it happens. Wrecks! Cowboys traveling the road from one rodeo to another, in the dead of night, is a major killer of cowboys, and yet what better or safer solution is there? To keep the pace that a serious competitor must keep, it is impossible to stay at the top if you don't "pull out all the stops." It helps to have a traveling partner, and often a competitor travels with one cowboy for awhile, finds another cowboy headed his way, and he ends up traveling with a different partner. It certainly breaks the monotony of those long roads between rodeos. The ideal, however, is when two traveling cowboys meet and find that elusive connection that makes them more than just traveling partners. They become friends of the very best kind.

Stran Smith of Tell, Texas, and Shawn McMullen from Iraan, Texas, were such friends. They totally enjoyed each other's company and traveled together like brothers. Both were calf ropers and enjoyed competing against each other. On the night of August 17, 1996, around 2:40 A.M., on Interstate 84 in Oregon between Portland and

Stran Smith, competitive roper and ambassador to rodeo.
—Photo by and courtesy of Dan Hubbell

Heppner, a drunken woman driving without lights and on the wrong side of the road hit head-on the rig with McMullen, Smith, and their driver, Jarod Grieve, of Australia. McMullen was killed instantly. Grieve sustained head injuries and was airlifted to a Portland hospital. Smith was asleep in the trailer and was uninjured—physically. The loss of his friend took much from Smith and it took a long time for him to process the accident before he could deal with it. Smith's faith in God and his knowledge that he will see McMullen again has sustained him. The two horses in the trailer were shaken and had minor cuts, but were relatively all right.

Shawn McMullen, who began his PRCA career in 1991, was ranked eighth in the calf roping event at the time of the accident. He was the National Intercollegiate Rodeo Association calf roping champion for four years, from 1988 through 1991, runner-up to Brent Lewis for PRCA Rookie of the Year in 1991, and had finished 1993, 1994, and 1995 in third place overall in calf roping. He had won the calf roping at Cheyenne Frontier Days and Houston in 1993. His future in the sport was bright and he was expected to be a world champion in the future.

McMullen loved calf roping and what he was doing. Those who knew him said he was one of the nicest people they ever met. I interviewed him at the Austin rodeo and I can certainly concur that he was most polite, courteous, and willing to take time with a reporter like myself during the hustle and bustle of the rodeo. Not all contestants give what he was willing to give to the media. The Texas Legislature honored Shawn on May 8, 1997, at 10 A.M. when resolutions by Representative Pete Gallegos and Proclamations by Senator Bill Sims (retired) were read and presented to the family on the House and Senate floors.[A11]

A DOZEN WINS

Guy Allen won his twelfth World Champion Steer Roping title at the Lazy E Arena in Guthrie, Oklahoma, in 1997. It was a close race between Allen, Rocky Garnett, who in the ninth round led the average by one tenth of a second, and first time qualifier Trevor Brazile. Allen placed in seven rounds, won four of those rounds and the average with a time for ten steers of 136.2 seconds.

A GOOD NIGHT FOR ROPERS

When calf ropers ride into the sixteen-foot box and make sure their horse is as focused on the business at hand as they are, the results can end in many ways. One of the best National Finals calf roping competitions happened in 1997 during the eighth and ninth rounds. In the eighth round Ronnie Hyde of Bloomington, Indiana, roped his calf in 7.1 seconds, two seconds less than the NFR record, held jointly by Cody Ohl and Blair Burk. Shawn Franklin had a time of 7.7, Fred Whitfield tied his calf in 7.2 seconds, the second fastest time in NFR history. Ohl tied his calf in 7.7, and Jeff Chapman had a 7.4 seconds run, followed by Marty Becker with a 7.5 time. That night it took a time of 7.7 seconds or better to be in the money. However, the ninth round was just as exciting. Blair Burk roped his calf in 7.0 seconds, giving Hyde's record breaking 7.1 seconds run the night before a very short reign as the NFR record. Just two ropers later, Fred Whitfield came up with a 6.9 seconds tie, ANOTHER RECORD! But before the crowd was back in their seats, Jeff Chapman, of Athens, Texas, wrapped his calf in 6.8 seconds! ANOTHER RECORD! Cody Ohl won the championship that year by placing in eight rounds with 87.0

Bucky Heffner the 1995 Steer Roping Champ at Cheyenne Frontier Days.
—Photo by and courtesy of Randall Wagner

Fred Whitfield set NFR calf roping average record in 1997 with 84.0 seconds on ten head.

—Photo by and courtesy of Dan Hubbell

seconds on ten calves. Whitfield won the NFR average with 8.4 on ten head.

An article in the *ProRodeo Sports News* the following year evaluated the innovations in calf roping that helped this sport trim the seconds off a winning run. It included various parts of the competition, including the flanking, the right-sided dismount, and slack. The article included a graph showing that in just seven years, from 1990 to 1997, the average time of first place NFR runs decreased from just below 9.0 to 7.5 seconds. Another graph showed that the NFR calf roping average time, based on ten calves, decreased from just over 120 seconds to just above 80 seconds. Extreme improvement in such a short time.[A11]

NEW RULES?

The Houston Livestock Show & Rodeo advertised their criteria for entering the 1998 event. They would have 64 entries per event, with three go-rounds, with the top twelve in each event in the finals. From the 1997 PRCA standings, the forty highest ranked contestants in each event would qualify. Additionally, the top ten ranked in the 1998 unofficial PRCA standings would be eligible. Others also available were former World Champions in the event they were entering, three time National Finals qualifiers in the event they were entering, and qualifiers for the 1995, 1996, and 1997 National Finals in the event they were entering. This was the first PRCA rodeo, with the exception of the National Finals Rodeo, that limited the contestants according to ranking. Previously it was always promoted by the association that if a cowboy was a PRCA member in good standing, he was eligible to contest against any other member at PRCA rodeos. The one thing that we can count on is that nothing remains the same.

Judging seminars for PRCA and NIRA were held in January and February of 1998. They were taught by Jack Hannum, supervisor of Wrangler ProOfficials, and at least one full time Wrangler official. They were held at colleges in Lubbock, Texas, Great Falls, Montana, Pocatello, Idaho, San Luis Obispo, California, Rapid City, South Dakota, Wichita, Kansas, Tucson, Arizona, and Laramie, Wyoming.

Jay Mattson throwing his calf at Cheyenne Frontier Days, 1997.
—Photo by and courtesy of Randall Wagner

Blair Burk at Pikes Peak or Bust, Colorado Springs, 2000.
—Photo by and courtesy of Louise Serpa

The main purpose of the seminars was to continue to improve and have as much consistency in the judging throughout rodeos as possible.

The PRCA Board of Directors amended the rule for the heeler in team roping, to also have the same barrier-breaking penalty of ten seconds as the header. The new rule was to take effect June 1, 1998. However, if both the header and the heeler break the barrier, only one ten second penalty will be imposed.[A11]

Prime time television was secured for ten PRCA top rodeos on ESPN2 for Sunday evenings. It gave the public a consistency of time slots so the public would know when and where to look for rodeo on television. Steven Hatchell, PRCA commissioner, said it gave rodeo the recognition as a legitimate sport.

As unusual as it is, it can happen. A steer roper, Colby Goodwin, age 32, of Lovington, New Mexico, was injured in an accident in the ninth round of the National Finals Steer Roping, when his horse stepped over the slack rope and tripped. The horse rolled on Goodwin. He was rushed from the Lazy E Arena to the hospital in Oklahoma City, then transported to another hospital where he died of massive head injuries the following morning, October 31, 1999.

The decade closed with National Finals crowning Fred Whitfield the All-Around Cowboy of the World, the first black cowboy to earn the prestigious title. He also again took the Calf Roping Championship and the NFR average winner, as well. Blair Burk was on the verge of winning his first gold buckle when a bit of bad luck in the tenth round of the calf roping ended that dream. Team Roping greats Speed Williams and Rich Skelton did it again, although they lost their run for the NFR average on the first of their ten steers at NFR. This was the second year in a row the Williams/Skelton team missed their first catch at NFR. The Steer Roping was won by none other than Guy Allen, who only missed one year, 1990, to call it a clean sweep for the nineties. It was his fourteenth title. Talk about a monopoly! The nineties ended the Twentieth Century with a Super Loop! It was a great time for ropers.

ROPERS AND THEN SOME

FRED WHITFIELD. Born August 5, 1967, in Houston, Texas, to Willie and Joyce Whitfield. Soon divorced Joyce worked diligently to

Fred Whitfield won his eighth world title in 2005.
—Photo by and courtesy of Dan Hubbell

make a life for her three children, Anthony, Tammy, and Fred, in the small town of Cypress, Texas. At age six Fred and Anthony rode two Shetland ponies all over town and used whatever they could find as a rope. Three years later Fred was competing in Little Britches rodeos. Roy Moffatt, employer of Fred's industrious mom, saw Fred's talent early. Moffatt saw to it that Fred was well mounted and had the calves, the place and the time to practice his roping skill, as well as seeing to it that he got to as many roping competitions as possible.

Whitfield was offered a job as a horse trainer in 1987 at $300 a week and the use of a truck. That was mighty appealing for a young man. He rode fifteen to thirty horses a day and roped 150 to 200 calves a day. *"I got tired of just roping to train horses and I missed not going to rodeos,"* he admitted.

Whitfield joined PRCA in 1990 and won the calf roping at Cheyenne Frontier Days that year. Whitfield is a record setter. He was the first African American to become the World Champion Calf Roper (1991) and the first to become the All-Around Champion of the World (1999). He also set a record in winning $100,000 faster than any cowboy ever had at that time. He has eight World Championships under his belt, so far, including seven in the Calf Roping and one All-Around. He has taken on team roping as well. *"I believe in whatever improves the roping sport,"* says the champ. He lives in Hockley, Texas, with wife Cassie and two daughters.

SPEED WILLIAMS and RICH SKELTON. After eight Team Roping World Championships, these two phenomenal ropers have mastered their trade, winning from 1997 through 2004. Their records are extensive. In 1999 they won six rounds during the National Finals.

In 2003 despite having the flu, Williams, whose wife gave birth to their first child just hours before they were crowned champs, also celebrated his birthday that day.

In 2004 they only spent one day in first place in the team roping event. They didn't win a dime until the Austin rodeo in March. They weren't in the top fifteen until summer. Williams was discouraged enough to offer Skelton the option of finding another partner, which Skelton would not consider.

Both entered PRCA in 1986. Williams began his career from Jacksonville, Florida, and Skelton called Llano, Texas, home. Today they are neighbors in Llano. Many things go into a finely tuned partnership such as this one. Skelton once said that Speed was fast roping

Speed Williams and Rich Skelton, team roping at NFR.
—Photo by and courtesy of Dan Hubbell

the head which allowed him more time to shoot his rope accurately and try not to make a mistake.

GUY ALLEN. Born September 5, 1958, in Chousatta, Louisiana, to James and Ann Allen. He graduated from Santa Anna (Texas) High School, one of twenty-six people. Allen knew he wanted to be a roper all his life. He joined the PRCA in 1976 and became the youngest steer roping world champion in 1977 at nineteen years of age. To date he holds eighteen World Championships in Steer Roping, and has won the average at the National Finals Steer Roping five times. He has qualified for the National Finals twenty nine times. His most exciting win was the first World Championship. He has been called "The Legend," by his peers, due to his numerous wins.

Allen's primary roping horses have been Jeremiah, who took him to five or six championships. The twenty-year-old horse has been turned out now for six to eight months, but Allen refuses to say he's retired. Rocky, Guy's dad's bay horse, also helped him win three or four world championships. Floppy was a back-up horse. Allen said, *"Generally I get a horse that is trained green and I finish him. It's real important to find one you can win on. Right now I don't have one."* Guy is a fourth generation to rope. His great-grandfather, James C. Allen, was quite a roper, as was grandfather, Orville, and, of course, his dad, James.[27]

Allen said he doesn't practice as much as he once did. *"I still practice in the winter when the weather is good. Right now the steers are so ex-*

pensive, and diesel is so high, we've cut practices down." Allen said there seems to be less steer ropings right now, possibly because PRCA is regrouping. Allen and wife, Lizzy, have three girls, ages 22, 18, and one. The oldest girl, Cigi, is a roper.

J. J. HAMPTON. Winner of seventeen World Championships in a short seven years is phenomenal, to say the least. Jackie Johnette, better known as J. J., of Stephenville, Texas, was born June 1, 1971, to Johnny Wayne and Barbara Hampton.

Her first competition was at four years of age when she competed in a flag race. She didn't do too well but her destiny was cast and rodeo became her game. Mother, Barbara, hauled all three of her offspring to many a youth rodeo during their tender years. J. J. joined Professional Women's Rodeo Association (PWRA) in 1993 and won her first two championships in 1994—All-Around and Tie Down Roping. All together she has won six All-Around titles, four Tie Down Roping championships, four Team Roping (Header) titles and three Breakaway Roping titles, all in seven years. Her last championship was in 2000. Her horse, Sara Rey Lynx, was picked as the All Women's Horse of the Year for Breakaway Roping in 1996 and 1998. It took

Guy Allen was named "The Legend" by his fellow ropers.
—Photo by and courtesy of Dan Hubbell

approximately 30 PWRA rodeos a year to qualify for the finals and to win the honors. She said the prize money yearly would be in the five to six thousand dollar range. But she also went to as many as seventy open rodeos per year, in addition to the PWRA events. J. J. admits, *"I don't like to lose. But the experience gave me so much more, something money can't buy."* After the loss of her horse she didn't compete for awhile, but presently she has a good mount and continues to rope. When not roping she sells real estate in Stephenville.[A24]

GOOD ROPING HORSES

SANTA CLAUSE. This white horse started his life with an injury to his shoulder and his owner was told he would probably never recover. He was sold for $600 at auction and was shuffled around until Lionel Burns introduced him to competitive roping in 1991. Arnold Felts, 1981 Steer Roping World Champion, bought him for $10,000 in 1992 and there wasn't a more perfect match. Felts won three out of four averages at the National Steer Roping Finals, 1992 through 1995. *"Roper styles and horse styles sometimes conflict,"* said Felts. *"He felt good the first time I got on him, and he just fit my style."*[A11]

WHIT. This bay horse helped cowboys earn more than one million dollars during his career. Whit was ridden by Roy Cooper, Joe Beaver, and Fred Whitfield, just to name a few. When Cooper was revolutionizing the calf roping sport, it was Whit he rode.

DUTCH. A 14.1 hands tall, 1,300 pound horse that won the American Quarter Horse Association Steer Roping Horse of the Year four different times. He is owned by Tee Woolman. *"Dutch had consistency and sense and he listens well, he's always alert,"* said Woolman when asked about his assets as a steer roping partner. An offer of $60,000 at the 1993 Steer Roping Finals for fifteen-year-old Dutch didn't phase Woolman, who had steer roped off him for seven years. He expected at least five or six more good years from the savvy steer roping partner.[A11]

FREEWAY. Todd Slone had just finished roping his first calf at the Fort Madison, Iowa, rodeo the evening of September 11, 1987. He had to rope another calf in the slack after the rodeo. The foggy, damp air determined he needed to take his ropes to the truck and warm them before his next calf. He left Freeway tied to the fence, with dozens of other timed event mounts, in an enclosed area guarded by security. When he returned Freeway was missing! No one had seen a thing. Stealing a cowboy's horse is seldom heard of in rodeo circles, but it happened to Slone. It was very untimely, as the Canyon Lake, Texas, cowboy was working toward his first National Finals qualification and he and Freeway were a real "fit," one not every contestant has the luxury of finding. Everyone was notified, police reports were made, everyone was on the lookout for this fine horse. No leads, no one saw a thing. Slone went on to his next rodeo, then returned to Fort Madison to continue his search. Absolutely no luck!

A week after the horse was stolen Slone received a call from the Fort Madison police saying they thought they had found his horse. A man, living in town, had a horse in his backyard, which he had never had before, informants had told the authorities. The police said they would call as soon as they had questioned the man. Unfortunately, when they called Slone back they said it was not his horse. The man in question had been a good citizen and bought a raffle ticket from a local 4H group and the prize was a horse. He had won! He offered to sell the horse to Slone as he had absolutely no use for his prize.

Years passed with no sign of the horse. It was as if the sorrel, flaxen-maned horse had vanished off the face of the earth. Meanwhile, in Savannah, Missouri, Roy Durfey was looking for a good calf roping horse for his son Wes, who had gotten his PRCA card and was ready to "break out." A horse, ridden by an acquaintance of the Durfeys, caught Roy's eye. When he inquired of the rider, he found he had borrowed the horse. The "owner" lived a couple of hours away in Iowa. When Roy Durfey called the owner, he was informed that he didn't actually own the horse. It had been left in his pasture by someone else, who had since skipped the country, leaving a wife and family, and had disappeared. Durfey pursued the purchase and the keeper of the horse decided this might be his only way of paying for the upkeep of this animal. He sold him to Durfey for $3,000.

The Durfeys called the horse Slack, and he and Wes proved to be a good team. In just a few short weeks, Wes won the United Rodeo Association Finals riding Slack, and won several thousand dollars on him at the Quarter Horse Congress in Ohio that fall.

Roy and Wes headed to Indianapolis to the rodeo on snow-packed roads. When they arrived they were ready to unload the horses and work them in the arena. Shortly Johnny Tibbetts rode up to Roy and told him he knew that was the horse Todd Slone had lost seven and a half years ago. Tibbetts had started the horse and knew him well. Slone was not at the Indianapolis rodeo.

The next rodeo the Durfeys went to was the National Western Stock Show & Rodeo in Denver in January 1995. When they arrived Durfey immediately looked for Todd Slone. It was time to resolve this question. Was Slack really Freeway, the horse stolen from Slone seven plus years ago? Slone identified marks on his shoulder and had his wife fax all identifying papers to them. *"Roy Durfey was quite honorable about the whole incident,"* recalled Slone. *"We had to go through a brand inspector, who was not accustomed to dealing with horses but cattle, and his suggested way of resolving the problem was not acceptable, and would take weeks to complete. When Roy Durfey refused to claim ownership to the brand inspector, the whole thing was dropped, and I had my horse back."* Slone told Wes Durfey to go ahead and ride Freeway at Denver in competition. Durfey tried to buy him back from Slone, *"I even asked if we could lease him, but Slone wasn't ready to let him out of his sight again. I don't think he ever fit anyone else like he did my son."*

When discussing this incident with Slone recently, I asked how many horses he had heard about that had been stolen at rodeos and he could only recall one. Horse-napping is not a concern at a rodeo, and yet it did happen. Slone did go to the National Finals in 1987 and six more times, winning the average in 1994. Slone never competed on Freeway again, as he felt the full time rodeo schedule was more than the eighteen-year-old horse could take. He eventually sold him to Mike Beers, who in turn sold him to Butch Knowles' boys. Today Slone has a saddle business in Cuero, Texas, and helps his teenage son, Ace, compete in roping. *"I wish I had a horse like Freeway for him to ride,"* said Slone.

CHAPTER 11

LASERS, IPODS & LAPTOPS— BUT A ROPE IS STILL A ROPE

The twenty-first century started with $$$ signs for some ropers. Ohl and Skelton hit the million dollar mark in wins, and Roy Cooper and Joe Beaver hit two million in earnings. J. B. Whatley tied the world record for the fastest steer roping run at the Walker County Fair and ProRodeo in Huntsville, Texas, with an 8.1. Guy Allen had the first 8.1 seconds run in 1986 at Coffeyville, Kansas.

Records were changed at the San Angelo Stock Show and Rodeo in 2001 when team ropers Speed Williams and Rich Skelton tied the record time made in 1986 by Tee Woolman and Bobby Harris of 3.7 seconds. But that lasted a short time, as Blaine Linaweaver and Jory Levy had a good steer that broke good and they topped the record with a 3.5 seconds time.[A11]

LARGEST RECREATIONAL SPORT IN AMERICA INVOLVING HORSES

Team Roping has become the biggest equine recreational sport in America, but it didn't start out that way. For a long time team roping was strictly a west coast rodeo event. But as it grew and moved eastward, more and more weekend ropers, as well as professional ropers, have found the sport to be challenging and satisfying. In the last fifteen years, it has become the fastest growing equine sport in the nation, and has outgrown many of rodeo's older events.

Shortly after college in the mid-1980s, Denny Gentry went to work for the New Mexico Cattle Growers Association. He found that getting cattlemen to become members was a major hurdle. The $40 membership dues was hard to come by. His entrepreneurial spirit directed him to offer, through the Association, a team roping event which proved extremely successful. The fund-raising event found people hesitant to pay $40 for a membership, but very willing when the

April Pablo, Navajo teenager, gets after her calf at Indian Junior Rodeo Association event at Window Rock, Arizona. She qualified for the Indian National Rodeo Finals that year.

—Photo by and courtesy of Gene Peach

team roping competition went with it. In fact, people from other states were joining the association just to team rope.

In 1990 Gentry started the United States Team Roping Championship (USTRC). He had done his research and had found that no one had been able to form a successful team roping organization because the ropers that roped for fun were always beat out by the professionals who came to the events when the purse was a fair amount of money. Gentry, with the design expertise of Gary Poythress, began a number-based handicap system that allowed a lesser capable roper to have a more qualified partner, which in turn gave the team a fairer chance to win a team roping. Admitting it is a complicated system, it encouraged professionals to help train and sponsor ropers less qualified. At first Gentry only planned to hold events in New Mexico, Texas, and Arizona. The finals the first year were at Oklahoma City with sixteen states being represented. Membership in the organization didn't start until 1993 with about 1,200 members.

Denny Gentry sold USTRC in 1998 to Equibrand. Kirk Bray became the president, succeeding Gentry. The national headquarters are located in Stephenville, Texas, and the organization has grown to more than 140,000 members. Approximately 30,000 are active, participating and competing members, including youngsters and oldsters. Bray explained that eventually the original handicapping system maxed out and it was necessary to design a more sophisticated system. USTRC hired Gary Poythress again and he designed a new and improved system called the TRIAD. TRIAD stands for Team Roping Information and Data. The system is the only nationally recognized handicapping system and objectively classifies ropers by performance, entries, wins, consistency, and so on. USTRC has members in forty-five states. They have three events in Hawaii. *"This is a very family oriented sport. Fourteen percent of our members are women. Dads and grandfathers compete against their youngsters. The roper who grew up in the country is now in the minority. We have all types of people and professions team roping,"* said Bray.

The membership dues to join USTRC are $80. Junior loopers, age twelve and under, are free. At most sanctioned events the entry fee is $50 per person. Ninety sanctioned events in 2006 qualify the competitors for the USTRC National Finals, held at Oklahoma City in late October. In 2005 over four and a half million dollars was paid in prize money at this event, where 6,200 teams competed over an eight day period. More than $19,000,000 was paid out at all USTRC sanctioned events during 2005.

THE FIRST FRONTIER

People in the west think the east, especially New York state, is asphalt and smoke stacks, hustle and bustle, and crowds everywhere. I learned in 2001 that this is a wrong assessment. I spent three weeks during the summer in the Adirondack Mountains of upstate New York, and if you stay away from Lake George and the tourist attractions, it is a very laid-back rural area. I based at Lake Luzerne, and within a short distance there was a rodeo, jackpot roping, or some western competition every night of the week.

We attended the Saratoga County Fair and Rodeo held in Ballston Spa. Providing the stock was the All American PRCA Rodeo Company of Ron and Cathy Martin, who also held rodeos throughout the summer on weekends in an arena behind their western wear store. Calf ropers and team ropers were in abundance, including the

Trevor Brazile and Rich Skelton heading and heeling.
—Photo by and courtesy of Dan Hubbell

Nastri boys and the Reynolds family. Ridin' Hy, a dude ranch, put on a rodeo for their guests on Tuesday nights during the summer, with roping being the main attraction. Painted Pony Rodeo at Lake Luzerne was held every Friday and Saturday night, with quite an attendance.

Dave Reynolds of Hudson Falls, New York, was the sixty-eight-year-old patriarch of the Reynolds clan. He is father to competitors Jeff, Benn, and Troy, and grandfather to Olin and Lee, who all rope. One grandson, Lee, was still in Texas where both grandsons attend college. The other five were all competing at Ridin' Hy. As we visited about the deep family love of the sport and how it has been carried on by the youngest generation, Dave remarked, *"In what other sport can a sixty-eight-year-old man compete against youngsters still in their teens and occasionally out-rope them?"* The night we met son Jeff, who was the First Frontier circuit Rookie of 1983, he won the roping with an 8.5 seconds time. The last few days of our eastern visit were spent at Cowtown, New Jersey, owned and operated by the Harris family. They have been in the rodeo business consistently since the 1950s, however, grandfather and great-grandfather produced an occasional rodeo long before that. Cowtown, New Jersey, is in the heart of truck farming country, and produces a weekend rodeo during the summer. It started many a cowboy on his road to professional rodeo.

Cheyenne Frontier Days held team roping as one of their events in 2001 for the first time in the history of the rodeo. Muleys, steers without horns, were used in the event with Blair Burk and Preston Williams winning the event. AQHA Roping Horses of that year were Herbert Theriot's calf roping horse, Easy; Jeremiah, Guy Allen's steer roping mount; team roping header horse Calhoon, owned by Richard Eiguren, and heeler horse Roany, owned by Rich Skelton.

A special Olympic Command Performance Rodeo was held in February, in conjunction with the 2002 Winter Olympic Games in Salt Lake City, Utah. This was only the second time a rodeo had been held in conjunction with the Olympics. The earlier venue was during the 1988 Calgary, Alberta, Canada, Olympics. PRCA Commissioner Steve Hatchell said it was the intent to showcase the sport with the best of the best. When all scores were tallied, Team USA won with 1,364 points to Team Canada's 737 points. Tom Reeves accepted the winning team trophy for the USA group. Eight individual gold medallions were awarded to bareback winner Lan LaJeunesse, bull rider Blue Stone, steer wrestler Rope Myers, saddle bronc champion Denny Hay,

The clock is ticking for Matt Petrus at 2000 Cheyenne Frontier Days Finals.
—Photograph by and courtesy of Randall Wagner

calf roper Jerome Schneeberger, barrel racer Molly Powell, and team ropers Murray Linthicum and Rocky Dallyn.

The Timed Event Championship of the World, held at the Lazy E Arena in Guthrie, Oklahoma, in March 2002, saw Daniel Green of Oakdale, California, break a record that had been in place for fourteen years. He roped and steer wrestled his twenty-five head of stock in 287.6 seconds. The previous record, set by Jimmie Cooper in 1986, was 318.3 seconds. Green, a team roping header by profession, left the event $45,500 richer.[A11]

The fans at the Steer Roping National Finals in October 2002 saw a real upset. After eleven straight championships, and sixteen titles in all, Guy Allen relinquished the World Championship to Buster Record, who earned $57,575. In second place was Trevor Brazile, who ended the year with $47,871, only $82 more than Guy Allen's 2002 earnings.[A11]

Cody Ohl suffered a serious knee injury during the National Finals in 2001 and was sidelined most of the 2002 season. But in February 2003 he proved he was back in the saddle by winning the calf roping aggregate title in a tie with Stran Smith and Johnny Emmons at the Southwest Exposition & Livestock Show in Fort Worth.[A11]

Calf roping's name was changed by the ProRodeo Cowboys

Association to "tie down roping" by 2003. Since then other organizations also changed the name to tie down roping. However, many continue to call it calf roping. There was no big hoopla or announcement when the change was made, it just happened. It has been thought to have been a more humane title. Evidently it has long been forgotten that calf roping came into rodeo and took the place of steer roping when steer roping was criticized as being inhumane.

World Champions are special. Their abilities to rise above and reach the heights of a title holder put them in a class of few. But don't think they aren't human just like the rest of us. Cody Ohl proved that when he had an altercation with a PRCA employee during the Pace Picante ProRodeo Chute-Out in Las Vegas on May 13, 2004. Ohl stated, *"People don't realize that just because we've won a World Championship we are treated any differently than other cowboys. When things happen that directly affect my family and our income, with sponsors, and such, I can get a little 'hot.'"* A grievance procedure was put into motion by the PRCA and it was reported he would serve a 30 day suspension, however he did apologize to PRCA members and fans. In spite of the suspension and not being allowed to compete, he finished fourth for the year.[A11]

PASSING THE TORCH

There is no better feeling than to pass on the torch to the next generation, and Mike Beers can attest to that. He assisted his son, Brandon, at the Great NW ProRodeo in Klamath Falls, Oregon, in May 2004, when they roped a steer in 5.3 seconds to earn $1,034 each, allowing Brandon to get his PRCA permit at his first rodeo.[A11]

Clint Cooper, son of champ Roy Cooper, started 2004 with a bang by winning the calf roping title at the National Western Stock Show & Rodeo in Denver with a score of 26.3 seconds on three head. That summer at Cheyenne Frontier Days he also took home $19,722 for winning the calf roping aggregate title with a 36.4 seconds time on three head.

June Ivory died in November 2004. Her rodeo credits were many, from early days of competition to being a crack rodeo secretary, and much more. She devoted her life to rodeo, but she was tough. She knew everyone in rodeo and everything that was going on. She was hard on cowboys if they didn't act right or look presentable. She was

Bryce Runyon, age eight, from Grant County, New Mexico, has his mouth set "just right" for the throw in break-away roping at a New Mexico Junior Rodeo Association event in Las Cruces.
—Photo by and courtesy of Gene Peach

Emerson Long, Jr., age eight, third generation Navajo rodeo cowboy, has his own "down-sized" stirrups to help him make his catch at a Smith Lake Chapter event, Indian Junior Rodeo Association, McKinley County, New Mexico.
—Photo by and courtesy of Gene Peach

a force to be reckoned with. At a memorial service for June in Las Vegas during National Finals, Joe Beaver spoke. He said, *"I thought I was young enough that I wouldn't have to put up with the likes of June Ivory. When I was ready to go 'pro,' I asked a friend what I needed to do to get along. He told me that if June Ivory was the secretary, I'd better cut my hair, and do everything she said. Sure enough the first rodeo, there she was, behind the secretary's desk, taking entries. When I went in she looked me up and down and told me to sit down, 'she'd get to me in a little while.' Well I sat there and time was ticking, it was getting close to rodeo time, and she just kept entering other guys. I got nervous and stood up*

Cutter Parsons in first go-round, Prescott, Arizona, 2003.

—Photograph by and courtesy of James Fain

to say something, and she told me to sit down again. I did. She finally got around to entering me and from that time we have been good friends. I will miss her."

The Southwest Exposition & Livestock Show in Fort Worth announced in 2005 that it had added team roping to its 2005 schedule, to comply with the PRCA mandatory requirement that beginning with the 2006 season, to be recognized as a PRCA-sanctioned rodeo, team roping will be required as a sixth standard event. The announcement went on to say it would be a one day event, in nearby Terrell, Texas, with two rounds and 116 teams.[A11]

RECORD BREAKERS

The Bob Feist Invitational Team Roping Classic, held in Reno, was won by Clay Tryan and Patrick Smith in 2005. They roped six steers in 43.87 seconds and left with more than $120,000 in cash and prizes. Their individual checks for the event were $46,696. Later in the year they won their first World Champion title at the NFR, *and* tied the world record with their 3.5 seconds run in Round 9. The first 3.5 seconds record was set in 2001 by Blaine Linaweaver and Jory Levy at the San Angelo Stock Show and Rodeo. Ricky Canton also broke the calf roping record with a 6.3 seconds run at the Strathmore Stampede on July 29, 2005. Cody Ohl and Clint Robinson had both held the record with 6.5 prior to Canton's Alberta, Canada, run.

GREEN GROWS THE GRASS—BE CAREFUL!

Pendleton RoundUp always has an abundance of timed event contestants, and the 2005 event was no different. Slack lasted three

"He who hesitates is lost . . ." doesn't apply to this roper, Rooster Ogg, at Omak, Washington.
—Photograph by and courtesy of Jon Millard

A wreck in the making.
—Photograph by and courtesy of Arthur Frank

mornings, starting at 9 A.M., giving the grass in the infield time to dry out from the overnight dew. Six hundred eighty-six contestants were in this eastern Oregon hamlet to test their ability. The best in the world were there including Trevor Brazile, Guy Allen, Cash Myers, and so on.

It was a treat watching these ropers as their stock was chased by a man on horseback up the alleyway, from under the bleachers. These calves and steers shot out of the chute in a dead run, over the score-line, across the angled part of the racetrack onto the grassy infield. Announcer Justin McKee said some of the competitors even re-shoed their roping horses, using *ice nails*, used in the north for traction and to prevent slippage. The grassy infield could give a roper a hard time if his mount slipped. This additional difficulty is not encountered in most arenas where the basic footing is dirt. But it doesn't stop the best of the best from competing at RoundUp. The winners in the roping events were Fred Whitfield in the calf roping with a total time of 29.4, Tee Woolman and Cory Petska in the team roping with a final time of 19.5 seconds, and Doug Clark in the steer roping with a final time of 42.7 seconds, one tenth of a second less than All-Around winner, Cash Myers.

A BUCK SIXTY SEVEN!!!

The National Finals Steer Roping held in Amarillo, Texas, November 18 through 20, 2005, was full of surprises for everyone. The first surprise was that Guy Allen did NOT win his nineteenth World Championship. Going into the Finals, having earned $63,680.11 throughout the year, he was sitting $16,148.33 ahead of the next competitor, Scott Snedecor—a sizeable margin. But Allen was quoted in a November 9th *ProRodeo Sports News* article as saying, *"I've got a real good shot, but it's not done yet. Amarillo kind of fits Snedecor pretty good, and he always does good there. He ropes fast and ties good."* Allen was right, Snedecor's consistency and ability to focus was uncanny. In ten rounds his times were 11.9, 10.7, 12.2, 15.6, 10.5, 11.9, 10.8, 13.6, 12.6, and 13.6 for a total of 123.4 seconds. Allen just didn't have a very good Finals, getting a "no time" in five rounds. When the final tally was made, Snedecor, who also won the Finals average and won money in seven rounds, added $21,850 to his previous total for a final count of $69,381.77. Guy Allen, who only placed in three rounds, had a total year earnings of $69,380.10—$1.67 behind Snedecor.

Steer roping in 2005 has changed considerably from the beginning

Guy Allen missed winning his 19th World Championship in steer roping by a mere $1.67.

—Photograph by and courtesy of Dan Hubbell

of the sport a hundred and some odd years before. As one old-timer said while watching a steer roping, *"Those early day steer ropers would turn over in their grave if they could see the way these guys are roping these steers. They used to lay 'em down easy, but they didn't have those fast times, either."* Times do change.

Jake Barnes, header, and Allen Bach, heeler, were competing at their 20th and 24th NFR, respectively, and were 2nd and 3rd, coming into the 2005 end-of-the-year event. In the fifth round Barnes lost part of his right thumb in his dally. He was taken to the University Medical Center in Las Vegas where he underwent surgery immediately to graft his thumb to his abdomen, to maintain a strong blood flow to his thumb. On December 30 he had a second surgery to remove the thumb from the abdomen at the Mayo Clinic in Scottsdale, Arizona. By February 10, 2006, only two months after the accident, Barnes and partner, Brock Hanson, were competing at the Silver Spur Rodeo in Yuma, Arizona, placing second in the first round and fourth in the average. Barnes also suffered a tear in his shoulder at the time he lost his thumb. He said he isn't affected in his roping by the thumb injury as much as he is by the limited range of motion he has in his shoulder. *"The money we won at Yuma was certainly a confidence builder,"* said Barnes, seven times World Champion Team Roper.[A11]

INSTANT REPLAY IN RODEO

Charles Pogue and Dennis Gatz were leading the average up until the final round of team roping at the National Western Stock Show & Rodeo in January 2006. A penalty, directed at them, which was allegedly considered a "bad call," cost them the average. Needless to say, they were extremely disappointed, especially since the judge's decision was controversial. This concern is not one that is an isolated case. There has been an interest in having instant replay in rodeo for some time, just to alleviate this problem. John Davis, who took over from Jack Hannum in 2004 as head of the PRCA judging group, said, *"Any good official in any sport should welcome the chance to get everything right. Our judges want to get it right and don't want to make any mistakes that cost anybody money."* Presently the possible use of instant replay in rodeo is being considered and will probably be tested at some selected rodeos.[A11]

A SPEEDY WIN

Speed Williams has been at the top of the Team Roping heap for some time. He and Rich Skelton have enough World Championships to start their own country. But that doesn't mean once you reach the pinnacle you can sit back in the glory of it—not if you are Speed or Rich. The 2006 George Strait Team Roping Classic was held in March at the Rose Palace in Leon Springs, just outside San Antonio. Speed headed with multiple heeling partners for this event, which is not unusual. At the end of the first two rounds he was sitting first, with Brad Culpepper from Tifton, Georgia. In second place was Speed with his more familiar partner, Rich Skelton. During the short go, he and Skelton had a 5.29 second time on their run, giving them a total aggregate score of 16.48 seconds. Williams followed it with his run with Culpepper and they had a 5.15 second time, and a total score of 15.82 to win the event and split $111,000.[A18]

The following day Williams spent the day heading again with multiple partners during the Brent Justus Memorial Roping at Llano, Texas, his home town. The entry fees weren't nearly as big, but neither were the payoffs, but that doesn't matter that much to avid ropers like Speed Williams. It is another chance to spend the day doing what he loves, and he was practically in his backyard.

Williams and Skelton won eight world titles during their career team roping together. The 2005 National Finals Rodeo was their last time to rope as a team.

—Photograph by and courtesy of Dan Hubbell

Unknown rider hustles as his horse stops short
—Photograph by and courtesy of Dan Hubbell

A first came to the twenty-second annual Wrangler 2006 Timed Event Championship, at the Lazy E Arena in Guthrie, with a tie between Trevor Brazile and K. C. Jones. The leaders became evident after all stock was roped and bulldogged. Both cowboys had a final time on 25 head of 337.5 seconds. After deliberating and going to the rule book, they went to a 6th sudden death round by swapping out five calves and steers they had from round five. Brazile won with 50.5 seconds to Jones 75.4 seconds.[A30]

Time is important to ropers. In fact, time is the ruler with which each and every roper is evaluated. An article appeared in a recent *ProRodeo Sports News* regarding the minimal monies a timer in rodeo is paid, compared to the responsibility the timer carries. Barbara Duggan, long time rodeo secretary and timer, representative for timers and secretaries on the Executive Council of the PRCA, was quoted as saying, *"Timers are grossly underpaid. What people need to realize is that the timer is important to every dollar won at that rodeo."*

There are two timers working each PRCA rodeo, using digital handheld watches, to record the official times in the timed events. The PRCA Timers Handbook directs the timer to watch from flag to flag, during all timed events. It also directs both timers to watch the barrier judge for penalties, watch the field flag judge for "no time" signals, and watch the field flag judge for penalties in team roping. The timers should know the time limit in each timed event (steer wrestling—60 seconds; tie-down roping—25 seconds; team roping and steer roping—30 seconds). One timer should be responsible for blowing the time limit whistle in all timed events. When there is a discrepancy of time between the timers, such as one timer has 5.9 seconds and the other timer has a 6.0 second time, the contestant gets a 5.9 time. At times there will be a slight difference because the two timers saw the flags differently. The responsibility of the timers and the importance of their positions is imperative to professional rodeo. PRCA annual dues for a timer, as a contract person, is $45. A new applicant must have their application signed by a Timer, one PRCA Rodeo Secretary and a PRCA Stock Contractor. Insurance is also required. Most timers are hired by the stock contractor or the rodeo committee.[49, A11]

RETURN TO COMPETITION

Walt Woodard started his team roping career in PRCA in 1975 and became the PRCA World Co-Champ in 1978, and the World Champion Team Roper in 1981. After a ten year absence in professional rodeo, Woodard returned in 2006 with partner, Matt Sherwood, to win the San Antonio team roping and the Dixie National at Jackson, Mississippi. Their horses were both honored with the State Farm Athlete Award at San Antonio. Nick, Sherwood's horse, and Little Gray, of Woodard, were both given $1,500 bonus checks.

A WELL TRAINED HORSE

Having a well trained roping horse is essential to winning. It has been necessary since the first cowboy threw a piece of hemp at a head of stock, but today the competition is fierce. Some ropers train their own mounts, but most of the time it is a better use of their time to have it done by a professional horse trainer. Finding the right horse for each and every roper is a major magic act and one that the trainer can often see better than the roper.

Doug Clark of Wayne, Oklahoma, is such a trainer. He grew up as part of a fourth generation rodeo family and when he graduated from high school he knew that his passion would take him down the rodeo trail and that he would train horses. His dad, Duke Clark, had done the same, and he had a good teacher. His great-grandfather, Monroe Veach, made saddles and tack, his grandfather and grandmother, Charley and Imogene Beals, also built saddles. His upbringing had given him a strong respect for not only the horse, but also the right tack as well.

Duke Clark had also shod horses and Doug grew up knowing how important the proper shoes were to a horse's performance. *"The right shoes give the horse a good foundation. If the shoes are not right—too little, wrong angle—it can cause a horse to get sore, then that sore moves up into his legs and he is constantly compensating for those sore spots. I try and keep him pain free,"* reported Clark. Horses that Doug Clark has either owned or trained have been performing their duties in the roping events at the National Finals and the National Steer Roping Finals every year for the past twenty years.

Clark says the biggest change in roping horses and the training of them is that in today's arena the emphasis is more on the back end of the horse than the front. *"In the earlier time the cattle used were fresh, not trained, as they are today. Ropers used to jerk 'em down harder. Today there*

The well-trained horse of Chip Porterfield does his job as they win the calf roping at Cheyenne Frontier Days in 1988.

—Photograph by and courtesy of Randall Wagner

is more need for a horse to 'be on his butt,' he is sliding a little farther," explained the trainer. *"I look at a horse's hocks and hind legs and their loin, over the top of their back."*

A criteria that confirms Clark's ability at training horses is the few injuries incurred by the horses he trains. It isn't luck, and everyone knows horses are notorious for injury. Clark realizes that a good exercise regime is important. *"We keep a horse in good shape and ride him a lot before we ever go in the pen or think about roping on him."* When asked about older horses brought to him with problems, such as being mean, he admitted, *"I really enjoy working with them, and changing them to be a better roping horse when they are returned to their owner. A horse doesn't learn bad habits 'eating out of the feed bucket.' Some person has caused them to be that way,"* said Clark.

The expert started handling Tom Ferguson's horses when he was only fifteen or sixteen years of age. Since then he has trained horses for numerous other world champions. Today he trains fifteen to eighteen horses at a time. However, he also competes in roping events throughout the year. He tries to make thirty rodeos a year, mainly the big ones and those close to home. He won the All-Around at Cheyenne Frontier Days in 1995 and the Steer Roping at Pendleton RoundUp in 2005, just to name a couple of his major wins.

ROPERS OF TODAY

CODY OHL. Born September 21, 1973, in Rosenberg, Texas. Dad, Leo Ohl, helped Cody practice for hours, even when it meant staying up late into the night. Both Cody's parents roped for fun, and went to many jackpot ropings in the area. Ohl says his dad was truly his mentor, although he watched all the big-name ropers.

The only roping school he ever attended was Roy Cooper's school when he was nine. Also at nine years of age he won his first saddle and at fourteen his first trailer. As a high school freshman he won the Texas state team roping championship. He went to the High School Finals every year, and won the calf roping championship as a junior. As a senior he qualified for the finals in three events: team roping, steer wrestling, and calf roping.

As a PRCA rookie in 1994, only Ohl and Mark Gomes, bareback rider, represented the Rookie class at the National Finals. He has won four Calf Roping Championships, in 1997, 1998, 2001, and 2003, and one All-Around Championship in 2001. Ohl's injury to his leg in the 9th round of the 2001 National Finals put him out of commission for half of the following year, however by June he and Mack Altizer won the Coleman, Texas, PRCA rodeo team roping average. Presently he participates in all three roping events, doesn't travel to as many rodeos as he once did, and admits he sure likes to be home to see his son play T-ball.

Ohl says, *"In twelve years of professional roping I feel I have had three or four unbelievable horses, two I bought. Some people will say that in roping 50% of the credit should go to the horse. I'm convinced they should have 80% of the credit because when you are riding a horse that is right for you there is no effort. It all works right. Hustler, my bay horse I won the World on in 2001, when he was 19, is one of those 'perfect horses.' I got him from Trent Walls, who in turn got him from Grady Lockhart. He's retired now but my son still rides him."*

When Ohl was asked what was the most thrilling win of his career, he didn't hesitate. *"Winning my first World Championship in 1997, and having my dad see me win, and the pride that my mom and dad had. My dad lived his goals through me. They didn't just help me, they lived their life for me and what I wanted to achieve."*

Cody Ohl won the first round of the 2005 National Finals Rodeo in calf roping, but strained his left groin when dismounting. He continued to compete and won the seventh and tenth go-rounds. He left Las Vegas earning $85,817, more than any other calf roper during the Finals.
—Photograph by and courtesy of Dan Hubbell

Ohl lives with his wife Jennie and two sons, Hunter, age six, and Cody Blake, three and a half, and has a new four-month-old daughter named Saylor. They call Hico, Texas, home.

TREVOR BRAZILE. Born November 16, 1976, in Amarillo, Texas. When Jimmy Brazile, Trevor's dad, began his roping career, no one in the Brazile family had ever competed in rodeo. Jimmy became the 1977 Steer Roping Rookie of the Year.

When Trevor was a year and a half old his granddad put a 30 gallon drum in the living room, put a calf head on it and there were lots of "matched ropings" in the living room. The rest is history! At first Trevor and his dad competed in team roping and the youngster always had a goal to become the All Around Cowboy of the World. His dad kept him active and practicing equally in all three events. *Trevor grew up knowing how to rope,* said Jimmy Brazile. *"When he finally got as good as he could be, it all seemed to come about at the same time."*

Twenty years later Trevor followed his dad into the world of professional rodeo and never looked back. There was a brief moment

Trevor Brazile is one of the most versatile champions of any era.
—Photograph by and courtesy of Dan Hubbell

Trevor Brazile in 2003 was the first contestant to ever qualify in four events for the National Finals: calf roping, team roping–header, team roping–heeler, and steer roping.

—Photograph by and courtesy of Dan Hubbell

when Trevor was in college that Jimmy had a concern. *"Trevor bought a saddle bronc saddle and brought it home. I talked as hard as I could and even had thoughts of chaining that bronc saddle to the saddle rack, but he eventually put that thought to rest,"* chuckled his dad.

"He wears everybody out when it comes to practicing with him," said Jimmy about his son, who won the same Steer Roping Rookie of the Year title in 1996. Roy Cooper has said about Brazile, *"It's his work ethic that separates him from the rest. If it rains at his arena, he comes over and practices in my indoor arena. By eight he has his horses saddled, and at 10:30 at night he might stop roping."* Brazile is the first cowboy in ProRodeo history to qualify for the National Finals in all four roping events.[A33] When I asked Jimmy Brazile what his son did for fun, he said, *"I don't know. If you find out, let me know."*

Although he has many horses in training, Brazile considers his two best currently to be Texaco, a Duo Pep bred little chestnut horse, and Duffus. Trevor and his wife Shada are building a new home near Decatur, Texas.

JERRY LONG. Born in eastern New Mexico. His dad Alex, a farmer turned rancher, had a special ability with horses plus he competed in rodeos. Jerry followed in his dad's footsteps and won his first competition at the age of eight. By the time he was nineteen he had won a dozen saddles.

Jerry's dad had health problems including diabetes. He lost his eyesight and died at the early age of 46. As Jerry aged he realized his health was following the same path as his father's. He, too, had diabetes and lost his eyesight, and had to have a kidney transplant. Jerry had become a school teacher and fortunately had pursued his education and received a master's degree and worked toward his doctorate. Eventually he was forced to get an educational retirement. He worked for a time with the Texas School for the Blind as a counselor. Who better than someone not sighted to advise youngsters with the same problem.

It was a downhill spiral for this competitive roper. With no eyesight except to see light and dark, Long became very depressed. A

Jerry Long, legally-blind roper, uses bells on the horns to locate his catch.
—Photographer unknown. Courtesy of Jerry Long

Jerry Long and wife Glenda at the Dean Smith Celebrity Rodeo, Abilene, Texas, 2004. When first invited to a celebrity roping, Long said, "I'm not a celebrity." Tuffy Cooper said, "Well, you're durn shore different."

—Photo by Gail Woerner

friend, Delbert McKenzie, forced him to a roping—just to get out. McKenzie introduced Long to a horse named Trace, who he assured his friend was trustworthy and steady. When Long first mounted Trace he remembered, *"I couldn't see the ground, or the horse's head—it felt so strange."* Slowly he rode around the arena, and eventually began to feel more confident. McKenzie then goaded Long to try team roping. He tied a bell on the steer's tail and Long heeled by aiming his loop toward the tinkle of the bell. Long felt he would never get the rope to make its mark on the steer's heels, but once it happened Long was hooked. Eventually Long started heading. By the time I met him at Dean Smith's Celebrity Rodeo in Abilene in November 2004, he was a header and the bells are attached to the steer's horns. He roped two steers at that event and never missed his mark.

This amazing man often gives motivational speeches, and is such a shining example to others who feel their challenges are too great. He has spoken to FFA conventioneers in several states and was featured on *Peter Jennings' Nightly News.*

When Tuffy Cooper approached him the first time to participate in a Celebrity Roping at Ruidoso, New Mexico, Long said, *"But, Tuffy, I'm not a celebrity."* Cooper was silent for a minute then responded in his inimitable way, *"Well, you're durn shore different."* Long has been invited to numerous "celebrity" events ever since, and rightly so. Long's motto is, Just *TRY, TRY, and TRY AGAIN.*

PROLOGUE

Cowboys will continue to swing a rope, throw a loop and tie their stock. They will continue to practice, practice, and practice. They'll go to jackpot ropings, as well as compete at full fledged competitions with high dollar stakes as often as possible. A few will continue to figure out ways to shorten their time, a millisecond here and another there, and if it works, other ropers will copy them. But there will always be that calf that runs with exceptional speed, or kicks like the devil when the contestant tries to tie him. The steer that gets thrown will jump to his feet just before the cowboy reaches him. The horse will loses his focus or forget to keep the rope tight until his rider has made the tie. All to the disappointment of the contestant.

Roping is a sport that has many variables, both human and animal. The cowboy thinks the next loop he throws will be straighter, faster, more perfect. Will they ever get it the way they want it—exactly right? The possibility is there, but it is elusive, and most will never get there. But that is the challenge to the roper, and he's up for it.

APPENDIX

PRORODEO RECORDS

CHAMPION ALL-AROUND COWBOYS

1929/Earl Thode, Belvedere, SD
1930/Clay Carr, Visalia, CA
1931/John Schneider, Livermore, CA
1932/Donald Nesbitt, Snowflake, AZ
1933/Clay Carr, Visalia, CA
1934/Leonard Ward, Talent, OR
1935/Everett Bowman, Hillside, AZ
1936/John Bowman, Oakdale, CA
1937/Everett Bowman, Hillside, AZ
1938/Burel Mulkey, Salmon, ID
1939/Paul Carney, Galeton, CO
1940/Fritz Truan, Long Beach, CA
1941/Homer Pettigrew, Grady, NM
1942/Gerald Roberts, Strong City, KS
1943/Louis Brooks, Pittsburg, OK
1944/Louis Brooks, Pittsburg, OK
1945/No Award
1946/No Award
1947/Todd Whatley, Hugo, OK
1948/Gerald Roberts, Strong City, KS
1949/Jim Shoulders, Henryetta, OK
1950/Bill Linderman, Red Lodge, MT
1951/Casey Tibbs, Fort Pierre, SD
1952/Harry Tompkins, Dublin, TX
1953/Bill Linderman, Red Lodge, MT
1954/Buck Rutherford, Lenapah, OK

1955/Casey Tibbs, Fort Pierre, SD
1956/Jim Shoulders, Henryetta, OK
1957/Jim Shoulders, Henryetta, OK
1958/Jim Shoulders, Henryetta, OK
1959/Jim Shoulders, Henryetta, OK
1960/Harry Tompkins, Dublin, TX
1961/Benny Reynolds, Melrose, MT
1962/Tom Nesmith, Bethel, OK
1963/Dean Oliver, Boise, ID
1964/Dean Oliver, Boise, ID
1965/Dean Oliver, Boise, ID
1966/Larry Mahan, Brooks, OR
1967/Larry Mahan, Brooks, OR
1968/Larry Mahan, Salem, OR
1969/Larry Mahan, Salem, OR
1970/Larry Mahan, Brooks, OR
1971/Phil Lyne, George West, TX
1972/Phil Lyne, George West, TX
1973/Larry Mahan, Dallas, TX
1974/Tom Ferguson, Miami, OK
1975/Tie: Tom Ferguson, Miami, OK
　　　　　Leo Camarillo, Oakdale, CA
1976/Tom Ferguson, Miami, OK
1977/Tom Ferguson, Miami, OK
1978/Tom Ferguson, Miami, OK
1979/Tom Ferguson, Miami, OK

1980/Paul Tierney, Rapid City, SD
1981/Jimmie Cooper, Monument, NM
1982/Chris Lybbert, Coyote, CA
1983/Roy Cooper, Durant, OK
1984/Dee Pickett, Caldwell, ID
1985/Lewis Feild, Elk Ridge, UT
1986/Lewis Feild, Elk Ridge, UT
1987/Lewis Feild, Elk Ridge, UT
1988/Dave Appleton, Dallas, TX
1989/Ty Murray, Odessa, TX
1990/Ty Murray, Stephenville, TX
1991/Ty Murray, Stephenville, TX
1992/Ty Murray, Stephenville, TX

1993/Ty Murray, Stephenville, TX
1994/Ty Murray, Stephenville, TX
1995/Joe Beaver, Huntsville, TX
1996/Joe Beaver, Huntsville, TX
1997/Dan Mortensen, Manhatten, MT
1998/Ty Murray, Stephenville, TX
1999/Fred Whitfield, Hockley, TX
2000/Joe Beaver, Huntsville, TX
2001/Cody Ohl, Stephenville, TX
2002/Trevor Brazile, Anson, TX
2003/Trevor Brazile, Decatur, TX
2004/Trevor Brazile, Decatur, TX
2005/Ryan Jarrett, Summerville, GA

CHAMPION STEER ROPERS

1929/Charles Maggini, San Jose, CA
1930/Clay Carr, Visalia, CA
1931/Andy Jauregui, Newhall, CA
1932/George Weir, Okmulgee, OK
1933/John Bowman, Oakdale, CA
1934/John McEntire, Kiowa, OK
1935/Richard Merchant, Kirkland, AZ
1936/John Bowman, Oakdale, CA
1937/Everett Bowman, Hillside, AZ
1938/Hugh Bennett, Fort Thomas, AZ
1939/Dick Truitt, Stonewall, OK
1940/Clay Carr, Visalia, CA
1941/Ike Rude, Buffalo, OK
1942/King Merritt, Federal, WY
1943/Tom Rhodes, Sombrero Butte, AZ
1944/Tom Rhodes, Sombrero Butte, AZ
1945/Everett Shaw, Stonewall, OK
1946/Everett Shaw, Stonewall, OK
1947/Ike Rude, Buffalo, OK
1948/Everett Shaw, Stonewall, OK
1949/Shoat Webster, Lenapah, OK
1950/Shoat Webster, Lenapah, OK

1951/Everett Shaw, Stonewall, OK
1952/Buddy Neal, Van Horn, CA
1953/Ike Rude, Buffalo, OK
1954/Shoat Webster, Lenapah, OK
1955/Shoat Webster, Lenapah, OK
1956/Jim Snively, Pawhuska, OK
1957/Clark McEntire, Kiowa, OK
1958/Clark McEntire, Kiowa, OK
1959/Everett Shaw, Stonewall, OK
1960/Don McLaughlin, Ft. Worth, TX
1961/Clark McEntire, Kiowa, OK
1962/Everett Shaw, Stonewall, OK
1963/Don McLaughlin, Ft. Collins, CO
1964/Sonny Davis, Kenna, NM
1965/Sonny Wright, Alto, NM
1966/Sonny Davis, Kenna, NM
1967/Jim Bob Altizer, Del Rio, TX
1968/Sonny Davis, Kenna, NM
1969/Walter Arnold, Silverton, TX
1970/Don McLaughlin, Ft. Collins, CO
1971/Olin Young, Peralta, NM
1972/Allen Keller, Olathe, CO

1973/Roy Thompson, Tulia, TX
1974/Olin Young, Peralta, NM
1975/Roy Thompson, Tulia, TX
1976/Charles Good, Elida, NM
1977/Guy Allen, Santa Anna, TX
1978/Kenny Call, Norman, OK
1979/Gary Good, Elida, NM
1980/Guy Allen, Santa Anna, TX
1981/Arnold Felts, Mutual, OK
1982/Guy Allen, Lovington, NM
1983/Roy Cooper, Durant, OK
1984/Guy Allen, Lovington, NM
1985/Jim Davis, Bandera, TX
1986/Jim Davis, Bandera, TX
1987/Shaun Burchett, Pryor, OK
1988/Shaun Burchett, Pryor, OK
1989/Guy Allen, Lovington, NM

1990/Phil Lyne, Cotulla, TX
1991/Guy Allen, Vinita, OK
1992/Guy Allen, Vinita, OK
1993/Guy Allen, Vinita, OK
1994/Guy Allen, Vinita, OK
1995/Guy Allen, Lovington, NM
1996/Guy Allen, Lovington, NM
1997/Guy Allen Lovington, NM
1998/Guy Allen, Lovington, NM
1999/Guy Allen, Lovington, NM
2000/Guy Allen, Lovington, NM
2001/Guy Allen, Santa Anna, TX
2002/Buster Record, Buffalo, OK
2003/Guy Allen, Santa Anna, TX
2004/Guy Allen, Santa Anna, TX
2005/Scott Snedecor, Uvalde, TX
2006/Trevor Brazile, Decatur, TX

CHAMPION CALF ROPERS

1929/Everett Bowman, Hillside, AZ
1930/Jake McClure, Lovington, NM
1931/Herb Meyers, Okmulgee, OK
1932/Richard Merchant, Kirkland, AZ
1933/Bill McFarlane, Red Bluff, CA
1934/Irby Mundy, Shamrock, TX
1935/Everett Bowman, Hillside, AZ
1936/Clyde Burk, Comanche, OK
1937/Everett Bowman, Hillside, AZ
1938/Clyde Burk, Comanche, OK
1939/Toots Mansfield, Bandera, TX
1940/Toots Mansfield, Bandera, TX
1941/Toots Mansfield, Bandera, TX
1942/Clyde Burk, Comanche, OK
1943/Toots Mansfield, Bandera, TX
1944/Clyde Burk, Comanche, OK
1945/Toots Mansfield, Bandera, TX
1946/Royce Sewalt, King, TX

1947/Troy Fort, Lovington, NM
1948/Toots Mansfield, Bandera, TX
1949/Troy Fort, Lovington, NM
1950/Toots Mansfield, Bandera, TX
1951/Don McLaughlin, Ft. Worth, TX
1952/Don McLaughlin, Ft. Worth, TX
1953/Don McLaughlin, Ft. Worth, TX
1954/Don McLaughlin, Ft. Worth, TX
1955/Dean Oliver, Boise, ID
1956/Ray Wharton, Bandera, TX
1957/Don McLaughlin, Ft. Worth, TX
1958/Dean Oliver, Boise, ID
1959/Jim Bob Altizer, Del Rio, TX
1960/Dean Oliver, Boise, ID
1961/Dean Oliver, Boise, ID
1962/Dean Oliver, Boise, ID
1963/Dean Oliver, Boise, ID
1964/Dean Oliver, Boise, ID

1965/Glen Franklin, House, NM
1966/Junior Garrison, Marlow, OK
1967/Glen Franklin, House, NM
1968/Glen Franklin, House, NM
1969/Dean Oliver, Boise, ID
1970/Junior Garrison, Duncan, OK
1971/Phil Lyne, George West, TX
1972/Phil Lyne, George West, TX
1973/Ernie Taylor, Hugo, OK
1974/Tom Ferguson, Miami, OK
1975/Jeff Copenhaver, Spokane, WA
1976/Roy Cooper, Durant, OK
1977/Jim Gladstone, Cardston, Alberta
1978/Dave Brock, Pueblo, CO
1979/Paul Tierney, Rapid City, SD
1980/Roy Cooper, Durant, OK
1981/Roy Cooper, Durant, OK
1982/Roy Cooper, Durant, OK
1983/Roy Cooper, Durant, OK
1984/Roy Cooper, Durant, OK
1985/Joe Beaver, Victoria, TX

1986/Chris Lybbert, Argyle, TX
1987/Joe Beaver, Victoria, TX
1988/Joe Beaver, Victoria, TX
1989/Rabe Rabon, San Antonio, FL
1990/Troy Pruitt, Lennox, SD
1991/Fred Whitfield, Cypress, TX
1992/Joe Beaver, Huntsville, TX
1993/Joe Beaver, Huntsville, TX
1994/Herbert Theriot, Wiggins, MS
1995/Fred Whitfield, Hockley, TX
1996/Fred Whitfield, Hockley, TX
1997/Cody Ohl, Orchard, TX
1998/Cody Ohl, Orchard, TX
1999/Fred Whitfield, Hockley, TX
2000/Fred Whitflield, Hockley, TX
2001/Cody Ohl, Stephenville, TX
2002/Fred Whitfield, Hockley, TX
2003/Cody Ohl, Stephenville, TX
2004/Monty Lewis, Hereford, TX
2005/Fred Whitfield, Hockley, TX

CHAMPION TEAM ROPERS

1929/Charles Maggini, San Jose, CA
1930/Norman Cowan, Gresham, OR
1931/Arthur Beloat, Buckeye, AZ
1932/Ace Gardner, Coolidge, AZ
1933/Roy Adams, Tucson, AZ
1934/Andy Jauregui, Newhall, CA
1935/Lawrence Conley, Prescott, AZ
1936/John Rhodes, Sombrero Butte, AZ
1937/Asbury Schell, Camp Verde, AZ
1938/John Rhodes, Sombrero Butte, AZ
1939/Asbury Schell, Camp Verde, AZ
1940/Pete Grubb, Salmon, ID
1941/Jim Hudson, Willcox, AZ
1942/Verne Castro, Livermore, CA

1942/Vic Castro, Livermore, CA
1943/Mark Hull, Stockton, CA
1943/Leonard Block, Denair, CA
1944/Murphy Chaney, Shandon, CA
1945/Ernest Gill, Madera, CA
1946/Chuck Sheppard, Phoenix, AZ
1947/Jim Brister, Lordsburg, NM
1948/Joe Glenn, Douglas, AZ
1949/Ed Yanez, Newhall, CA
1950/Buck Sorrels, Tucson, AZ
1951/Olan Sims, Madera, CA
1952/Asbury Schell, Camp Verde, AZ
1953/Ben Johnson, Hollywood, CA
1954/Eddie Schell, Camp Verde, AZ

1955/Vern Castro, Richmond, CA
1956/Dale Smith, Chandler, AZ
1957/Dale Smith, Chandler, AZ
1958/Ted Ashworth, Phoenix, AZ
1959/Jim Rodriguez, Jr., Castroville, CA
1960/Jim Rodriguez, Jr., Castroville, CA
1961/Al Hooper, Escalon, CA
1962/Jim Rodriguez, Jr., Castroville, CA
1963/Les Hirdes, Turlock, CA
1964/Bill Hamilton, Phoenix, AZ
1965/Jim Rodriguez, Jr., Paso Robles, CA
1966/Ken Luman, Merced, CA
1967/Joe Glenn, Phoenix, AZ
1968/Art Arnold, Buckeye, AZ
1969/Jerold Camarillo, Oakdale, CA
1970/John Miller, Pawhuska, OK
1971/John Miller, Pawhuska, OK
1972/Leo Camarillo, Donald, OR
1973/Leo Camarillo, Donald, OR
1974/H. P. Evetts, Hanford, CA
1975/Leo Camarillo, Oakdale, CA
1976/Bucky Bradford, Sylmar, CA
1976/Ronnie Rasco, Lakeside, CA
1977/David Motes, Fresno, CA
1977/Dennis Motes, Mesa, AZ
1978/Brad Smith, Prescott, AZ
1978/George Richards, Humbolt, AZ
1979/Allen Bach, Queen Creek, AZ
1980/Tee Woolman, Llano, TX
1981/Walt Woodard, Stockton, CA
1981/Doyle Gellerman, Oakdale, CA
1982/Tee Woolman, Fredonia, TX
1983/Leo Camarillo, Lockeford, CA
1984/Dee Pickett, Caldwell, ID
1984/Mike Beers, Rufus, OR
1985/Jake Barnes, Bloomfield, NM
1985/Clay O. Cooper,
      Chandler Hgts, AZ
1986/Clay O. Cooper,
      Chandler Hgts, AZ
1986/Jake Barnes, Bloomfield, NM
1987/Clay O. Cooper, Gilbert, AZ

1987/Jake Barnes, Bloomfield, NM
1988/Jake Barnes, Bloomfield, NM
1988/Clay O. Cooper, Gilbert, AZ
1989/Jake Barnes, Bloomfield, NM
1989/Clay O. Cooper, Gilbert, AZ
1990/Allen Bach, Merced, CA
1991/Bob Harris, Gillette, WY
1991/Tee Woolman, Llano, TX
1992/Jake Barnes, Higley, AZ
1992/Clay O. Cooper, Gilbert, AZ
1993/Bobby Hurley, Ceres, CA
1994/Jake Barnes, Cave Creek, AZ
1994/Clay O. Cooper, Gilbert, AZ
1995/Bobby Hurley (hdr), Ceres, CA
1995/Allen Bach (hlr), Toltec, AZ
1996/Steve Purcella (hdr), Hereford, TX
1996/Steve Northcott (hlr), Odessa, TX
1997/Speed Williams (hdr),
      Jacksonville, FL
1997/Rich Skelton (hlr), Llano, TX
1998/Speed Williams (hdr),
      Jacksonville, FL
1998/Rich Skelton (hlr), Llano, TX
1999/Speed Williams (hdr),
      Jacksonville, FL
1999/Rich Skelton (hlr), Llano, TX
2000/Speed Williams (hdr),
      Jacksonville, FL
2000/Rich Skelton (hlr), Llano, TX
2001/Speed Williams (hdr),
      Jacksonville, FL
2001/Rich Skelton (hlr), Llano, TX
2002/Speed Williams (hdr),
      Jacksonville, FL
2002/Rich Skelton (hlr), Llano, TX
2003/Speed Williams (hdr), Amarillo, TX
2003/Rich Skelton (hlr), Llano, TX
2004/Speed Williams (hdr), Llano, TX
2004/Rich Skelton (hlr), Llano, TX
2005/Clay Tryan (hdr) Billings, MT
2005/Patrick Smith (hlr) Midland, TX

AMERICAN QUARTER HORSE ASSOCIATION HORSE OF THE YEAR

EVENT	NICKNAME	NAME	OWNER
1989——			
Calf Roping		Doc's Desperado	Paul Zanardi
			Joe Parsons
Steer Wrestling	"Doc"	Doc Bee Quick	Larry Ferguson
TR—Heading		Mr. Ruby Clerk	Matt Tyler
TR—Heeling		Flint's Friend	J. D. Yates
Steer Roping	"Dutch"	Cody Bar Skip	Mack Yates
			Tee Woolman
WPRA Barrel Race	"Scamper"	Gill's Bay Boy	Charmayne Rodman
1990——			
Calf Roping	"Mr. Tee"	Power Key	Johnny Emmons
Steer Wrestling	"Doc"	Doc Bee Quick	Larry Ferguson
TR-Heading		Yellow Bar Smug	Bobby Hurley
TR—Heeling	"B. J."	Jet Interruption	Dennis Watkins
Steer Roping	"Rocky"	Barley Needs Rivet	Mack Yates
WPRA Barrel Race	"Scamper"	Gill's Bay Boy	Charmayne Rodman
1991——			
Calf Roping	"Boogie Man"	Broadway Tar Baby	Mike & Paula Arnold
Steer Wrestling	"Doc"	Doc Bee Quick	Larry Ferguson
TR—Heading	"Scooter"	Oklahoma Top Hat	Charles Pogue
TR—Heeling	"Dunny"	Bar Five Keys Dun	Steve Northcott
Steer Roping	"Dutch"	Cody Bar Skip	Mack Yates/
			Tee Woolman
WPRA Barrel Race	"Scamper"	Gill's Bay Boy	Charmayne Rodman
1992——			
Calf Roping	"Malachi"	Tommy's Blue Bag	Brent Lewis
Steer Wrestling	"Skippy"	Skip D Sack	Harrison Halligan
TR—Heading	"Scooter"	Oklahoma Top Hat	Charles Pogue
TR—Heeling	"Iceman"	Flit's Smokin Dream	Kory Koontz
Steer Roping	"Dutch"	Cody Bar Skip	Tee Woolman
WPRA Barrel Race	"Scamper"	Gill's Bay Boy	Charmayne Rodman
1993——			
Calf Roping	"Boogie Man"	Broadway Tar Baby	Mike & Paula Arnold
Steer Wrestling	"Hank"	Hank Bar Binion	Bill Cresta
TR—Heading	"Scooter"	Oklahoma Top Hat	Charles Pogue
TR—Heeling	"Iceman"	Flit's Smokin Dream	Kory Koontz
Steer Roping	"Dutch"	Cody Bar Skip	Tee Woolman
WPRA Barrel Race	"Scamper"	Gill's Bay Boy	Charmayne Rodman
1994——			
Calf Roping	"Prime Time"	Grand Rapid Return	Jim Farris
			J. D. Tadlock

Steer Wrestling	"Yellow Dog"	Too Vee	Jimmy & Allison Powers (Steve Duhon)
TR—Heading	"Spiff"	Tres Spiffy Dude	Bobby Hurley
TR—Heeling	"Dunny"	Bar Five Keys Dun	Steve Northcott
Steer Roping	"Santa Clause"	Gray Baldy	Arnold Felts
WPRA Barrel Race	"Brown"	Special Agreement	Bubba & Deb Mohon

1995——

Calf Roping	"Orejas"	Cowboy Marine	Jerry Jetton
Steer Wrestling	"Whitey"	Mr. Light Star	Bill Duvall (Bill, Sam, Roy)
TR—Heading	"Rooster"	Ayes Have It	Eddie Wilkerson (Jake Barnes)
TR—Heeling	"Blue"	Wills Budha	Cody Cowden
Steer Roping	"Refuse"	Flaxy Flash	H.L. Todd (& Jimmy Hodge)
WPRA Barrel Race	"Bozo"	French Flash Hawk	Kristie Peterson

1996——

Calf Roping	"Art"	Little Ring	Junior Lewis (Brent Lewis)
Steer Wrestling	"San Wood"	Super San Wood	Jerry & Todd Suhn
TR—Heading	"Butterbean"	Mark My Dream	Steve Purcella
TR—Heeling	"Iceman"	Flit's Smokin Dream	Kory Koontz
Steer Roping	"Chubs"	Van's Lad	Mel Potter
WPRA Barrel Race	"Bozo"	French Flash Hawk	Kristie Peterson

1997——

Calf Roping	"Rifleman"	Kido Doc	Stran Smith
Steer Wrestling	"Blue"	Mama's Jr.	Byron Walker/ George Strait
TR—Heading	"Scooter"	Oklahoma Top Hat	Charles Pogue
TR—Heeling	"Roany"	Boons Smooth Val	Rich Skelton
Steer Roping	"Bullet"	Jack Bart Tender	Guy Allen
WPRA Barrel Race	"Bozo"	French Flash Hawk	Kristie Peterson

1998——

Calf Roping	"Deuce"	Merry Two Bar	Trent Walls
Steer Wrestling	"Scooter"	Bad Motor Scooter	Jimmy Powers
TR—Heading	"Scooter"	Oklahoma Top Hat	Charles Pogue
TR—Heeling	"Roany"	Boons Smooth Val	Rich Skelton
Steer Roping	"Rocky"	Dr. Rocky Bob	Bucky Hefner
WPRA Barrel Race	"Bozo"	French Flash Hawk	Kristie Peterson

1999——

Calf Roping	"Smoky"	Smokin Dee	Clay Cade/ Jerome Schneeberger
Steer Wrestling	"Preacher"	Padres Perfection	Wayne Jennings
TR—Heading	"Scooter"	Oklahoma Top Hat	Charles Pogue
TR—Heeling	"Roany"	Boons Smooth Val	Rich Skelton
Steer Roping	"Jeremiah"	Two D Ole Man	Guy Allen

| WPRA Barrel Race | "Bozo" | French Flash Hawk | Kristie Peterson |

2000——

Calf Roping	"Grumpy"	Kid Taurus	Brent Lewis
Steer Wrestling	"Becky"	Becky My Loop	Brent Arnold
TR—Heading	"Viper"	Keep on Flushing	Speed Williams
TR—Heeling	"Dinero"	Nifty Jacks Back	Kyle Lockett
Steer Roping	Jeremiah"	Two D Ole Man	Guy Allen
WPRA Barrel Race	"Fiesta"	Firewater Fiesta	Kelly Yates

2001——

Calf Roping	"Easy"	Leos Sen Bar	Herbert Theriot
Steer Wrestling	"Scooter"	Bad Motor Scooter	Jimmy Powers/ Steve Duhon
TR—Heading	"Calhoon"	Smoothly Anchored	Richard Eiguren
TR—Heeling	"Roany"	Boons Smooth Val	Rich Skelton
Steer Roping	"Jeremiah"	Two D Ole Man	Guy Allen
WPRA Barrel Race	"Fiesta"	Firewater Fiesta	Kelly Yates

2002——

Calf Roping	"Tweeter"	Tinys Clipso	Trevor Brazile
Steer Wrestling	"KO Jak"	Sort of Like Fast	Clyde Himes
TR—Heading	"Calhoon"	Smoothly Anchored	Richard Eiguren
TR—Heeling	"Wick"	Smokin Holly 045	Allen Bach
Steer Roping	"Boudreaux"	Tee Sue Jr.	Jim Evans
WPRA Barrel Race	"Llave"	The Key Grip	Robert & Kay Blandford

2003——

Tie-Down Roping		Topofthemarket	Stran Smith
Steer Wrestling		Ima Star O Lena	Bryan Fields
TR—Heading		Precious Speck	Travis Tryan
TR—Heeling		Marvins Wonder	Dugan Kelly
Steer Roping		Fannin War Leo	Vin Fisher
WPRA Barrel Race		Top Tally	Nathan Williams/ Darlene Kasper

2004——

Tie-Down Roping		IR Still Dry	Monty Lewis
Steer Wrestling		FF Zans A Baron Jack	James Burks/ Ronnie Fields
TR—Heading		Megazord	Tee Woolman
TR—Heeling		Pets Ten	Rich Skelton
Steer Roping		Two D Ole Man	Guy Allen
WPRA Barrel Race		Krimps Ready To Go	Paula Seay

2005——

Tie-Down Roping		Topofthemarket	Stran Smith
Steer Wrestling		FF Zans A Baron Jack	James Burks/ Ronnie Fields
TR—Heading		Docalickin	Pauline Robertson/ Clay Tryan

TR—Heeling	Pets Ten	Rich Skelton
Steer Roping	Bobs Lena	Cash Myers
Barrel Racing	Sparky Impression	June Holeman

The award for the horse chosen for first place is $2,000, second place is $1,000, and third is $500, plus the winner gets a beautiful bronze Quarter Horse statue.

LINDERMAN AWARD WINNERS

(Award named for Bill Linderman, a timed event and roughstock competitor. Winner must win the most monies in three events, including timed events and roughstock)

1966/Benny Reynolds, Melrose, MT
1967/Kenny McLean, Okanagan Falls, British Columbia
1968/Paul Mayo, Grinnell, IA
1969/Kenny McLean, Okanagan Falls, British Columbia
1970/Phil Lyne, George West, TX
1971/Phil Lyne, George West, TX
1972/Phil Lyne, George West, TX
1973/Bob Blandford, San Antonio, TX
1974/Bob Blandford, San Antonio, TX
1975/Chip Whitaker, Chambers, NE
1976/Phil Lyne, Artesia Wells, TX
1977/Chip Whitaker, Chambers, NE
1978/Chip Whitaker, Chambers, NE
1979/Chip Whitaker, Chambers, NE
1980/Steve Bland, Trent, TX
1981/Lewis Feild, Peoa, UT
1982/Tom Eirikson, Innisfail, Alberta
1983/Marty Melvin, Holabird, SD
1984/Marty Melvin, Holabird, SD
1985/Tom Eirikson, Innisfail, Alberta
1986/Bob Schall, Arlee, MT

1987/Tom Eirikson, Priddis, Alberta
1988/Lewis Feild, Elk Ridge, UT
1989/Philip Haugen, Williston, ND
1990/Bernie Smyth Jr., Crossfield, Alberta
1991/Lewis Feild, Elk Ridge, UT
1992/Bernie Smyth Jr., Crossfield, Alberta
1993/Casey Minton, Redwood Valley, CA
1994/No contestant qualified
1995/Chuck Kite, Montfort, WI
1996/No contestant qualified
1997/Kyle Whitaker, Chambers, NE
1998/Kyle Whitaker, Chambers, NE
1999/Dan Erickson, La Junta, CO
2000/Jesse Bail, Camp Crook, SD
2001/Jesse Bail, Camp Crook, SD
2002/Dan Erickson, La Junta, CO
2003/Kyle Whitaker, Chambers, NE
2004/Mike Outhier, Utopia, TX
2005/Kyle Whitaker, Chambers, NE

PRCA OVERALL RESISTOL ROOKIE OF THE YEAR

1956/John W. Jones, San Luis
   Obispo, CA
1957/Bob A. Robinson, Tuttle, ID
1958/Benny Reynolds, Melrose, MT
1959/Harry Charters, Melba, ID
1960/Larry Kane, Big Sandy, MT
1961/Kenny McLean, Okanagan Falls,
   British Columbia
1962/Jim Houston, Omaha, NE
1963/Bill Kornell, Salmon, ID
1964/Jim Steen, Glenn's Ferry, ID
1965/Dan Willis, Aquilla, TX
1966/Tony Haberer, Muleshoe, TX
1967/Jay Himes, Beulah, CO
1968/Bowie Wesley, Wildorado, TX
1969/Phil Lyne, George West, TX
1970/Dick Aronson, Tempe, AZ
1971/Kent Youngblood, Lamesa, TX
1972/Dave Brock, Goodland, KS
1973/Bob Blandford, San Antonio, TX
1974/Lee Phillips, Carseland, Alberta
1975/Don Smith, Kiowa, OK
1976/Roy Cooper, Durant, OK
1977/Jimmy Cleveland, Hollis, OK
1978/Dee Pickett, Caldwell, ID
1979/Jerry Jetton, Stephenville, TX

1980/Jimmie Cooper, Monument, NM
1981/John W. Jones, Jr., Morro Bay, CA
1982/Clark Hankins, Rocksprings, TX
1983/Jacky Gibbs, Ivanhoe, TX
1984/Sam Poutous, Julian, CA
1985/Joe Beaver, Victoria, TX
1986/Jim Sharp, Kermit, TX
1987/Tony Currin, Heppner, OR
1988/Ty Murray, Odessa, TX
1989/David Bailey, Tahlequah, OK
1990/Fred Whitfield, Cypress, TX
1991/Brent Lewis, Pinon, NM
1992/Rope Myers, Athens, TX
1993/Blair Burk, Durant, OK
1994/Cody Ohl, Orchard, TX
1995/Curt Lyons, Ardmore, OK
1996/Shane Slack, Idabel, OK
1997/Mike White, Lake Charles, LA
1998/Danell Tipton, Spencer, OK
1999/Cash Myers, Athens, TX
2000/Luke Branquinho, Los Alamos, CA
2001/Matt Robertson, Augusta, MT
2002/Will Lowe, Gardner, KS
2003/Matt Austin, Wills Point, TX
2004/Clayton Foltyn, El Campo, TX
2005/Steve Woolsey, Spanish Fork, UT

PRCA STEER ROPING ROOKIE OF THE YEAR

1977/Jimmy Brazile,
1978/Bob Harren
1979/??
1980/Clark Victory
1981/Shaun Burchett
1982/Tommy Pearson, Eunice, NM

1983/Jerry Bailey, Washington, OK
1984/Roy Brooks, Amarillo, TX
1985/Kress Jones, Hobbs, NM
1986/Philip Berry, Lovington, NM
1987/Vance McNeil, Pecos, TX
1988/Ben Ingham, Sonora, TX

1989/Bucky Hefner, Chelsea, OK
1990/Scott Stickley, Denton, TX
1991/Todd Casebolt, Sinton, TX
1992/Rocky Patterson, Pratt, KS
1993/J. Paul Williams, Ponca City, OK
1994/Kenyon Burns, Lovington, NM
1995/Jimmy Vaughan, Argyle, TX
1996/Trevor Brazile, Decatur, TX
1997/Paul Patton, Abilene, TX

1998/Clay Cameron, Claude, TX
1999/Bobby Brock, Cushing, OK
2000/Scott Bliss, Sheridan, WY
2001/John McDaniel, Adair, OK
2002/Jarrett Blessing, Paradise, TX
2003/Neal Wood, Guy, TX
2004/Brady Garten, Pawhuska, OK
2005/Cody Scheck, Buffalo, OK

PRCA CALF ROPING ROOKIE OF THE YEAR

1977/Steve Bland
1978/Dee Pickett
1979/Jerry Jetton
1980/Jimmie Cooper
1981/Jim Light
1982/Clark Hankins, Rocksprings, TX
1983/James Zant, Harper, TX
1984/Puddin Payne, Stillwater, OK
1985/Joe Beaver, Victoria, TX
1986/David Bowen, Yoakum, TX
1987/Ricky Canton, Houston, TX
1988/David Felton, Weatherford, TX
1989/Morris Ledford, Comanche, OK
1990/Fred Whitfield, Cypress, TX
1991/Brent Lewis, Pinon, NM

1992/Marty Lindner, Giddings, TX
1993/Blair Burk, Durant, OK
1994/Cody Ohl, Orchard, TX
1995/Chad Johnson, Cut Bank, MT
1996/Shane Slack, Idabel, OK
1997/Clay Cerry, Eagle Lake, TX
1998/Chance Tinney, Winnsboro, TX
1999/Josh Crow, Lovington, NM
2000/Kyle Hughes, Model, CO
2001/Brady Brock, Springtown, TX
2002/Scott Kormos, Mexia, TX
2003/Clint Robinson, Farmington, UT
2004/Caddo Lewallen, Morrison, OK
2005/Jerrad Hofstetter, Athens, TX

PRCA TEAM ROPING ROOKIE OF THE YEAR

1977/Brian Murphy
1978/Brian Burrows
1979/Bill E. Parker
1980/Tee Woolman

1981/Bret Beach
1982/(tie) Mike Fuller, Clarkston, WA
    Chris Henderson, Coulee City, WA
1983/Joel Maker, Poteau, OK

1984/Rusty Wright, Mt. Pleasant, TX
1985/Jerry Buckles, Scotts Bluff, NE
1986/Dennis Gatz, Oakdale, CA
1987/Charles Pogue, Ringling, OK
1988/Flynn Farris, Dalhart, TX
1989/Andy Anaya, Tucson, AZ

1990/Liddon Cowden, Merced, CA
1991/Martin Lucero, Villa Nueva, NM
1992/Britt Bockius, Dewey, OK
1993/Nick Sarchett, Scottsdale, AZ
1994/Brye Sayer, Phoenix, AZ
1995/Shad Chadwick, Mesa, AZ

PRCA TEAM ROPING HEADER ROOKIE OF THE YEAR

(In 1996 PRCA began honoring both header and heeler Rookie)

1996/Scooter Nolen, Jr., Whitesboro, TX
1997/Kit Sherwood, Snowflake, AZ
1998/Charly Crawford, Canby, OR
1999/Ty Thomas, Idabel, OK
2000/Nick Sartain, Yukon, OK

2001/Reese Kerr, Cotulla, TX
2002/Travis Gallais, Olds, Alberta
2003/Jason Adams, Logandale, NV
2004/Jake Cooper, Monument, NM
2005/Brandon Beers, Powell Butte, OR

PRCA TEAM ROPING HEELER ROOKIE OF THE YEAR

1996/Mickey Gomez, Salado, TX
1997/Kyle Lockett, Ivanhoe, CA
1998/John Paul Cuero, Villanueva, NM
1999/Craig Branham, Canyon
     Country, CA
2000/Trey Johnson, Lovington, NM

2001/Matt Robertson, Augusta, MT
2002/Randon Adams, Logandale, NV
2003/Patrick Smith, Midland, TX
2004/Jimmie Cooper, Stephenville, TX
2005/Douglas Gillespie, Arrowhead,
     Alberta

PRCA NATIONAL FINALS

NFR Average Steer Roping Champion	Seconds	Roped
1959/Jim Snively Sr., Pawhuska, OK	170.4	6
1960/Don McLaughlin, Fort Collins, CO	125.2	6
1961/Joe Snively, Pawhuska, OK	145.6	6
1962/Everett Shaw, Stonewall, OK	124.3	6
1963/Glenn Nutter, Thedford, NE	114.9	6
1964/Don McLaughlin, Fort Collins, Co	178.2	6
1965/Walt Arnold, Silverton, TX	124.4	6
1966/Kelly Corbin, Delaware, OK	108.1	6
1967/Olin Young, Peralta, NM	127.5	6
1968/Sonny Davis, Kenna, NM	120.8	6
1969/Tim Prather, Post, TX	125.5	6
1970/Dewey Lee David, Riverton, WY	214.5	6
1971/James Allen, Santa Anna, TX	117.1	6
1972/Joe Snively, Sedan, KS	131.7	6
1973/Eddie Becker, Ashby, NE	197.7	8
1974/Olin Young, Peralta, NM	149.1	8
1975/Dewey Lee David, Riverton, WY	150.8	8
1976/Charles Good, Elida, NM	182.2	10
1977/Olin Young, Peralta, NM	204.0	10
1978/Walt Arnold, Silverton, TX	228.2	10
1979/Gary Good, Elida, NM	208.3	10
1980/Terry McGinley, Keystone, NE	200.4	10
1981/Terry McGinley, Keystone, NE	194.4	10
1982/Wade Lewis, Hereford, TX	222.8	10
1983/Phil Lyne, Cotulla, TX	176.7	10
1984/Roy Cooper, Durant, OK	146.7	10
1985/Roy Cooper, Durant, OK	153.2	10
1986/Phil Lyne, Cotulla, TX	184.8	10
1987/Rod Pratt, Sharon Springs, KS	148.6	10
1988/Jim Davis, Bandera, TX	155.0	10
1989/Guy Allen, Lovington, NM	144.2	10
1990/Neil Worrell, Fredonia, KS	175.2	10
1991/Guy Allen, Vinita, OK	160.8	10
1992/Arnold Felts, Sonora, TX	172.8	10
1993/Roy Cooper, Childress, TX	147.8	10
1994/Arnold Felts, Sonora, TX	159.4	10
1995/Arnold Felts, Sonora, TX	148.8	10
1996/Roy Cooper, Childress, TX	131.5	10
1997/Guy Allen, Lovington, NM	136.2	10

	Seconds	Head
1998/Tee Woolman, Llano, TX	168.7	10
1999/Rocky Patterson, Pratt, KS	146.7	10
2000/Guy Allen, Lovington, NM	139.3	10
2001/Rocky Patterson, Pratt, KS	114.5	10
2002/Chet Herren, Pawhuska, OK	223.2	10
2003/Ora Taton, Rapid City, SD	159.9	10
2004/Guy Allen, Santa Anna, TX	128.2	10
2005/Scott Snedecor, Uvalde, TX	123.4	10

NFR Average Calf Roping Champion

	Seconds	Head
1959/Olin Young, Albuquerque, NM	191.3	10
1960/Don McLaughlin, Fort Collins, CO	161.6	10
1961/Dean Oliver, Boise, ID	124.0	8
1962/Olin Young, Albuquerque, NM	122.1	8
1963/Olin Young, Albuquerque, NM	112.6	8
1964/Jim Bob Altizer, Del Rio, TX	120.3	8
1965/Jim Bob Altizer, Del Rio, TX	114.6	8
1966/Lee Cockrell, Panhandle, TX	124.5	8
1967/Glen Franklin, House, NM	131.4	9
1968/Junior Garrison, Marlow, OK	128.6	9
1969/Mark Schricker, Sutherlin, OR	125.0	9
1970/Richard Stowers, Duncan, OK	134.7	10
1971/Olin Young, Peralta, NM	139.6	10
1972/Phil Lyne, George West, TX	129.7	10
1973/Barry Burk, Duncan, OK	144.8	10
1974/Ronnye Sewalt, Chico, TX	137.6	10
1975/Bobby Goodspeed, High Ridge, MO	140.6	10
1976/Roy Cooper, Durant, OK	133.4	10
1977/Jim Gladstone, Cardston, Alberta	119.7	10
1978/Gary Ledford, Comanche, OK	134.9	11
1979/Roy Cooper, Durant, OK	107.9	10
1980/Chris Lybbert, Coyote, CA	123.5	10
1981/Chris Lybbert, Coyote, CA	113.4	10
1982/Mike McLaughlin, Saginaw, TX	122.2	10
1983/Roy Cooper, Durant, OK	109.1	10
1984/Dee Pickett, Caldwell, ID	114.9	10
1985/Mike McLaughlin, Fort Worth, TX	102.6	10
1986/D. R. Daniel, Okeechobee, FL	102.6	10
1987/Joe Beaver, Victoria, TX	112.3	10
1988/Joe Beaver, Victoria, TX	117.1	10
1989/Dave Bowen, Yoakum, TX	110.6	10
1990/Herbert Theriot, Wiggins, MS	106.8	10
1991/Fred Whitfield, Cypress, TX	91.7	10

	Seconds	Head
1992/Joe Beaver, Huntsville, TX	96.8	10
1993/Troy Pruitt, Minatare, NE	96.4	10
1994/Todd Slone, Canyon Lake, TX	99.5	10
1995/Roy Cooper, Childress, TX	101.8	10
1996/Joe Beaver, Huntsville, TX	101.9	10
1997/Fred Whitfield, Hockley, TX	84.0	10
1998/Cody Ohl, Stephenville, TX	91.6	10
1999/Fred Whitfield, Hockley, TX	87.0	10
2000/Brent Lewis, Pinon, NM	86.9	10
2001/Jerome Schneeberger, Ponca City, OK	109.6	10
2002/Fred Whitfield, Hockley, TX	88.8	10
2003/Mike Johnson, Henryetta, OK	86.4	10
2004/Monty Lewis, Hereford, TX	87.8	10
2005/Ryan Jarrett, Summerville, GA	89.0	10

NFR Average Team Roping Champions

	Seconds	Head
1959/Jim Rodriguez, Jr., San Luis Obispo, CA		
Gene Rambo, Shandon, CA	121.8	6
1960/Jim Rodriguez, Jr., San Luis Obispo, CA		
Gene Rambo, Shandon, CA	134.8	8
1961/Sam Edmondson, Fresno, CA		
R. D. Rutledge, Tulare, CA	124.1	8
1962/Les Hirdes, Turlock, CA		
Julius Boschi, Patterson, CA	134.5	8
1963/Les Hirdes, Turlock, CA		
Al Hooper, Reno, NV	100.9	8
1964/Byron Gist, Lakeside, CA		
Gary Gist, Lakeside, CA	114.2	8
1965/Bronc Curry, Thousand Oaks, CA		
Billy Darnell, Rodeo, NM	100.6	8
1966/Ken Luman, Merced, CA		
Jim Rodriguez, Jr., Paso Robles, CA	116.2	8
1967/Ace Berry, Modesto, CA		
Bucky Bradford, Jr., Tucson, AZ	141.7	9
1968/Leo Camarillo, Donald, OR		
Billy Wilson, Arroyo Grande, CA	104.6	9
1969/Leo Camarillo, Donald, OR		
Reg Camarillo, Mesa, AZ	115.6	9
1970/Leo Camarillo, Donald, OR		
Reg Camarillo, Mesa, AZ	126.9	10
1971/Leo Camarillo, Donald, OR		
Reg Camarillo, Mesa, AZ	154.5	10
1972/John Miller, Pawhuska, OK		

Ace Berry, Modesto, CA	124.7	10
1973/Ken Luman, Visalia, CA		
Jim Rodriguez, Jr., Paso Robles, CA	100.4	10
1974/Jim Wheatley, Hughson, CA		
John Rodriguez, Castroville, CA	104.3	10
1975/Reg Camarillo, Oakdale, CA		
Jerold Camarillo, Oakdale, CA	106.7	10
1976/Doyle Gellerman, Oakdale, CA		
Frank Ferreira, Sr., Fresno, CA	102.2	10
1977/David Motes, Fresno, CA		
Dennis Motes, Mesa, AZ	94.6	10
1978/Brad Smith, Prescott, AZ		
George Richards, Humbolt, AZ	105.8	11
1979/Allen Bach, Queen Creek, AZ		
Jesse James, Porterville, CA	107.5	10
1980/Tee Woolman, Llano, TX		
Leo Camarillo, Lockeford, CA	98.7	10
1981/David Motes, Fresno, CA		
Dennis Watkins, Chowchilla, CA	91.6	10
1982/Tee Woolman, Fredonia, TX		
Leo Camarillo, Lockeford, CA	80.8	10
1983/Lee Woodbury, Nampa, ID		
Jake Milton, Torrington, WY	99.2	10
1984/David Motes, Fresno, CA		
Dennis Watkins, Taft, CA	82.4	10
1985/Jake Barnes, Bloomfield, NM		
Clay O'Brien Cooper, Chandler Hts, AZ	87.8	10
1986/Monty Joe Peska, Carlsbad, NM		
Paul Petska, Carlsbad, NM	90.2	10
1987/(tie) Bob Harris, Voca, TX		
Tee Woolman, Llano, TX	77.2	10
Jake Milton, Torrington, WY		
Walt Woodard, Stockton, CA	77.2	10
1988/Charles Pogue, Ringling, OK		
Rickey Green, Burbank, CA	99.7	10
1989/Bret Boatright, Conway Springs, KS		
Steve Northcott, Odessa, TX	78.0	10
1990/Tee Woolman, Llano, TX		
Bobby Harris, Gillette, WY	78.8	10
1991/David Motes, Fresno, CA		
Bret Tonozzi, Fruita, CO	85.9	10
1992/Mark Simon, Florence, AZ		
Bret Tonozzi, Fruita, CO	80.8	10

1993/Kevin Stewart, Glen Rose, TX		
Jacky Stephenson, Charlotte, TX	100.5	10
1994/Jake Barnes, Cave Creek, AZ		
Clay O'Brien Cooper, Higley, AZ	59.1	10
1995/Kermit Maass, Snook, TX		
Tyler Magnus, Manor, TX	62.9	10
1996/Steve Purcella, Hereford, TX		
Steve Northcott, Odessa, TX	70.9	10
1997/Bret Boatright, Mulhall, OK		
Kory Koontz, Sudan, TX	83.0	10
1998/Jimmy Tanner, Tifton, GA		
Brad Culpepper, Poulan, GA	68.0	10
1999/Jimmy Tanner, Tifton, GA		
Brad Culpepper, Poulan, GA	83.9	10
2000/Charles Pogue, Ringling, OK		
Britt Bockius, Claremore, OK	73.3	10
2001/Speed Williams, Jacksonville, FL		
Rich Skelton, Llano, TX	92.8	10
2002/J. D. Yates, Pueblo, CO		
Bobby Harris, Gillette, WY	96.6	10
2003/Matt Tyler, Dennis, TX		
Patrick Smith, Midland, TX	62.3	10
2004/Clay Tryan, Billings, MT		
Michael Jones, Stephenville, TX	77.8	10
2005/Tee Woolman, Llano, TX		
Cory Petska, Lexington, OK	71.7	10

PRCA RECORDS

PRCA Career Earnings Leaders (Through 2005)
Joe Beaver (TD, TR, SR) $2,597,896
Fred Whitfield (TD, TR) $2,497,417
Dan Mortensen (SB, BR) $2,392,167
Billy Etbauer (SB) $2,377,662
Tee Woolman (TR, SR) $2,284,783

Highest Single Year Earnings
$320,766, Matt Austin, 2005

Most Money Won at a Rodeo
$126,412, Lee Graves at 2005 Wrangler NFR

Most Money Won at a Regular Season Rodeo
$35,130, Wade Wheatley/Kyle Lockett at USSTC Cup
Finale in Dallas, 2002

Most Money Won in Rookie Year
$197,646, Steve Woolsey (BR) 2005

WRANGLER NFR RECORDS

Youngest World Champion
Jim Rodriguez, Jr., 1959, TR, age 18

Oldest World Champion
Ike Rude, 1953, SR, age 59

Youngest Qualifiers
J. D. Yates, TR, 1975, 15 years, 4 months
Ace Berry, TR, 1962, 15 years, 11 months

Oldest Qualifier
Everett Shaw, SR, 1965, age 57

Only Father-Son-Daughter to Compete at NFR in Same Year
Dick Yates (TR), J. D. Yates (TR), Kelly Yates (barrel racing), 1984

Only Mother-Son Combination to Compete at NFR in Same Year
Terri Kaye Kirkland (LBR) and Clay and Travis Tryan (TR)

Three-Brother Sets to Qualify in Same Year
Butch (BR), Kaye (BB), and Sandy Kirby (BB, BR), 1994-1997
Robert, Billy, Dan Etbauer (SB)

Only Three Brothers to Qualify in the Same Event in the Same Year
Robert, Billy, and Dan Etbauer (SB), 1989-1992, 1994-1997

Only Left-handed Tie Down Ropers to Qualify
Grady Allen, 1960
Bob Ragsdale, 1961-1975
Ronnye Sewalt, 1961, 1963-1975, 1977-1978
Butch Bode, 1976
Tom Walker, 1986, 1998
James Zant, 1987-1988, 1990, 1995

Most Consecutive Qualifications
29—Guy Allen (SR), 1977-2005
21—Roy Duvall (SW), 1966-1986

Most NFR Qualifications in All Events Combined
41—Tee Woolman (SR), 1985-2001, 2004-2005;
    (TR), 1980-1984, 1986-1988, 1990-1993, 1995-2000, 2002-2005
32—Roy Cooper (TD), 1976-1987, 1989, 1991-1993, 1995-1996, 2000;
    (SR), 1980-1981, 1983-1988, 1990, 1992-1993, 1996, 1999
27—Larry Mahan (SB), 1964, 1966-1971, 1973, 1975;
    (BB), 1966-1971, 1973-1975, (BR), 1965-1973
26—Olin Young (TD), 1959-1971; (SR), 1966-1972, 1974-1978,
    1980 (alt. SR 1979)

Cowboys Qualifying in Four Events
Trevor Brazile—TD, SR, TR (heading and heeling)

Cowboys Qualifying in Three Events

Joe Beaver, SR, TD, TR	Larry Mahan, SB, BB, BR
Mike Beers, TD, TR, SR	Ty Murray, SB, BB, BR
Bobby Berger, SB, BB, BR	Cash Myers, SW, TD, SR
Jimmie Cooper, TD, SW, TR	Benny Reynolds, BB, BR, SW
Tom Ferguson, TD, SW, SR	Lyle Sankey, SB, BB, BR
Phil Lyne, BR, TD, SR	Dale Smith, TD, TR, SR

Cowboys Qualifying in Three Events in One Year
Bobby Berger, SB, BB, BR, 1971
Trevor Brazile, TD, TR, SR, 2003
Tom Ferguson, TD, SW, SR, 1979
Larry Mahan, SB, BB, BR, 1966-1970, 1971, 1973
Ty Murray, SB, BB, BR 1990-1994
Dale Smith, TD, TR, SR, 1959-1960

PRCA DODGE NATIONAL CIRCUIT FINALS WINNERS

Twelve Circuits of PRCA

Columbia River	Montana	Badlands	Great Lakes
California	Mountain States	Prairie	Southeastern
Wilderness	Turquoise	Texas	First Frontier

Dodge National Circuit Finals Rodeo Champions
(Roping Events & All Around Only Listed)

1987   Team Roping   Jake Barnes/Clay O'Brien Cooper .... Turquoise Circuit
      Calf Roping   D. R. Daniel.......................... Southeastern

1988   Team Roping   Dennis Gatz/ David Motes .... Sierra (California)
      Calf Roping   D. R. Daniel.......................... Southeastern

1989   All-Around   Lewis Feild .... Wilderness
      Team Roping   Jake Barnes/Clay O'Brien Cooper .... Turquoise
      Calf Roping   Herbert Theriot...................... Southeastern

1990   All Around   Joe Parsons .... Turquoise
      Team Roping   Dennis Watkins/David Motes........ Sierra (California)
      Calf Roping   Darryl Crowley .... Montana

1991   All Around   Dee Pickett .... Wilderness
      Team Roping   Bob Harris/Jake Milton .... Mountain States
      Calf Roping   Maury Tate .... Prairie

1992   All Around   Dan Mortensen .... Montana
      Team Roping   Dennis Gatz/Bobby Hurley .... Sierra (California)
      Calf Roping   Nate Kayser .... Columbia River

1993   All Around   Ty Murray................................. Texas
      Team Roping   Will Schmidt/Scott English............ Columbia River
      Calf Roping   Kyle Kosoff.............................. Wilderness

1994   All Around   Ty Murray................................. Texas
      Team Roping   Jay Wadhams/Jay Ellerman............ Mountain States
      Calf Roping   Dave Cannon .... Columbia River

1995   All Around   Speed Williams...................... Southeastern
      Team Roping   Jake Barnes/Clay O'Brien Cooper .... Turquoise
      Calf Roping   Brian Fulton .... Badlands

1996   All Around   Brian Fulton .... Badlands
      Team Roping   Jake Barnes/Clay O'Brien Cooper .... Turquoise
      Calf Roping   Bud Ford................................. Texas

1997	All Around	Tony Currin .... Columbia River
	Team Roping	Tee Woolman/Rich Skelton..................... Texas
	Calf Roping	Cody Ohl .... Texas

1998	All Around	Brad Goodrich .... Columbia River
	Team Roping	Steve Purcella/Steve Northcott .... Texas
	Calf Roping	K. C. Jones .... Prairie

1999	All Around	Fred Boettcher .... Great Lakes
	Team Roping	Jason Stewart/Bucky Campbell......... Columbia River
	Calf Roping	Brad Goodrich .... Columbia River

2000	All Around	Mark Garrett .... Badlands
	Team Roping	Bret Boatright/Mickey Gomez................. Prairie
	Cal Roping	Herbert Theriot...................... Southeastern

2001	All Around	Felipe Aragon .... Turquoise
	Team Roping	Speed Williams/Rich Skelton .... Texas
	Calf Roping	Shawn Franklin............................. Prairie

2002	All Around	Kyle Whitaker.............................. Prairie
	Team Roping	Richard Eiguren/B. J. Campbell .... Columbia River
	Calf Roping	Bill Huber .... Great Lakes

2003	All Around	Carmine Nastri....................... First Frontier
	Team Roping	Speed Williams/Rich Skelton .... Texas
	Calf Roping	Fred Whitfield .... Texas

2004	All Around	Wade Kreutzer/Ryan Zurcher .... Mountain States
	Team Roping	Wade Kreutzer/Ryan Zurcher .... Mountain States
	Calf Roping	Nate Baldwin........................... Wilderness

2005	All Around	Ryan Jarrett .... Southeastern
	Team Roping	Rube Woolsey/Matt Sherwood .... Turquoise
	Calf Roping	Casey Branquinho .... California

PROFESSIONAL WOMEN'S RODEO ASSOCIATION CHAMPIONS

| 1948 | All Around/Margaret Owens | Calf Roping/Betty Dusek |
| | Team Roping/Blanche Smith | Ribbon Roping/Judy Hays |

| 1949 | All Around/Amy McGilvray | Calf Roping/Betty Dusek |
| | Team Roping/Margaret Owens | |

| 1950 | All Around/Jackie Worthington | Calf Roping/Blanche Smith |
| | Team Roping/Blanche Smith | Ribbon Roping/Jackie Worthington |

1951 All Around/Jackie Worthington　Calf Roping/Wanda Harper Bush
Ribbon Roping/Wanda Harper Bush

1952 All Around/Wanda Harper Bush　Calf Roping/Wanda Harper Bush
Team Tying/Judy Hays　Ribbon Roping/Ruby Goble

1953 All Around/Jackie Worthington　Calf Roping/Wanda Harper Bush
Team Tying/Ruby Goble　Ribbon Roping/Wanda Harper Bush

1954 All Around/Jackie Worthington　Calf Roping/Wanda Harper Bush
Team Tying/Betty Dusek　Ribbon Roping/Wanda Harper Bush

1955 All Around/Jackie Worthington　Calf Roping/Wanda Harper Bush
Team Tying/Blanche Smith

1956 All Around/Jackie Worthington　Calf Roping/Wanda Harper Bush
Ribbon Roping/Wanda Harper Bush

1957 All Around/Wanda Harper Bush　Calf Roping/Fay Ann Horton Leach
Team Tying/Jane Mayo　Ribbon Roping/Wanda Harper Bush

1958 All Around/Wanda Harper Bush　Calf Roping/Betty Dusek
Team Tying/Jane Mayo　Ribbon Roping/Wanda Harper Bush

1959 All Around/Jane Mayo　Calf Roping/Fay Ann Horton Leach
Team Tying/Jane Mayo　Ribbon Roping/Wanda Harper Bush

1960 All Around/Fay Ann Horton Leach　Calf Roping/Wanda Bush

1961 All Around/Betty Combs Johnson　Calf Roping/Betty Dusek

1962 All Around/Wanda Bush　Calf Roping/Wanda Bush
(incomplete records)

1963 All Around/Wanda Harper Bush

1964 All Around/Wanda Harper Bush　Calf Roping/Wanda Harper Bush

1965 All Around/Wanda Harper Bush　Calf Roping/Rosalyn Mitchell
Ribbon Roping/Rosalyn Mitchell

1966 All Around/Florence Youree　Calf Roping/Wanda Harper Bush

1967 All Around/Betty Dusek　Calf Roping/Wanda Harper Bush
Ribbon Roping/Betty Dusek

1968 All Around/Wanda Harper Bush　Calf Roping/Betty Dusek
Ribbon Roping/Joyce Burk Loomis

1969 All Around/Wanda Harper Bush　Calf Roping/Betty Dusek
Ribbon Roping/Terry Lewis

1970 All Around/Bonnie McPherson　Calf Roping/Betty Dusek

Ribbon Roping/Annette Duncan

1971 No records kept

1972 No records kept

1973 All Around/Sheila Bussey   Calf Roping/Sheila Bussey
      Team Roping/Cindy Dodge   Goat Tying/Kay Huddleston
      Ribbon Roping/Sheila Bussey

1974 All Around/Sue Pirtle   Calf Roping/Sue Pirtle
      Breakaway/Becky Berggren   Team Roping/Gail Higgins
      Goat Tying/Pam Simon   Ribbon Roping/Sue Pirtle

1975 All Around/Jimmie Gibbs Munroe   Calf Roping/Jimmie Gibbs Munroe
      Breakaway/Becky Fuchs   Team Roping/Gail Higgins
      Goat Tying/Bonny Pleasant

1976 All Around/Sue Pirtle   Calf Roping/Bonny Pleasant
      Team Roping/Becky Fuchs   Goat Tying/Bonny Pleasant

1977 All Around/Jennifer Haynes   Calf Roping/Jennifer Haynes
      Team Roping/Jennifer Haynes   Goat Tying/Becky Fuchs

1978 All Around/Judy Robinson   Calf Roping/Twyla Rutherford
      Team Roping/Kathy Kennedy   Goat Tying/Bonny Pleasant

1979 All Around/Jennifer Haynes   Calf Roping/Betty Gayle Cooper
      Team Roping/Jennifer Haynes   Goat Tying/Bonny Pleasant

1980 All Around/Gloria Paulsen   Calf Roping/Gloria Paulsen
      Team Roping/Roxy McIntosh   Goat Tying/Gloria Paulsen

1981 All Around/Betty Gayle Cooper   Calf Roping/Betty Gayle Cooper
      Team Roping/Nancy Hammons   Goat Tying/Bonny Blassingame

1982 All Around/Betty Gayle Cooper   Calf Roping/Betty Gayle Cooper
      Breakaway/Pam Minick   Team Roping/Twyla Rutherford
      Goat Tying/Betty Gayle Cooper   Ribbon Roping/Ronda Harrison

1983 All Around/Betty Gayle Cooper   Calf Roping/Betty Gayle Cooper
      Breakaway/Heather Hodson   Team Roping/Denema Merrell
      Goat Tying/Sherri Hernandez

1984 All Around/Jan Howell   Calf Roping/Jan Howell
      Team Roping/Cheri Berthoud

1985 All Around/Twyla Rutherford   Calf Roping/Ronda Harrison
      Team Roping/Twyla Rutherford

1986 All Around/Nancy Peirce   Calf Roping/Jeana Brooks
      Team Roping/Twyla Rutherford

1987   All Around/Gayle Brittain   Calf Roping/Jeana Brooks
       Team Roping/Nancy Peirce

1988   All Around/Viki Williamson   Calf Roping/Jeana Brooks
       Team Roping/Cindy Waters

1989   All Around/Ronda Harrison   Calf Roping/Edee Hurst
       Breakaway/Betty Gayle Cooper   Team Roping/Denema Merrell

1990   All Around/Ronda Harrison   Calf Roping/Ronda Harrison
       Breakaway/Jayme Reaves   Team Roping/Denema Merrell

1991   All Around/Ronda Harrison   Calf Roping/Jeana Brooks
       Breakaway/Jimmi Jo Martin   Team Roping/Lori Merrell-Patterson

1992   All Around/Jeana Brooks   Calf Roping/Jeana Brooks
       Breakaway/Jimmi Jo Martin   Team Roping/Lori Merrell-Patterson

1993   All Around/Jimmi Jo Martin   Calf Roping/Jayme Reaves-Marcrum
       Breakaway/Lisa Pulse-Gasperson   Team Roping/Angie Ritchie

1994   All Around/J. J. Hampton   Calf Roping/J. J. Hampton
       Breakaway/Lisa Gasperson   Team Roping/Cindy Waters

1995   All Around/J. J. Hampton   Calf Roping/Jeana Brooks
       Breakaway/J. J. Hampton   Team Roping/Tami Vaught Kemp

1996   All Around/Lisa Gasperson   Calf Roping/Jeana Brooks
       Breakaway/J. J. Hampton
       Team Roping—Heading/J. J. Hampton
       Team Roping—Heeling/Melissa Brillhart

1997   All Around/J. J. Hampton   Calf Roping/J. J. Hampton
       Breakaway/Lisa Gasperson
       Team Roping—Heading/J. J. Hampton
       Team Roping—Heeling/Melissa Brillhart

1998   All Around/J. J. Hampton   Calf Roping/J. J. Hampton
       Breakaway/Rhonda Harrison
       Team Roping—Heading/J. J. Hampton
       Team Roping—Heeling/Melissa Brillhart

1999   All Around/J. J. Hampton   Calf Roping/J. J. Hampton
       Breakaway/J. J. Hampton
       Team Roping—Heading/J. J. Hampton
       Team Roping—Heeling/Melissa Brillhart

2000   All Around/J. J. Hampton   Calf Roping/Sandy Hodge
       Breakaway/Ashlee Miller
       Team Roping—Heading/Patti McCutchen

Team Roping—Heeling/Kim Williamson

2001   All Around/Dedee Crawford   Calf Roping/Kelly Lawrence
Breakaway/April Harms
Team Roping—Heading/Penny Conway
Team Roping—Heeling/Melissa Brillhart

2002   All Around/Teresa Bilyeu   Calf Roping/Teresa Bilyeu
Breakaway/Nora Hunt
Team Roping—Heading/Teresa Bilyeu
Team Roping—Heeling/Cathy Johnson

2003   All Around/Tami Noble   Calf Roping/Nora Hunt
Breakaway/Tami Noble
Team Roping—Heading/Tami Noble
Team Roping—Heeling/Michelle Owens

2004   All Around/Kim Williamson   Calf Roping/Kelly Lawrence
Breakaway/Kim Williamson
Team Roping—Heading/Kim Williamson
Team Roping—Heeling/Kera Washburn

2005   All Around/Kim Williamson   Calf Roping/Kim Williamson
Breakaway/Kim Williamson
Team Roping—Heading/Lora Pierson
Team Roping—Heeling/Kim Williamson

NATIONAL COWBOY & WESTERN HERITAGE MUSEUM
RODEO HALL OF FAME

Oklahoma City, Oklahoma

HONOREES

Aber, Doff	Austin, Tex	Blancett, Bertha
Adams, Leon	Baldwin, Tillie	Blevins, Earl
Akridge, Eddy	Barmby, Bob	Boen, Ken
Akers, Ira	Beeson, Fred	Bolen, Bernice Dossey
Alexander, Joe	Bell, Ray	Bond, Paul
Altizer, Jim Bob	Bennett, Hugh	Boucher, C. R.
Ambler, Jerry	Berry, Ace	Bowman, Everett
Appleton, Dave	Beutler, Elra	Bowman, John
Arnold, Carl	Beutler, Lynn	Bowman, Louis Ed
Askin, Bob	Blackstone, Vick	Brady, Buff

Brennan, Harry
Brooks, Louis
Brown, Freckles
Burk, Clyde
Burmeister, A. H. "Hippy"
Burrell, Cuff
Buschbom, Jack
Bush, Wanda
Byers, Chester
Bynum, James
Caldwell, Lee
Camarillo, Jerold
Camarillo, Leo
Canutt, Yakima
Carney, Paul
Carr, Clay
Carroll, J. Ellison
Carter, Barton
Christensen, Hank
Clancy, Foghorn
Clark, Bobby
Clark, Gene
Clennon, Bart
Colborn, Ava
Colborn, Everett E.
Combs, Benny
Combs, Willard
Connelly, Edith Happy
Connelly, Lex
Cook, Bob
Cooper, Felix
Cooper, Jimmie B.
Cooper, Roy
Cooper, Tuffy
Copenhaver, Deb
Cornish, Cecil
Cox, Breezy
Crosby, Bob
Curtis, Andy
Curtis, Eddie
Davis, Gordon
Davis, Sonny
Decker, Jo

Decker, Tater
Dightman, Myrtis
Doak, George
Dollarhide, Ross, Jr.
Doubleday, Ralph R.
Douthitt, Buff
Dunafon, Wayne
Duvall, Roy
Elliott, Verne
Eskew, Colonel Jim
Eskew, Junior
Estes, Bobby
Feild, Lewis
Ferguson, Tom
Fletcher, George
Fletcher, Kid
Fort, Troy C.
Fulkerson, Jasbo
Gale, Floyd
Gamblin, Amye
Gardner, Joe
Garrett, Sam
Gaudin, D. J. "Kajun Kidd"
Goodspeed, Buck
Goodspeed, Jess
Grammer, Henry
Greenough, Turk
Griffith, Dick
Groff, Buddy
Hadley, Tom
Hancock, Bill
Hancock, Sonny
Harris, Howard III
Hastings, Fox
Hastings, Mike
Hatley, John
Haverty, Del
Hefner, Hoytt
Helfrich, Devere
Hennigh, Duane
Henson, Margie
    Greenough
Holcomb, Homer

Hopkins, Ethel "Ma"
Irwin, C. B.
Ivory, Buster
Ivory, Petty
Ivory, June
Jauregui, Andy
Johnson, Ben Sr
Johnson, Bernis
Johnson, Clint
Johnson, Sherry Combs
Jones, Cecil
Jones, John
Justin, John
Kirnan, Tommy
Knight, Harry
Knight, Pete
Lambert, Mel
Lefton, Abe
Leuschner, C. O.
    "Dogtown Slim"
Lewallen, G. K.
Like, Jim
Linder, Herman
Linderman, Bill
Linderman, Bud
Lindsey, John
Logan, Pete
Long, Hughie
Lowry, Fred
Lucas, James E. "Buck"
Lucas, Tad
Lybbert, Chris
Lyne, Phil
McCarroll, Bonnie
McCarty, Eddie
McLean, Kenny
McClure, Jake
McCrory, Howard
McEntire, Clark
McEntire, John
McGinnis, Vera
McGinty, Rusty
McGonagill, Clay

McLaughlin, Don
McSpadden, Clem
Maggini, Charles
Mahan, Larry
Mansfield, Toots
May, Harley
Mayo, Don
Meek, Junior
Merchant, Richard
Merritt, King
Miller, Clyde S.
Mills, George
Montana, Montie
Mosley, Dixie Lee Reger
Mulhall, Lucille
Mulkey, Burel
Mullens, Johnnie
Murray, Leo "Pick"
Murray, Ty
Nesbitt, Don
Nesbitt, Pauline
Nesmith, Tom
Oliver, Dean
Oropeza, Vincente
Orr, Alice Greenough
Pickens, Slim
Pettigrew, Homer
Pickett, Bill
Pickett, Dee
Porter, Willard H.
Privett, "Booger Red"
Pruett, Gene
Purdy, Ikua
Ragsdale, Bob
Rambo, Gene
Randall, Glenn
Randolph, Florence
Reynolds, Benny
Richardson, Nowata Slim
Riley, Doyle
Riley, Lanham

Riley, Mitzi Lucas
Roach, Ruth
Roberds, Coke T.
Roberts, E. C.
Roberts, Gerald
Roberts, Ken
Robinson, Lee
Roddy, Jack
Rollens, Rufus
Ross, Gene
Rowell, Harry
Rowell, Maggie
Rude, Ike
Rutherford, Buck
Ryan, Paddy
Salinas, Juan
Sawyer, Fern
Schell, Asbury
Schneider, Frank
Schneider, Johnnie
Scudder, Pat
Sewalt, Ronnye
Shaw, Everett
Shelton, Dick
Shelton, Reine Hafley
Sheppard, Chuck
Sheppard, Lynn
Sheppard, Nancy Kelley
Shoulders, Jim
Shultz, Charley
Slocum, Tex
Smith, Bill
Smith, Dale D.
Smith, Velda Tindall
Snyder, Smokey
Sorenson, Doc
Sorrels, Buckshot
Sowder, Thad
Stahl, Jesse
Steele, Fannie S.
Steiner, Buck

Steiner, Tommy
Stillings, Floyd
Stoker, J. W.
Strickland, Hugh
Strickland, Mabel
Stroud, Leonard
Sundown, Jackson
Taillon, Cy
Tegland, Howard
Tescher, Jim
Thode, Earl
Tibbs, Casey
Tierney, Paul
Todd, Homer
Tompkins, Harry
Trickey, Lorena
Truan, Fritz
Truitt, Dick
Tucker, Harley
Tureman, Sonny
Veach, C. Monroe
Walker, Enoch
Ward, Leonard
Ward, William "Bill"
Weadick, Guy
Webster, Shoat
Weeks, Billy
Weeks, Guy
Welch, Joe
Whaley, Everett "Slim"
Wharton, Ray
Whatley, Todd
White, Vivian
Whiteman, Hub
Whiteman, Jim
Wilcox, Don
Witmer, Nancy Bragg
Worrell, Sonny
Yoder, Phil
Young, Rick
Zumwalt, Oral

PRORODEO HALL OF FAME HONOREES
Colorado Springs, Colorado
(By category)

All-Around Cowboy

Chris Lybbert, 2006
Jimmie Cooper, 2005
Dee Pickett, 2003
Todd Whatley, 2003
Joe Beaver, 2002
Paul Carney, 2001
Ty Murray, 2000

Chuck Sheppard, 2000
Tom Ferguson, 1999
Fritz Truan, 1995
Benny Reynolds, 1993
Lewis Feild, 1992
Louis Brooks, 1991
Gerald Roberts, 1990

Gene Rambo, 1989
Everett Bowman, 1979
Clay Carr, 1979
Bill Linderman, 1979
Phil Lyne, 1979
Larry Mahan, 1979
Jim Shoulders, 1979

Bareback Riding

Chris LeDoux, 2005
Clint Corey, 2004
Clyde Vamvoras, 2002
Marvin Garrett, 1998
Jack Ward, 1995

J. C. Trujillo, 1994
Bruce Ford, 1993
Jim Houston, 1979
Eddy Akridge, 1979

Joe Alexander, 1979
Jack Buschbom, 1979
Jack Hawkins, 1979
Sonny Tureman, 1979

Steer Wrestling

Bob A. Robinson, 2006
Steve Duhon, 2003
C. R. Boucher, 2001
Ote Berry, 1998
John W. Jones, Jr., 1996

Gene Ross, 1994
Bill Pickett, 1989
Hugh Bennett, 1979
James Bynum, 1979
Roy Duvall, 1979

John W. Jones, 1979
Harley May, 1979
Homer Pettigrew, 1979
Jack Roddy, 1979

Team Roping

Charles Maggini, 2005
Tee Woolman, 2004
Asbury Schell, 2004
Les Hirdes, 2001

Jake Barnes, 1997
Clay O'Brien Cooper, 1997
Leo Camarillo, 1979
Ben Johnson, 1979

John Miller, 1979
Jim Rodriguez, 1979
Dale Smith, 1979

Saddle Bronc Riding

Joe Marvel, 2005
Alvin Nelson, 2004
Dennis Reiners, 2003
Guy Weeks, 2001
Mel Hyland, 1999
Brad Gjermundson, 1995
Monty Henson, 1994

Deb Copenhaver, 1992
Clint Johnson, 1992
Marty Wood, 1991
Bobby Berger, 1990
Winston Bruce, 1989
Shawn Davis, 1979
Sharkey Irwin, 1979

Pete Knight, 1979
Gene Pruett, 1979
Bill Smith, 1979
Mike Stuart, 1979
Earl Thode, 1979
Casey Tibbs, 1979

Tie Down Roping

Fred Whitfield, 2004
Jake McClure, 2002
Barry Burk, 1994
Clyde Burk, 1979

Roy Cooper, 1979
Troy Fort, 1979
Glen Franklin, 1979

Toots Mansfield, 1979
Don McLaughlin, 1979
Dean Oliver, 1979

Bull Riding

Jim Sharp, 2006
Gary Leffew, 2002
Richard "Tuff"
   Hedeman, 1997
Charles Sampson, 1996

John Schneider, 1992
Lane Frost, 1990
Dick Griffith, 1989
Freckles Brown, 1979
Don Gay, 1979

George Paul, 1979
Ken Roberts, 1979
Smokey Snyder, 1979
Harry Tompkins, 1979

Steer Roping

Guy Allen, 1996
Jim Bob Altizer, 1979
Sonny Davis, 1979

Clark McEntire, 1979
Ike Rude, 1979
Everett Shaw, 1979

Shoat Webster, 1979
Olin Young, 1979

Contract Personnel

Rob Smets, 2006
Slim Pickens, 2005
Bob Tallman, 2004
June Ivory, 2004
Nancy Sheppard, 2003
Cecil Cornish, 2003
Quail Dobbs, 2002
Edith Happy Connelly,
   2002
Jay Sisler, 2002
Jo Decker, 2001

Tom Hadley, 2001
Jerry Olson, 2001
George Doak, 2000
Junior Meek, 2000
Hadley Barrett, 1999
Andy Womack, 1998
Gene Clark, 1997
Bobby Clark, 1997
Pete Logan, 1996
Ellen Backstrom, 1995
Chuck Henson, 1995

Montie Montana, 1994
Glenn Randall, 1993
Mel Lambert, 1990
Wilbur Plaugher, 1990
Chuck Parkison, 1989
Jasbo Fulkerson, 1979
Dudley J. Gaudin, 1979
Homer Holcomb, 1979
George Mills, 1979
Wick Peth, 1979
Jimmy Schumacher,
   1979

Notables

John and Mildred Farris,
   2006
Chris LeDoux, 2005
Dr. J. Pat Evans, 2004
Myron "Doc" Etienne,
   2001
Cecil Jones, 2000
Bob Thain, 1999

John Justin, 1998
Eldon Evans, 1997
Bill Hervey, 1997
John Burke, 1996
Buster Ivory, 1991
W. R. Watt Sr., 1991
Clem McSpadden, 1990
Malcolm Baldrige, 1988

Benny Binion, 1988
Lex Connelly, 1985
Bob Crosby, 1983
Josie Bennett, 1979
Harry Knight, 1979
Tad Lucas, 1979
Dave Stout, 1979
Cy Taillon, 1979

Stock Contractor

Doc Sorensen, 2006	Harry Vold, 1994	Gene Autry, 1979
Marvin Brookman, 2005	Neal Gay, 1993	Lynn Beutler, 1979
Mike Cervi, 2003	Reg Kesler, 1992	Everett Colborn, 1979
Joe Kelsey, 2000	Walt Alsbaugh, 1990	Leo J. Cremer, 1979
Swanny Kerby, 1997	Verne Elliott, 1990	C. B. Irwin, 1979
Tommy Steiner, 1996	Henry & Bobby	Andy Jauregui, 1979
Cotton Rosser, 1995	Christensen, 1989	Harry Rowell, 1979
Bob Barnes, 1994	James H. Sutton, 1982	

Media
Dave Smith, 2004

Lifetime Achievement
Charles "Lefty" Wilken, 1999
Sonny Linger, 1998

Livestock
Bareback Broncs

Three Bars, 2004	High Tide, 1993
Skoal's Sippin' Velvet, 2000	Come Apart, 1979

Saddle Broncs

Miss Klamath, 1998	Midnight, 1979
Descent, 1979	Steamboat, 1979
Hell's Angel, 1979	Tipperary, 1979
Five Minutes to Midnight, 1979	

Bulls

Bodacious, 1999	Old Spec, 1979
Crooked Nose (fighting bull) 1990	Oscar, 1979
Red Rock, 1990	Tornado, 1979

Timed Event Horses

Scamper, 1996	Bullet, 1979
Baby Doll, 1979	Peanuts, 1979
Baldy, 1979	Poker Chip Peake, 1979

Special Recognition
San Antonio Stock Show & Rodeo, 2003
Dodge National Circuit Finals Rodeo, 2004

RODEO ORGANIZATIONS

Professional Rodeo Cowboys Association
101 ProRodeo Drive
Colorado Springs, CO 80919

American Junior Rodeo Association
P O Box 481
Rankin, TX 79778

Canadian Professional Rodeo Association
223 2116 27th Ave., N. E.
Calgary, Alberta, Canada T2E 7A6

National High School Rodeo Association
11178 N. Huron St.,#7
Denver, CO 80234

National Intercollegiate Rodeo Association
2316 Eastgate N. St.,#160
Walla Walla, WA 99362

National Little Britches Rodeo
1045 W. Rio Grande
Colorado Springs, CO 80906

Women's Professional Rodeo Association
& Professional Women's Rodeo Association
1235 Lake Plaza Drive,#134
Colorado Springs, CO 80906

Senior ProRodeo National Old Timers Rodeo Association
P O Box 419
Roundup, MT

International Professional Rodeo Association
2304 Exchange Ave
Oklahoma City, OK 73108

USTRC
P O Box 1198
Stephenville, TX 76401

GLOSSARY

A.S.C.P.A.—organization that protects animals from cruelty.

Anti-Rodeo Cruelty Association—group formed to eliminate rodeo based on their cruelty to animals.

arena director—manager of happenings during a rodeo in the arena.

average—totaling the number of stock per each event by contestant and dividing it into the number of seconds for all stock (10 head divided into 125 seconds = 12.5 average).

barrier—string across roper's box to prevent roper from getting a head start on stock.

box—16 foot enclosure from which roper and horse leave to rope the designated stock at a rodeo.

branding—a ranch chore requiring putting ranch brand on cattle, plus doctoring of stock.

breakaway steer roping—a competition where the steer is roped, but not thrown, rope merely pulls away.

buckjumping—Australian term for bronc riding.

bulldogging—same as steer wrestling, jumping from a horse and grabbing the horns of a steer and attempting to twist his neck so that all four feet leave the ground.

bushmen—Australian term for cowboys.

busting—throwing a steer to the ground.

Calcutta—a game where people bid on ropers and high bidder gets money provided his roper wins in the event.

calf—a young bovine, usually less than a year old.

cannon—part of horse's leg between the hock (knee) and fetlock.

cantle—part of saddle, the upward curve behind the seat.

catch rope—the rope the roper uses to catch stock.

chute—the divided alleyway where one head of stock is released for the roper to rope.

circuit—in professional rodeo the United States is divided into twelve circuits, for competitors who chose to compete in their home area, and in which they can earn points and win on the circuit level.

competition—an event where the ropers pay an entry fee to be able to try and win.

contested—if a judge or someone questions the legality of a roper's catch or method of roping.

Cowboy's Turtle Association—the first group of cowboys organized in 1936 for the purposes of having higher purses, more qualified judges, and more uniform rodeos across the country.

cracker—a cowboy from the southeast part of the United States, primarily Florida and Georgia, who uses a whip instead of a rope when dealing with cattle, due to the heavy foliage.

crossfire—in team roping, when the heeler throws a loop before the header turns the steer.

dairymen—men who own and milk cows for a living.

dally—wrapping the catch rope around the saddle horn when a catch is made.

double rigged saddle—a saddle with a cinch around the belly and a second strap at the back of the saddle which keeps it from rising up in the back when a rope is tied around the horn and the calf or steer pulls tight on the rope.

eared down—in a wild horse race, one competitor will grab the horse's head and bite the ear, to distract the wild horse from realizing they are putting a saddle on him.

entry fee/entrance fee—the amount each contestant is required to pay to compete in an event.

exhibition—when cowboys and cowgirls perform for a salary or set amount and are not competing.

fairgrounding—a term used to mean steer roping, which in the earliest days was usually held at a local fairground, if one existed.

fetlock—part of horse's leg just above the hoof.

flag judge—the timed event judge who waves the flag when the steer or calf is tied, or the steer wrestler completes his throw with the steer's feet in the air, which is when the timers stop their watches.

flanking—to pick up a calf by grabbing the catch rope next to his neck with one hand, and grabbing his flank with the other hand, in order to lie him down on the ground, preparing for the tie.

grandstand—where the spectators sit to watch a rodeo or roping.

ground work—the part of calf or steer roping which is done after the rider has left his mount, usually to pick up and tie the calf or steer.

half-hitch—looping a rope around an object, then back around itself, bringing the end of the rope through the loop.

header—team roper who ropes the head of the steer first before the heeler ropes.

heeler—team roper who ropes after the header has roped the steer, and ropes to catch the hind feet.

hemp—another term for rope.

honda—the eye in one end of the catch rope. The other end of the rope is passed through the honda to make the loop.

Humane Society—international organization that watches to make sure animals are not treated in a cruel and harmful way.

jackpot roping—a gathering of cowboys for the purpose of roping, usually putting up some money to be divided among the winners.

jerked down—when a competitor ropes a calf and uses more force than required

lariat—a length of rope used to rope cattle or animals.

legging—a term used in picking up the front leg of a calf until the calf falls over, then the tie is made. This was eventually replaced by flanking the calf.

maguey—a type of rope made from fiber from the agave plant, native to tropical America.

matched roping—when one roper competes against another roper of like ability, usually with some type of "winner take all" purse involved; usually side bets are made by spectators.

mestizos—a man of mixed European and American Indian ancestry.

mollycoddlers—a term used by the British to define a weak-type individual unable to do the work of a cowboy.

mulattos—a person of mixed Caucasian and Negro ancestry.

no jerk down rule—a rule used to keep the calf roper from roping the calf and jerking it unnecessarily and allowing the horse to drag the calf more than three feet.

noose—a loop made in a rope.

PROCOM—form of entering professional rodeo used by PRCA.

pastern—part of a horse's foot, above the hoof.

permit—a cowboy can get permission to compete in PRCA until he wins a certain amount of money, then he must become a member of the organization.

pick up men—men riding horses who help in a rodeo arena, herding cattle out, helping riders off broncs, etc.

piggin' string—the piece of rope used by a roper to tie three legs of a steer or calf together.

purse—the amount of money set aside for the prizes in a contest.

rawhide—the untanned hide of cattle or other animals.

reata/riata—another word for lariat or lasso.

right-side dismount—as competitive roping improved it was determined getting off the horse on the right side would allow a quicker time in roping stock.

rookie—term used for a competitor in his first year of professional rodeo.

roughstock—the events in rodeo that pertain to riding saddle broncs, riding bareback, or riding bulls.

scoreline—a line drawn in front of the chute where the steer or calf must cross, before the barrier in front of the roper or steer wrestler is released. This varies in distance from rodeo to rodeo.

skid boots—covers for a horse's hooves, used for protection.

steer wrestling—same as bulldogging.

string a foreleg—the process of putting the piggin' string over the front leg, prior to tying the two back legs next.

three calf time/ten steer time—varies depending how many head of stock a roper gets during a competition; it is an accumulative time of all his stock in that event.

three bones crossed—tying three legs of a calf or steer.

timed events—events in rodeo that use a stop watch or timer, such as calf, steer and team roping, and steer wrestling.

trip—when steer roping the competitor must guide the rope from the horns down the body and maneuver the rope between the hip bone and the hock, then turn so the steer is thrown.

trip and bust—when a steer is roped, tripped, and then falls to the ground.

trick roping—when a cowboy does unusual things with a rope such as butterfly, Texas skip, etc., and performs for the audience.

vaquero—Spanish word for cowboy.

waddies—another name for cowboy.

wild west show—a western show that often includes rodeo events such as roping and bronc riding, but the performers are paid a salary; they do not compete.

RESOURCE MATERIALS

BOOKS

1. *My Fifty Years in Rodeo, Living with Cowboys, Horses and Danger* by Foghorn Clancy, Naylor Company, San Antonio, TX, 1952.
2. *Man, Beast, Dust, the Story of Rodeo* by Clifford P. Westermeier, University of Nebraska Press, 1947.
3. *Who's Who in Rodeo* by Willard Porter, Powder River Book Company, Oklahoma City, OK, 1983.
4. *Born to Rope, the Sam Garrett Story*, by Harriet Hinsdale, Aero Publishers, Inc., Fallbrook, CA, 1971.
5. *Calf Roping, A Western Horseman Book*, by Toots Mansfield, 1961.
6. *Bob Crosby, World Champion Cowboy*, by Thelma Crosby and Eve Ball, Clarendon Press, Clarendon, TX, 1966.
7. *Cowboy Roping, and Rope Tricks* by Chester Byers (originally published in 1928 under the name *Roping, Trick and Fancy Rope Spinning*) Dover Publications, NY, 1966.
8. *Cowboy Fun* by Frank Dean, Sterling Publishing Co., NY, 1980.
9. *A Brand of its Own, the 100 Year History of the Calgary Exhibition and Stampede*, by James H. Gray, Western Producer Prairie Books, Saskatoon, Saskatchewan, 1985.
10. *American Rodeo, from Buffalo Bill to Big Business*, by Kristine Fredriksson, Texas A&M University Press, College Station, TX, 1985.
11. *A Hundred Years of Heroes, a History of the Southwestern Exposition and Livestock Show*, by Clay Reynolds with Marie-Madeleine Schein, Texas Christian University Press, 1995.
12. *13 Flat, Tales of Thirty Famous Roping Rodeo Ropers and Their Great Horses*, by Willard Porter, A. S. Barnes & Co., Inc., Cranberry, NJ, 1967.
13. *Let 'Er Buck, the History of the Pendleton Roundup*, by Virgil Rupp, by Pendleton RoundUp Association, printed by Master Printers, Pendleton, OR, 1985.
14. *Cheyenne Frontier Days, a Marker from Which to Reckon All Events*, by Milt Riske, published by The Cheyenne Corral of Westerners International and Joy Riske, Cheyenne, WY, 1984.
15. *Roping*, by Bernard S. Mason, A. S. Barnes & Co., New York, 1937.
16. *Makin' Circles with a Rope, the Lore of the Lasso Wizards*, by Marv "Slim" Girard, Marshall Jones Company, Francestown, New Hampshire, 1985.
17. *Roping the 101 Ranch*, by Mike J. Sokoll, Limited Edition of 1,000, Collector's Autographed First Edition, 1973.
18. *Let 'Er Buck, a Story of the Passing of the Old West*, by Charles Wellington Furlong, G. P. Putnam & Son, London & New York, 1921.

19. *Montie Montana, Not Without My Horse! The Autobiography of the West's Living Legend*, by Montie Montana, Double M Company, Agua Dulce, CA, 1993.
20. *Trick & Fancy Roping in the Charro Style*, by Frank Dean and Nacho Rodriguez, published by Wild West Arts Club, Las Vegas, NV, 2003.
21. *R-o-d-e-o, Back of the Chutes*, by Gene Lamb, Official Publication of The Rodeo Cowboys Association, Inc., U.S.A., 1956.
22. *How to Trick Rope*, by Clare Johnson, published by Wild West Arts Club, U.S.A, 1994.
23. *Daddy of 'Em All, the Story of Cheyenne Frontier Days*, by Robert D. Hanesworth, Flintlock Publishing Co., Cheyenne, WY, 1967.
24. *Horseman, Brand of a Legend*, by Hugh L. Bennett, The Type-Smith of Colorado, 1992.
25. *World's Oldest Rodeo*, by Danny Freeman, published by Prescott Frontier Days, Inc., 1988.
26. *Let's Go, Let's Show, Let's Rodeo*, by Shirley Flynn, Wigwam Publishing Company, LLC, Cheyenne, WY, 1996.
27. *Rope Burns*, by Lee & Lela Karr, San Angelo, TX, Newsfoto Publishing Co, 1975.
28. *Fast Times, Super Looper, Roy Cooper*, by Kendra Santos, published by Roy Cooper, 1997.
29. *Fifty Years at the San Angelo Stock Show & Rodeo, Also Featuring 27 Years of Roping Fiesta History*, published by San Angelo Rodeo Foundation, 1982.
30. *Ten Days Every January, A History of the National Western Stock Show*, by Willard E Simms, published by The Western Stock Show Association and Willard E. Simms, 1982.
31. *Why We Win*, by Roy Cooper, Don Gay, Walt Woodard, Lynn McKenzie, Corriente Press, Amarillo (no date).
32. *Rodeo History and Records*, by Foghorn Clancy, 1948-1949.
33. *50 Years of Nebraska's Big Rodeo*, Clair Berney, editor, Rodeo Book Co., Burwell, NE, 1975.
34. *College Rodeo, from Show to Sport*, by Sylvia Gann Mahoney, Texas A&M University Press, 2004.
35. *Bridlewise and Otherwise*, by Rusty Bradley, Nortex Offset Publications, Inc., Wichita Falls, TX, 1972.
36. *The American Cowboy in Life & Legend*, by Bart McDowell, National Geographic Society, 1972.
37. *50 Years a Living Legend—Texas Cowboy Reunion and Old Timers Association*, by Hooper Shelton, published by Hooper Shelton in collaboration with the Texas Cowboy Old Timers Association, 1979.
38. *Roping and Riding, Fast Horses and Short Ropes*, by Willard H. Porter, A. S. Barnes & Co., 1975.
39. *The St Paul Rodeo, My Labor of Love*, by Gene Smith, Eagle Web Press, Salem, OR, 2000.
40. *Bumfuzzled*, by R. Lewis Bowman, published by author, 1995.
41. *Australian Cowboys, Roughriders and Rodeos*, by Jenny Hicks, Angus & Robertson, 2000.
42. *Lucille Mulhall, Wild West Cowgirl*, by Kathryn B. Stansbury, Homestead Heirloom Press, 1985.
43. *Cowgirls of the Rodeo*, by Mary Lou LeCompte, University of Illinois Press, 1993.

44. *Those Magnificent Cowgirls, a History of the Rodeo Cowgirl*, by Milt Riske, Wyoming Publishing, 1983.
45. PRCA Media Guides, printed yearly, 1983 to 2006.
46. *The Finals, a Complete History of the National Finals Rodeo, 40 Years*, editor Steve Fleming, published by Professional Rodeo Cowboys Association, 1998.
47. *Rodeo Champions, Eight Memorable Moments of Riding, Wrestling and Roping*, by Larry Pointer, University of New Mexico Press, 1985.
48. *Calf Roping* by Roy Cooper, A Western Horseman Book, 1984.
49. Professional Rodeo Cowboys Association 2005 Rule Book.
50. Ibid.
51. *Memoirs of a Cow Pony As Told by Himself*, by John H. Burns, published by Eastern Publishing Co., Boston, 1906.
52. *A Flavor of Texas*, by J. Frank Dobie, Jenkins Publishing Company, 1975.
53. *Western Words, a Dictionary of the Range, Cow Camp & Trail*, By Ramon F. Adams, published by University of Oklahoma Press, 1944.

ARTICLES

A1. The *Billboard* magazine, The Corral Column, December 1925 through 1936, various articles.
A2. "Rodeo 100—Looking Back," compiled by Bruce Claussen.
A3. Boots & Saddles, by Imogene Veach Beals, columns appeared in *Ranchman* magazine, Tulsa, OK, 1953 to 1958.
A4. *Hoofs & Horns*, A Western Range publication, various articles.
A5. "'A Look Back at the Old Boys" by Willard H. Porter, *Quarter Horse Journal*, April 1973
A6. "Lea County, Champion Cowboy Capitol of the World," by Douglas Kent Hall, *New Mexico* magazine, August 1985.
A7. "Drifter," by Hughie Long, *The Texas and Southwestern Horseman*, July 1965.
A8. "How Roping Came To Be," by D. L. Frazier, *Cowboy* magazine, June 2004.
A9. "Leo & Stick," by Anna Robertson, *Horse & Rider All-Western Yearbook*, 1982.
A10. Madison Square Garden Rodeo Program, 1935.
A11. *Rodeo Sports News*, Official Publication of the Rodeo Cowboys' Association (after 1974); *Prorodeo Sports News*, Official Publication of the ProRodeo Cowboy's Association.
A12. Paper on "Accounts of a Cowboy," by Junior Turner.
A13. "McLaughlin's Roping School," by Chuck King, *The Western Horseman*, August 1966.
A14. "Speed in the Rope Horse," by Mark Herra, *Hoofs & Horns*, January 1962.
A15. "Strong Man from Stonewall Hogs Dewey Roundup Prizes," by Bobby Vincent, *The Ranchman*, August 1946.
A16. "La Chavinda," by Dick Glenn, *The Western Horseman*, August 1969.
A17. "Old Time Cow Show," by Ross Santee, *Arizona Highways*, February 1960.
A18. "Williams Ropes in Top Prizes at Strait," by Tim Skaggs, *San Antonio Express News*, March 12, 2006.
A19. "A Cowboy's Rope Horse," by Richard Schaus, *The Quarter Horse Journal*, December 1951.
A20. "Troy Fort, Champion Roper," by Ray Davis, *The Western Horseman*, November 1966.
A21. "RAA News," *Rodeo Association of America* magazine, March 1940.

A22. "John Wheatley of Turlock, Calif.," *The Horse Lovers Magazine*, June-July 1954.

A23. "Olin Young," by Sidney R. Thompson, *The Western Horseman*, September 1967.

A24. Women's Professional Rodeo Association Media Guide, 2005.

A25. "Induction, the Ketch Pen," *Rodeo Historical Society Magazine*, Summer 2001.

A26. "Rodeo Life Before RVs, the Story of Cleo Crouch Rude," by Judy Goodspeed, *The Ketch Pen*, Autumn 2002.

A27. "RHS Induction Highlights," *The Ketch Pen*, Spring 2002.

A28. "National Cowboy Hall of Fame," by Flaxie Fletcher, EXTRA!, monthly newsletter for Rodeo Historical Society.

A29. "They're the Roughest Roper of Them All," by Willard Porter, *Argosy* magazine, July 1953.

A30. "No Time to Spare," by Kendra Santos, *American Cowboy* magazine, May/June 2006.

A31. "Ropers Who Were Horsemen, Fred Lowry," by Willard Porter, *The Ranchman*, November 1974.

A32. "The Calf Ropers" by Dean Oliver, *Rodeo* magazine, September-October 1971.

A33. Trevor Brazile, Wrangler Timed Event Champion of the World Program, 2006.

A34. "Shaw—the Ropers' Roper," by Willard H. Porter, Persimmon Hill, Volume 10, Number 4, 1981.

A35. "Texas Hill Country News" by Gardner Riley, *Rodeo Fans of America* magazine, January 1947.

A36. "Colorado Cowgirl Maybelle Wilson Puts a Cinch on Her Old Horse One More Time," by Ivan Wilson, Earl Anderson Memorial Rodeo Program, 2003.

A37. "Lady Steer Roper" by Judy Rush, Earl Anderson Memorial Rodeo Program, 2003.

INDEX

267

Berry, Ace, Jr., 120, 140
Beutler & Sons, 141
Big Red (horse), 70
Bigon, Ron, 123
Billboard, 33, 38, 40, 41
Binion, Benny, 161
Birchfield, Steve, 15-16
Bishop, Billy, 53
Bland, Steve, 147
Bode, Butch, 145
Bogust, Todd, 172
Bones (horse), 110
Bonnell, W. S., 20
Bowen, David, 177
Bowman, Dick, 40
Bowman, Everett, 31, 40, 42, 49, 53, 55,
    56, 62, 64, 65, 68, 76, 94, 96
Bowman, John, 31, 41, 42, 53, 60, 62, 94
Bowman, Lewis, 127
Bowman, Roger, 64
Bowman, Skeet, 40
Boyd Gaming Group, 161
Bradford, Bucky, 112
Bradley, Rusty, 136
Brannan, Leo, 69
Bray, Kirk, 203
Brazile, Jimmy, 147, 220, 221
Brazile, Shada, 221
Brazile, Trevor, 109, 189, 204, 206, 211,
    215, 220-221
Breeders & Feeders Show, 18
Bridlewise & Otherwise, 136
Brock, Dave, 148, 183
Brown, A. Clark, vi, vii, viii
Brown, Dorothy, vi, vii, viii
Brown, Freckles, 120
Brown, Ray, vii
Brownings, Alvin, 142
Brownings, Eddie, 142
buckjumping, 109, 147
Buddy Peak Roping, 111
Buffalo Bill, 10, 11, 42
Bugs (horse), 81, 82
bullock riding, 109
Burchett, Shaun, 171
Burk, Barry, 130, 139
Burk, Blair, 139, 190, 193, 194, 205
Burk, Clyde, 54, 56, 68, 69, 79, 90-91,
    93, 127

Burk, Dee, 79
Burk, Jiggs, 79, 80
Burk, Kathryn, 93
Burke, Bob, 33
Burns, Lionel, 198
Burns Rodeo Company, 179
Bush, Wanda Harper, 132
Buster (horse), 43
Butler, Ferrell, 131
Byers, Chester, 12, 19, 22, 26
Byers, Chet, 53

Caldwell, Lee, 127
Calgary Stampede, 38, 40, 63, 66, 130,
    155, 168
Calhoon (horse), 205
Callyn, Rocky, 172
Camarillo, Jerold, 159
Camarillo, Leo, 139, 144, 152-153, 155,
    156, 174
Camarillo, Ralph, 152
Canadian Rodeo Cowboy Association,
    139
Canton, Ricky, 210
Canutt, Yakima, 37
Card, Bob, 176
Carlson, Ervin, 130
Carney, Paul, 56, 58, 60, 127
Carr, Clay, 68, 81
Carroll, J. Ellison, 15, 30
Carroll, R. M., 30
Carter, Barton, 69
Casebolt, Kelly, 177
Cassidy, Greg, 168
Chapman, Jeff, 190
Charlie (horse), 81
Charters, Harry, 116
Cheyenne Frontier Days, 9, 10, 14, 20,
    21, 24, 31, 35, 36, 37, 40, 43, 44, 46,
    59, 68, 74, 85, 86, 88, 100, 128, 146,
    161, 177, 178, 183, 184, 205
Chicago World's Championship Rodeo,
    32
Chomistek, Guy, 172
Cindy (horse), 110
Circuit System, 143-144
Clancy, Foghorn, 16, 33, 38, 83
Clark, Doug, 211, 216-218
Clark, Duke, 217

About the Author

GAIL HUGHBANKS WOERNER was born in northeastern Colorado on a ranch homesteaded by her great-grandparents. She was a constant companion of her cowboy grandfather when growing up. She has been researching and interviewing rodeo people the last twenty years.

Her first book on rodeo history, *Fearless Funnymen: The History of the Rodeo Clown*, was published in 1993. *Belly Full of Bedsprings: The History of Bronc Riding* and *Cowboy Up! The History of Bull Riding* were her next two books. She and illustrator Gail Gandolfi published a children's book, *Charley & Amanda Meet Rusty the Rodeo Clown*, as the beginning of a series introducing wee ones, ages four to ten, to people in rodeo in a fun manner. She also writes an occasional article on rodeo history for various magazines, including periodicals in Australia, Canada, and France. Every other year she holds a Rodeo Clown Reunion to honor retired funnymen and bullfighters. National Geographic, TNN, and OLN "Cowboy" have covered the event for special television programs.

Gail is a member of Western Writers of America. She is the resident rodeo historian for a website at rodeoattitude.com. She also writes a column entitled "Behind the Chutes & Elsewhere," which covers positive events happening to rodeo people, as well as biographies and stories about rodeo persona, past and present. She is chairman of a Rodeo Historical Society program gathering oral histories of cowboys and cowgirls, which is housed at the National Cowboy and Western Heritage Museum in Oklahoma City.

She and husband Cliff presently live in Austin, Texas.

www.ingramcontent.com/pod-product-compliance
Lightning Source LLC
Chambersburg PA
CBHW070744270326
41927CB00010B/2090